LEARNING
TO HEAR

LEARNING TO HEAR

THE AUDITORY BASES OF EXCELLENCE IN PRACTICING MEDICINE, CLIMBING MOUNTAINS, MAKING MUSIC, AND COMMUNICATING IN MORSE CODE

SARAH MASLEN

Columbia University Press   *New York*

Columbia University Press
Publishers Since 1893
New York   Chichester, West Sussex
cup.columbia.edu

Library of Congress Cataloging-in-Publication Data
Names: Maslen, Sarah, author
Title: Learning to hear : the auditory bases of excellence in practicing
medicine, climbing mountains, making music, and communicating in
morse code / Sarah Maslen.
Description: New York : Columbia University Press, [2025] |
Includes bibliographical references and index.
Identifiers: LCCN 2024050302 | ISBN 9780231217880 hardback |
ISBN 9780231217897 trade paperback | ISBN 9780231561952 ebook
Subjects: LCSH: Hearing | Communication
Classification: LCC BF251 .M36 2025 | DDC 152.1/5—dc23/eng/20250325
LC record available at https://lccn.loc.gov/2024050302

Cover design: Julia Kushnirsky
Cover image: Amy Hutcheson, *We Have Been Listening All the Time*

GPSR Authorized Representative: Easy Access System Europe, Mustamäe tee 50,
10621 Tallinn, Estonia, gpsr.requests@easproject.com

To my girls, Genevieve and Juliette,

for their endless inspiration in the nature of human learning

CONTENTS

ACKNOWLEDGMENTS

This book has been a long time in the making, and I am indebted to many people who have taken the journey with me.

The form that the manuscript takes today owes much to the generous feedback and mentorship of Jack Katz. Jack saw something worthwhile in my work in its raw state and supported me to develop it in conversation with the long intellectual tradition of studying the backgrounded foundations of conduct. Countless drafts were always met by Jack with great enthusiasm and rigorous critique. Jack, I'm extremely thankful for your confidence in, and commitment to, the project.

The research came to life many moons ago as my doctoral thesis. I had wonderful supervisors at the Australian National University in Alastair Greig and Aat Vervoorn. Ally, you showed great trust in my unusual project and continued to mentor me well after my graduation. Thank you for the intellectual rigor and clarity that you brought to our discussions and for giving me a sociological imagination. Aat, you introduced me to many of the people and ideas that formed the basis of my original research and analysis. I will be forever grateful.

Many thanks to the editorial team at Columbia University Press, especially Eric Schwartz, Alyssa Napier, and Elliott Cairns, along with KGL's project manager Ben Kolstad and copyeditor Kara Cowan, as well as the anonymous reviewers who took the time to engage with my work.

Ideas grow in communities. I am grateful for the vibrant doctoral cohort that I was a part of at the Australian National University and for my research collaborators and faculty colleagues. Particular gratitude goes to those colleagues who read drafts or suggested resources and lines of inquiry, including Jan Hayes, Stephanie Kizimchuk, Katie Ley, and Kim Williamson. Thanks also to the Australian National University and the University of Canberra for their support during the preparation of the manuscript.

Most of all, thank you to my family and friends for all your support, patience, and encouragement. A special mention goes to Alex, Caroline, David, Debra, Emily, Genevieve, Juliette, Lisa, Paul and Robert. Some of you were instrumental in my access to the field, others have been sounding boards, and all of you have offered inspiration regarding the folk methods for the cultivation of the sensed unconscious. Without you, this wouldn't have been possible.

Last, a very big thank you to the people who participated in this research. I am indebted to you for generously sharing your experiences and expertise with me.

LEARNING
TO HEAR

INTRODUCTION

We typically experience our senses as passive windows on the world, not as sense-abilities that we are constantly creating. We open our eyes, and the world is there to be seen. Sound seems just to come in, independent of our volition. If we think about it, we know that our food preferences are inherited as we grow up in particular regions and families and that we "acquire" tastes. Still, when we eat, the taste seems to come from the food, not from our own backgrounds or choices. Something similar can be said for movement. As we walk about, we can attend to a conversation we are having, taking for granted that, without our attention, the ground will continue to stabilize our steps.

When things go wrong, as when the next step is not "there" as we descend a staircase, we turn to how we were using a pattern of sensation. We are craft practitioners of our senses. Each of us develops techniques of personal control, some idiosyncratic, some commonly used. Like when you do not want to taste what you are nevertheless determined to eat, you may block your nose or swallow mouthfuls whole. If you want to enjoy a fragrant smell as you enter your home, you might plant roses along the entryway. If you need to improve your vision, you can see an optometrist, get a lens prescription filled, clean your glasses, and keep them where you can find them easily. You might also sometimes choose not to see; perhaps you wear an eye mask to help you get to sleep on a plane. We readily recognize that if we want to play tennis or ride a bike, we may have to do a lot of work to build the necessary patterns of movement, some of it painful or awkward.[1]

Although we routinely experience our senses as passive, as members of communities we learn they are not. Communities pick up, share, and to varying extent give force to propriety and tricks in constructing the senses. Let's say you are shorter than others but still want to look down on people. Gang culture can show you how to do that: tilt your head back so that, when meeting the gaze of others, you will be casting your eyes down.[2] Or let's say you want to become an archaeologist. Your professors will provide you with a standardized schema for classifying dirt and help you to identify archaeological features by tracing the ground with you.[3]

We develop our sense-abilities via a great variety of communal aids. Family elders shape vision, as when parents encourage their children to make eye contact with others in the opening phases of an interaction[4] or not to stare at those who are different from them.[5] Protocols in some arenas govern when to look at others directly and when to avert one's gaze. For instance, handbooks of traditional manners detail norms like holding eye contact throughout a conversation, which can be useful in avoiding a social faux pas in formal situations such as meeting royalty.[6] Vision is also shaped by larger institutional forces. When they go to urinals, men know they need to practice civil inattention by directing their gazes to the wall rather than to the men standing beside them.[7] To make it natural to divert one's gaze in this setting, architects design partitions, and posters may be placed strategically to capture people's attention, so that individuals do not need to make a special effort.

This collective shaping is not limited to vision. Touch must not "just happen." Strict social rules dictate who can touch whom, when, where, and how. Through training and sharing practices, occupational cultures teach us how to touch others in a way that is cognitively effective but does not convey personal feelings. For example, police officers and security guards learn how to conduct body searches that allow them to discover concealed weapons effectively but in an entirely nonsexual way.[8] And physicians and nurses follow a script of sorts and use props to construct touch as medical, a practice that is especially necessary in cases such as vaginal examinations.[9]

The cultivation of touch is not limited to learning social rules and norms. Medical practitioners, for example, develop tactile knowledge to visualize what they cannot see. Learning the feel of body parts is a necessary part of medical training.[10] Where patients need to self-examine, clinicians adopt various strategies to help them navigate their bodies, for example, by providing explicit guidance and feedback and by referring to clock positions.[11] Other professions teach newcomers methods for interrogating material, as in the case of the palpation of cheese practiced by cheese connoisseurs.[12]

Our body positions and patterns of movement are also a collective accomplishment. Teachers of capoeira do not assume that students already know how to move their bodies in ways that are at once acrobatic, aesthetically pleasing as dance, and powerful in fighting. Teachers break down the rocking steps and kicks so that students can imitate their body positions.[13] In many activities, people become adept by learning to turn to their kinesthetic organizing aided by instruments offered by teachers. For example, rifle instructors put a dime on a rifle barrel to help students gauge their steadiness when shooting.[14] Ballet teachers direct dancers' attention to the studio mirrors to bring self-consciousness to their movements.[15]

We cannot help but experience our sense perceptions as natural and automatic. They seem to just happen to us. Yet we also know that we can change them. We are ingenious in the idiosyncratic ways we improve our sense-abilities, through the "tricks" we pass on to others, through the communal legacy of sense-aiding devices that we unselfconsciously appropriate, and, at the most formalized level through the pedagogies that we develop. This book is dedicated to opening a field of study into the dialectic of our actively and communally engendered but passively experienced sense-abilities.

Hearing, which is the focus of the original studies reported in the following chapters, usually strikes us as an especially passive sensory process. We open our eyes, but we do not open our ears.[16] We carefully choose what we will taste, but we can feel "bombarded" by sounds in our environments.[17] We have even created the word *eavesdropping* to avoid taking personal responsibility for listening in on others' conversations.[18] Touch, sometimes referred to as the haptic sense, seems to be more within our control, yet sound waves touch us without our consent.[19] We think of hearing as something done *to* us, except in specific situations in which we have more control, like turning off the radio to hear the person we are talking to or moving closer to hear someone who is speaking softly. It is the *object* of our hearing, rather than the experience of hearing itself, that takes our attention, such as whether we like a song that we hear, or the meaning of what is said in spoken communication.[20]

But hearing, too, is done; it is not just passively experienced. When we think about it, some of the active aspects of hearing are obvious, such as when we listen for wildlife or traffic or when we pay attention to the sounds we use to time our social lives.[21] While not used as commonly as glasses, devices like hearing aids and cochlear implants are used by many to improve their hearing.[22] Other devices reduce what is heard, as when workers exposed to hazardous levels of noise protect their hearing with earplugs or earmuffs.[23] Many in the general public also use noise-canceling headphones to block out ambient noise.

We hear in different ways and for different purposes. Listeners use music to adjust their physical and affective states, whether to motivate themselves at the gym or set the right mood in intimate moments.[24] Some music lovers and audiophiles talk about hearing music with varying acuity.[25] And when watching a film or television show in which the actors speak in our native language but in an unfamiliar accent, we often need a few moments to "tune in."

As with our other senses, hearing is a collective accomplishment. Observing novices reveals how expert knowledge underpins the operation of seasoned members of a vocation or profession. When newcomers join a group, they often interpret the skills of seasoned members as nearly magical. But magicians have their tricks, and those tricks can be taught to novices.

Novices need pathways to build knowledge, in the form of either access to formal education, or through social relationships that allow for mentorship and entry into traditions. While this book describes how this is done in certain fields, the larger implication of this work is that, beyond prejudices and barriers to entry based irrationally on personal attributes, overcoming the social distance between insiders and outsiders requires access to the collectively supported ways that seemingly natural sense-abilities are cultivated to competency. Too often, special abilities, such as moving and hearing as musicians do, are glossed over as a matter of "talent." Yet musicality is not so much genetic as a result of the socially available resources that children have at their disposal.[26] I hope that the studies presented in this book will show you that the same can be said for any form of embodied competency.

FOUR STUDIES OF HEARING

I have picked four social fields to study how competent and creative hearing is achieved collectively. These studies take us into very different contexts: the practices of medical doctors, musicians, outdoor adventurers, and Morse code operators. Hearing is crucial to competent practice in these cases, sometimes in surprising ways.

Of the four cases, the need for special skills in hearing is most obvious in the case of the musicians. Players, composers, conductors, and teachers all deal in the production and manipulation of sound. Yet hearing does not happen in the temporal direction that outsiders might assume. When audience members watch a performance or listen to a recording, they hear the end point of the musical action. Nonplayers may then understandably assume that this is the same for players; that is, that to make music, players hear the sound they have produced. In fact, what players need to do is "hear" the music that *will* sound if they play their instruments in one way or another. And conductors need to anticipate the sound that ensemble players *will* produce based on their conductorial gestures. Players and conductors alike partially disattend (i.e., turn their attention away from) the music that *has been* played to orient themselves toward how they need to organize their bodies to make the music they *will* play.

Music lovers sometimes like to play down their connoisseurship in deference to the superior perspective of the musicians they love. What those elite players do onstage is special, and by extension we might think that their ways of hearing overshadow that of the audience. However, it is the audience who judges the quality of the music that players produce.[27] This is perhaps expected in the case of professional connoisseurs like music critics, competition judges, or student examiners,[28] but players and their conductors must consider the perspective of the audience irrespective of their level of expertise. The trouble for players here is that, for many reasons, their experience of the sound they produce differs from what the audience hears. They cannot rely on what they hear as they sing or play their instrument to perfect what the audience will hear and so need other strategies to improve the sound that their audiences will experience.

In a medical consultation, we readily acknowledge that doctors do not hear as patients do. However, the displayed aspects of medical hearing obscure the strategies involved in doctors' hearing of patients' bodies. In auscultation (listening to bodily sounds using a stethoscope), the technology itself attracts much of the focus as if it is the application of a stethoscope to a body that makes intelligible what lies beneath the skin. But the sounds are not simply there for registration. To hear the body effectively, doctors and patients must collaborate in the animation of the sounds.[29] In this context, the sounds also lack an absolute meaning. Laypeople likely think of the formation of a diagnosis as the identification of cues—a heart sound, a breath sound—each signifying something specific to trained clinicians. But this is often not the case. The sounds produced depend on each patient's unique physiology. The same sound may also have various meanings depending on the patient's age and state of health. Doctors do not listen for a single definitive sound that tells them what they need to know.

Other reference points that laypeople have for medical practice are the many dramas and comedies set in hospitals or general practice that grace our screens. Whether set in an idyllic British hamlet, as in the television program *Doc Martin*, or an American metropolitan teaching hospital, as in the program *Grey's Anatomy*, the prerogatives of film and television make medical and surgical practice seem like one emergency after another. Some of a doctor's activities have the character of "action,"[30] as in difficult phases of surgeries in which a pause or delay may be fatally consequential. But doctors usually have the option to pause interactions with patients to focus on their hearing, as they do when they use a stethoscope in a clinical exam. They can stop and try to "replay" a sign they think they may have heard, as when they ask a patient to breathe deeply several times. Where musicians are plagued by the problem of time, doctors are less so, which allows for a fundamentally different approach to hearing: one in which the sound itself is the subject of interrogation.

The practices of Morse code operators raise further questions about how competent hearing is developed. Operators must translate a heard code into a typed message. What is most intriguing about this is that they are not listening to what you might think they are listening to. In film and television, Morse is typically transmitted by tapping on an inanimate object or through Morse systems that use an oscillator that emits beeps for each signal. When Morse systems were in common use, most operators used a device called a sounder that emits a click at the beginning and end of each signal that forms part of a character. Operators are thus challenged with reading the silence between the two clicks. They do not listen to sound; they learn to measure *silence*.

Thinking about the case of Morse code also reminds us that hearing needs frequent reinvention. Sets of social and technological circumstances give rise to new forms of aural competency, with strategies and aids emerging to meet these forms of competency over time. Cultivating hearing to send and receive Morse code followed the invention of this technology. In fact, the inventors did not anticipate that operators would hear the code being transmitted. Messages came through on paper tape via a machine that made small indentations for each signal, and it was expected that operators would translate those indentations into alphanumeric characters. It was later discovered that operators could hear messages as they were being transmitted by the clicks of the receiver, rendering the paper tape redundant. Thus, the inventors needed to develop training programs and tools to cultivate operators' abilities to interpret the aural signals. Morse was later superseded by other means of communication. But interestingly, it was first superseded by systems that could transmit Morse code at high speed using paper tape rather than relying on human operators.

Each case expands on what we consider hearing to mean and what purpose it serves. The case of adventurers is no different. *Adventurer* is the preferred term for people who practice mountaineering, rock climbing, bushwalking, cross-country skiing, canyoning, and other similar activities. The notion of cultivating listening for adventure seems at odds with the fundamental premise of the activity. Adventure brings to mind speed, bravado, risk, and an inward orientation to what a person can achieve—against the odds. But adventurers say that it is listening that is critical, meaning turning to the environment as a ground for action, including and beyond what the ear offers. Listening is a call to pause. Speed and bravado are the kind of hubris that get people killed.

As I learned about the craft of hearing in these four social and material contexts, I came to realize that there are some commonalities in aids and learning experiences. These include the need for teachers to bring consciousness to and reshape hearing through strategies as varied as abstract analogy, reference to (folk) theoretical knowledge, tools that help a person to perceive themselves as others do, imitation and other approaches that involve working off another's body, exercises that focus on a mini-process, and, conversely, efforts to communicate a "part" by attending to a longer sequence and by exploiting sensory intertwining. The four studies also demonstrate that hearing is considerably more varied than we often assume and extends far beyond what happens in the ear.

SOME KEY CONCEPTS

We are practiced at thinking of the senses as being connected to isolated body parts. In the West, we commonly acknowledge five senses: seeing with our eyes, hearing with our ears, smelling with our nose, tasting with our tongue, and touching with our hands and other body parts. Sometimes we remember a sixth sense, proprioception: our sense of body position and self-movement.[31] Physiologically, *proprioception* refers to the information that comes from the mechanoreceptors located in places like our muscles, joints, and skin that respond to internal and external stimuli, sending neural signals to the brain.[32] We often forget proprioception because it is mostly relegated to our unconscious. It is our sense of proprioception that ensures that we climb stairs without missteps, but so long as our steps are well placed, we have no sense of our body position from within.

While there are instances when we can isolate our senses to a degree, as when a clinician closes their eyes when auscultating or when we listen to music in the dark, our perceptual experience is mostly synesthetic. In cognitive neuroscience, *synesthesia* refers to a rare abnormal or clinical condition in which people experience cross-modal sense associations, such as grapheme-color synesthesia in which seeing letters or numbers elicits sensation of color.[33] A grapheme-color synesthete may experience colored photisms or overlays or see the associated color in their mind's eye.[34] The interest for cognitive neuroscientists here is how the experiences of synesthetes instruct on sensory processing in the normally functioning brain.[35]

These experiences are distinct from those expressed in the accounts of artists, especially in the nineteenth and early twentieth centuries, which suggest synesthetic experience but are likely more metaphorical in their meaning. For instance, the composers Alexander Scriabin and Nikolai Rimsky-Korsakov both claimed that musical pitches related to specific colors, yet their accounts are inconsistent with those of synesthetes.[36]

My use of *synesthesia* is neither clinical nor metaphorical. Following Maurice Merleau-Ponty, I use the term to refer to sensory intertwining as a common, even basic, aspect of the human perceptual experience. Merleau-Ponty outlined examples of synesthesia in which seeing an object triggered a tactile and aural awareness of its material properties. One such example concerned a perceptual encounter with glass: "One sees the hardness and brittleness of glass, and when, with a tinkling sound, it breaks, this sound is conveyed by the visible glass."[37] Synesthesia can prepare the body for action, as when it triggers caution in handling a fragile object. Seeing and simultaneously knowing an object in terms of its materiality constitutes a "quasi-sensory experience" with sensory stimuli engaged via one modality conjuring another.[38]

Synesthesia is not simply a matter of one sense experience conjuring another, as in relation to the example of seeing, touching, and hearing glass. To see an object better, we move toward it or bring it closer to us with our hands and arms. We sense through our active exploration.[39] Imagine you are a watchmaker trying to see almost imperceptibly small units of measurement to check for the placement of a component in the mechanism. You see that this will require you to manipulate the tweezers you are using to grasp the component, meaning that you are effectively seeing with your fingers.[40] Or let's say you are a working musician playing in an ensemble. You will need to rely on your gaze to coordinate your playing with that of the other musicians, in effect hearing with your eyes.[41] Such sensory intertwining is evident in tasting, which involves not only what we see and smell of our food but also how we manipulate our bodies to construct the perfect bite, even manually crushing the food with our fingers to combine flavors.[42]

My focus on hearing is not meant to close off or bracket the synesthetic nature of perception. I will show that cultivating one's hearing involves deliberately exploiting sensory intertwining. Proprioception is essential in work on the transformation of hearing because it provides pathways into the production of sound, what we might think of as a kind of "pre-hearing." Practitioners know what sound they will make based on their awareness of their bodily organizing. Armed with this knowledge, they can *change* the sound that they produce. This knowledge can also be recruited as a technique of learning by bootstrapping hearing to audible movements.

One final note on language. Studies of audition often use the language of listening as opposed to hearing. *Listening* is typically understood as the active use of the sense, meaning to give one's attention to a sound. *Hearing* typically implies the passive "detached registration and classification of phenomena"[43] or the physiological capacity to perceive sounds.[44] Theodor Adorno talked about the "musical expert" who listens actively as distinct from the "ear of the layman."[45] Hearing is thus often understood as a somehow innate or pre-social reality, in comparison to listening which is cultivated and done.

My preference is for the language of hearing because it is a reminder that we are talking about work done by and cultivated at the level of bodies with the resulting knowledge typically residing in our unconscious. It also serves as a challenge to the idea that aspects of our embodied selves are untouched by culture. That said, I use the term *listening* where it makes sense in the flow of the English language; that is, where I am describing a conscious practice like listening to traffic. I also use the language of listening as my interlocutors did. In these cases, listening does not have a single meaning. People may use it to refer to aural perception generically, to imply something more active, or even to refer to a synesthetic mode of attending.

HOW I DEVELOPED MY CASE STUDIES

I collected my data in Australia and New Zealand from 2008 to 2012 when I was a doctoral student. I came into my doctoral work interested in the perception of music. I am a classically trained pianist, so my orientation toward music has long had this embodied understanding as a backdrop. I cannot play by ear, but I trained for around twenty years to hear music analytically in terms of its tonality, timbre, instrumentation, harmonic structure, and form, as well as to attend to my own sound when playing as a ground to adjust my movements. Engaging with music in these ways does not come naturally and is not the result of some special gift that I have but is the product of sustained effort under the guidance of teachers at the conservatory where I trained.

As a counterpoint to this classical education, in my late teens, friends introduced me to metal. These forms of music are customarily conceived of as being at opposite ends of a taste continuum. The combination of playing classical piano and listening to metal in my spare time often raised eyebrows, especially those of people in my life involved in my classical education. People on the classical side regularly asked how I could find enjoyment in metal with my "highly skilled ears," the inference being that I should know better.

What intrigued me about this question was the attention that it drew to the acquired aspect of the ear. I could not shake the feeling that it was not only a matter of taste, that the people who asked me to explain my musical preferences were not hearing the music in the same way that I was. While it lacks the institutional prestige of the conservatory, metal can nonetheless be technically sophisticated.[46] Metal fans also do not typically experience their music as noise.[47] In talking with friends about various metal bands, I realized that they were not hearing the music in the same way that I was either given that I was able to apply my analytical resources from my classical training.

This hearing conundrum seemed to me to be a case of different ways of perceiving. As an undergraduate student I had read histories of the body and philosophies of embodiment, including those by Norbert Elias on the civilizing process, Marcel Mauss on techniques of the body, Pierre Bourdieu on habitus, Michel Foucault on disciplining and repressive institutions, Erving Goffman on self-presentation, and Judith Butler on performativity.[48] Among my reading in feminist philosophy, I came across Iris Marion Young and Elizabeth Grosz, and through them I found my way to Merleau-Ponty.[49] I became familiar with early contributions to sensory studies through Alain Corbin's writing on odor and Elaine Scarry's work on bodies in pain.[50] Each of these traditions of thought has its own concerns, yet all point to the cultivation of bodies and sensation.

My interest in the cultivation of hearing presented the challenge of how to investigate those mostly unconscious aspects of our perception and led me toward a graduate program in sociology. I needed to find methods to reach inside the bodies of my interlocutors to understand what and how they were hearing. My goal was not to provide a portrait of people involved in music-making or subcultures and what a form of music "means" to them. I was instead chasing something more in the comparative analytic genre of ethnography in which the focus is on situations and the tactics people develop to navigate them.[51]

Early on I became aware that I would have trouble investigating hearing musically. My musical background was advantageous in that I had a working knowledge of music-making in the classical tradition and some methods of cultivating hearing in conservatory environments. However, as our perceptual experience typically sits in our unconscious, my background was also a barrier to talking about and analyzing this form of embodied competency. Unlike the sociologist David Sudnow, who was learning the piano when he was writing about it, I was not in the early stages of taking up my instrument where it is easy to see things as strange.[52] The musicians I eventually met were also aware that I played, so we went deeply into some aspects as is possible with other insiders, and we skipped over some others. In those moments, no one in the room thought that some happening was remarkable enough to ask, "What's going on here?"

This personal challenge led to a self-reflective search for novel contexts in which to study hearing. I was looking for contrast in terms of the place and function of hearing, as well as in the learning strategies that I expected I might find. I quickly settled on the study of hearing medically. Doctors are trained in clinical skills, which include attention to the sounds that bodies make, with and without tools like the stethoscope. This sensory work has been a mainstay of medical training with textbooks detailing sensory cues of disease since the nineteenth century.[53]

I anticipated some productive contrasts to the case of hearing in music-making given that the nature of the activity is overtly different from that of doctors. In music-making, the musician is generating the sound and indeed almost endlessly refining its production. Doctors interrogate the sounds generated by patients' bodies and machines, which can include efforts to elicit the sounds and the use of devices to aid hearing. The institutions and techniques for cultivating hearing also differ. Many people who learn an instrument take private lessons with a teacher and become involved in ensemble playing. The medical field relies on universities and hierarchies of professional supervision.

Practically, I had an entry into this field of activity through family connections, so as a second case study, it felt doable.

Two cases quickly became three. In a previous life, one of my doctoral supervisors, Aat Vervoorn, was a professional mountaineering guide known for climbing Mount Cook in New Zealand. In our meetings, I would talk about hearing in music and what I was learning about hearing medically, and he would reflect on how that related to the domain he knew well. Aat talked about how mountaineering involves a process of tuning in to the surroundings, how above the snowline silence dominates making those sounds that do occur more acute, and how the silence takes some getting used to. These conversations showed further productive contrasts. Hearing in outdoor adventuring is considerably more informal than in music-making and medical practice. Further, adventurers do not routinely seek to elicit sounds as do doctors or to produce them as do musicians. They take what they hear in their environment as part of a synesthetic experience.

The fourth case was the product of happenstance. About a year into the project, I met some Morse operators while on a holiday. Making my way down the Great Ocean Road in Victoria, I came upon Cape Otway Lightstation, mainland Australia's oldest surviving lighthouse. That day, Cape Otway was celebrating International Lighthouse Day, and the site was teeming with volunteers eager to share their passion for the technologies and practices used during the lighthouse's history. Among the volunteers were two Morse operators, Albert and Alan, who were staffing the Cape's old telegraph station and sharing their stories with an audience of visitors. While the Morse lines were decommissioned, at the time around eighty operators from across Australia maintained Morse equipment in their homes to communicate with one another and volunteered in museums and historical sites to demonstrate Morse. I was particularly taken by Alan's description of how he developed his aural skills, so I mentioned the connection with my work.

Alan produced his business card, suggesting we could talk further. He also passed on the details of my research within his Morse networks, resulting in a list of operators keen to speak with me. As context for their enthusiasm, the group had a collective pride in their unique way of hearing and, in equal measure, a fear that this knowledge would soon die out. They wanted their special skills to be remembered, and they hoped that I would help capture their oral history while investigating my research questions. The case of Morse code differed from the others in some interesting ways. Morse operators produce sound in sending as do musicians, but the measure of excellence is not aesthetic. Their learning methods are concentrated on drills and exams.

My methods evolved alongside the four cases, but the general principle was to find ways of talking about the specific challenges and tactics for doing hearing in each context. My initial instinct was toward observation, but early attempts progressed less than fruitfully. The trouble was that in naturally occurring settings, people typically do not commentate on how they are experiencing and interpreting a situation.[54] In observational methods, field notes often tell more about what the researcher sees or hears, their own veils, rather than what others see or hear. Having an insider view as a researcher is equally problematic as their work may demonstrate more of what they have come to understand about the topic than others' experience of it.

One response to this challenge is the go-along method—part "hang out," part targeted discussion—which allows the researcher to "witness in situ the filtering and shaping of their subjects' perceptions."[55] I adopted a version of this approach, chatting with musicians around rehearsals and either side of their teaching activities. I spoke with physicians and surgeons in their consulting rooms and in hospitals. I met the Morsecodians at various historical reenactment sites, at telecommunications museums, and sometimes at their homes, which were filled with personal collections of equipment, allowing our conversations to involve demonstrations. Especially in New Zealand, the adventurers I met were often keen to take me places, resulting in a kind of interview on the move.

Our conversations were not only about a particular technique for working on hearing that they had experienced as students or one they used now as teachers. I was after the whole story: from student days to the skill refinement that continues to happen, even for practitioners who have been at it for forty years. It is not a single lesson or pedagogical device that leads to excellence. It is achieved over a long temporal scale, provided that students are committed to taking what they can from the help others provide. Speaking with experienced practitioners in each of the domains I was investigating also revealed how work on hearing reaches into professional practice. Their understanding builds from case to case, gig to gig, shift to shift, and one trip to the next.[56]

I took on a novice role where this made sense. At times, the unconscious aspects of our experience are more accessible. Practice phases have the space for dwelling in the body.[57] The physicians and surgeons I talked with typically treated me as a medical student who needed clinical skills demonstrated, which involved short role plays in which I was either the patient or the clinician conducting an exam. The adventurers treated me as a novice, too, pointing out features in the environment as we traveled so I might become attentive to the cues. A couple of the Morse operators encouraged me to work the key, but for the most part they were under no illusions about my ability to build competency in Morse.

In the following chapters, I address hearing in each field of activity. Each chapter describes various dilemmas that people confront in achieving competent hearing and the solutions that are collectively provided. Chapter 1 examines doctors' hearing and describes strategies to develop hearing that are used in medical schools and throughout clinicians' careers. Chapter 2 addresses the frameworks used to cultivate musical hearing. Chapter 3 addresses the adventurers and explains that narrative and embodied strategies for cultivating hearing in this context are necessarily intertwined. In chapter 4, the case of Morse code takes us back in time to early twentieth-century pedagogical approaches and work domains. In these discussions, the names that I give people are pseudonyms. I stick to the context of the research in my use of terminology, and put the word used in North America in parentheses where there is a difference.

The aim of this book is not only to offer a set of case studies of hearing but also to contribute to the appreciation of how social life is embodied more broadly. The variety of examples already used in this introduction demonstrates the scattered nature of the mass of keen observations of and insights into bodily learning that underlie occupational and nonoccupational competencies—that scattered nature is in part the warrant for this book. Ultimately, I draw my case studies back into these long-developing advances in theories of social action. My overall objective is to demonstrate that the strategies of communal support used to develop sense abilities could serve as a model for developing a better appreciation of hearing in other domains. I also hope to show that my approach could be applied equally to studies of haptic experience, our use of smell and taste, the doing of seeing, and perhaps the most foundational sense-ability, proprioception.

1

HOW DOCTORS HEAR

The saying goes that anesthetics is 95 percent boredom and 5 percent panic. Anesthetists (anesthesiologists in American English) are responsible for perioperative patient care, not only in terms of administering anesthetic but also providing pain management, monitoring patients' airways and circulation, and providing advanced life support when needed. During an operation, an anesthetized patient is connected to electronic monitoring devices, and the soundscape of the operating room is filled with a cacophony of beeps, tools clinking, blood being suctioned, the surgical team talking, and often music. The music may be anything from Mozart to The Clash. The surgeon selects it purposefully to regulate their own emotions or those of the surgical team.

Most of the time, this soundscape includes signifiers of a stable patient and the controlled progress of a given procedure. Matthew, one of the anesthetists I spent time with, told me, "These things [monitors] beat away, and they become a subliminal sound that everything is all right." Patient oxygenation is critical. Monitors emit pitched beeps that rise and fall with the amount of oxygen in the patient's bloodstream. Hearing the meaning of these beeps is a learned skill, though not one that Matthew entirely acknowledged in himself. He recalled a musically trained registrar (resident) who "could tell the actual note on the musical scale that he was listening to" and based on this know what a patient's oxygen saturation was without looking at the monitor. As if to suggest his ear was untrained, Matthew said that, not being a musician, he could tell without looking only whether a patient's oxygen saturation was above or below 90 percent or whether it had changed by 1 or 2 percent.

While Matthew framed his own hearing as less skilled than that of the musician, for an anesthetist, sensitivity to this change in sound is critical. Patients are defined as hypoxic (i.e., deprived of adequate oxygen supply) when their oxygen saturation drops below 90 percent. The ability to hear changes in the sound of the beeps of an oxygen saturation monitor is a key skill for anesthetists because such changes are one way that they are alerted to the 5 percent of cases that justify panic. "We hope that it [this skill] won't fail us because it would be dreadful to not notice that something vital has stopped," Matthew said. Noticing these changes is so important that when experienced anesthetists like Matthew work with registrars, they sometimes switch the monitors off "to test whether they notice the absence of that reliable sound." If the registrar notices, great. If not, an opportunity for growth is presented (figure 1.1).

Critically, building aural expertise in anesthetics is not achieved through methods that target musical pitch recognition. Anesthetists and other medical specialists have their own significant sounds and methods for refining their hearing. They work to develop aural skills that are defined by nonmusical measures of excellence.

Our bodies produce all sorts of diagnostically significant sounds: the heart beats audibly, and each breath brings with it the potential for various sounds according to our states of health and disease. Doctors' skillful investigation of these sounds with a stethoscope is perhaps the most recognizable form of medical hearing, although it involves ways of attending that mostly go unspoken. A cardiologist I spoke with named Samuel explained to me, "You don't just put a stethoscope on and hope that there is an answer." Bodies have unique physical

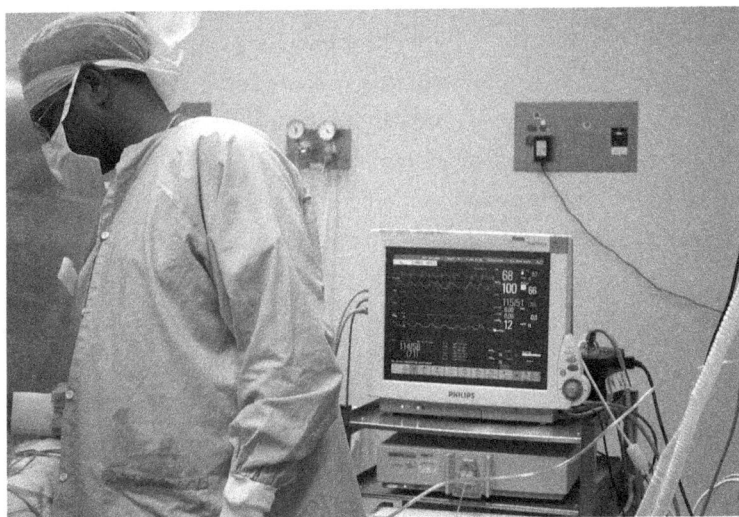

FIGURE 1.1 An anesthetist hearing monitoring devices in the operating room.

structures and conditions that affect how sounds pertinent to diagnosis manifest. Samuel said that he needs to hear "cleverly" for the opening and closing of the heart's four valves and be attentive to the volume of the sounds and their timing: "You are listening both to the gap between the first and second heart sound and [between] the second and the first. You are listening to the loudness of the first sound, especially for mitral heart disease. You're listening for the interval itself, what is called the 'split-second heart sound,' what the interval of closure is for the mitral and tricuspid valves, and the closure of the aortic and the pulmonary valves, and that can give you a hint about severity or the duration of the disease."

Regardless of the symbolic importance of the stethoscope, the difference between an experienced cardiologist's auscultatory skill and that of a novice is not the possession of this instrument. An expert's hearing like Samuel's is distinguished by how much he can make sense of patients' bodies from what he hears.

The body makes sounds without specific manipulation or without the patient's awareness that they are generating signs and symptoms. As we move, our bone structures may creak and grate when there is an abnormality such as damage to joint cartilage, producing sounds that orthopedic specialists become particularly sensitive to and pick up on without patients even noticing they are being heard. Of course, people often make sounds when they are in pain. For example, when a person is giving birth, the obstetrician will listen for cries, grunts, and silence to assess the progress of labor.[1]

For senior doctors, much aural diagnostic work happens in split-second encounters. Doctors called this the "foot-of-the-bed" or the "Hi, Doc" test. Cameron, a specialist physician and clinical skills educator, captured this process:

> The patient comes in to me with a particular problem, and as soon as he starts talking to me, I can hear the resonant voice of someone with emphysema. Immediately, while I am listening to his story, I am looking at his skin [and asking myself,] does he have the skin of a smoker? Do I see the tar staining on his fingers? Do I see a packet of cigarettes in his pocket? So within seconds I am not just listening to the resonant voice, but I am putting together a whole lot of other pieces of information that, before he has even told me, tells me that this guy is a smoker, and not only is he a smoker, but he also has emphysema.

Doctors constantly collect aural and other sensory information and refine their perceptual skills while seemingly doing other things.[2] They then use the information they glean to make care decisions for their patients. Such tacit decision-making distinguishes experts in many fields of activity.[3] However, this complex and largely hidden work is at risk of being overlooked in the design and management of health care delivery.[4]

The following analysis specifies some methods used to cultivate medical hearing, including and beyond the use of the stethoscope.

When I asked doctors about their learning, reflections such as the following from Joshua, an anesthetist, were common: "[There is] the academic side of things, but . . . I think the real way that we learn is on a one-to-one basis, with somebody actively teaching you how to do it, what to watch for, and what to listen for. At a later level, actually been left on your own and being supervised from afar . . . you then have to make your own decisions, and you have to live with them." We could stop here and say that developing medical hearing is a matter of mentoring and experience, but that would leave us without an understanding of exactly what makes up this experience doctors say they must acquire.

I asked senior doctors to reflect on the development of their medical hearing and their teaching of hearing. The fifteen doctors I met practiced in Australia and New Zealand. They practiced various specialties, which allowed me to gain insight into types of hearing beyond recognized clinical techniques such as auscultation.[5] Our conversations took place mostly in doctors' consulting rooms as part of their workday, which was a practical consideration but one that also allowed me to observe the doctors in work mode. They worked with me as if I were a medical student to illustrate the methods used to develop medical hearing. Aural knowledge was then often demonstrated to me through stories of cases and dramatizations of the patient exam.

I develop my analysis in two parts. First, I describe some devices used by clinical skills educators and clinicians who supervise and mentor learners in clinical practice to teach trainees how to hear correctly. Medical students first gain codified biomedical knowledge, which they then use as a ground to build knowledge in the body. Clinical skills educators and supervisors use onomatopoeic vocalizations and metaphors to direct and redirect students' ears to significant "sounds-within-a-sequence." They also encourage students to explore and experiment with their own bodies—rubbing their hair, pulling wet fingers apart—to simulate sounds that will later be encountered in patients' bodies.

Second, I examine the ways that doctors learn to hear through the course of their work. Once doctors start practicing, they have many patients to diagnose. As they progress, they come to identify differences patient by patient and situation by situation, simultaneously learning to use sound to support their interpretations in the moment and to refine their hearing over time. Assessing patients both clinically and via diagnostic technologies presents opportunities to extend perception where there is a difference in findings.

FOLK DEVICES USED BY CLINICAL SKILLS EDUCATORS AND SUPERVISORS TO DIRECT MEDICAL STUDENTS' HEARING

How Theory Learned in School Structures Doctors' Aural Competency

At the start of my conversations with doctors, I typically asked about their medical training in an open-ended way, and the flow of conversation tended to be predictable. They spoke about the approach their medical school took, which consistently began with preclinical studies of the human body as grounded in disciplines such as biochemistry. Their learning then progressed to clinical training at the bedside, which seemed to them much more relevant. They spoke about where they studied, the duration of their program, and their choice of specialty.

The difficulty with formally teaching hearing reflects broader challenges with mass education.[6] It is difficult to give sensorial experience to students, whether in medicine or other fields. While medical schools attempt to train through experience—at the bedside or in simulated environments—practice following formal education is essential.[7] The medical education system acknowledges this fact by requiring doctors to pursue often up to ten years of further scaffolded work under the guidance of supervisors and mentors before taking specialist exams.[8]

However, we should not dismiss medical students' early theoretical years as unimportant for medical hearing. Extrasensory medical knowledge is fundamental in structuring embodied understanding. Stories of diagnoses illustrate the many direct connections between biomedical knowledge and sounds that can be perceived. In a more pedagogical mode, clinical skills educators position the sounds of the body in the context of biomedical knowledge. A theoretical appreciation of how the body functions gives students a framework with which to hear and interpret sounds. As a neurologist named Nelson put it, "Knowing simplistically what generates the sound gives you a bit of a feel for why a sound happens."

The first doctor I met was Cameron. I told him I was interested in hearing medically, so he put his clinical skills educator hat on and explained sounds that are important in the context of biomedical knowledge, starting with those of the heart:

> The time-old description of the sound is "lub dub," which you probably would have read about or heard about, and it is a bit like that. In most normal hearts, that is all you will hear. The first heart sound is generated by the mitral and tricuspid valves closing. During systole, where the heart contracts and expels blood from the left and right ventricles, that [sound] is associated with the closing of the mitral and tricuspid valves, which stop blood flowing into the ventricles at the same time from the atria. As they close, that causes "lub," and blood is expelled from the heart. And then at the end of systole, or the contraction of the ventricles, the aortic and pulmonary valves close, and that gives the "dub." "Lub dub, lub dub." So the heart sounds are not due to blood flow; they're due to closing of the valves.

The heart is two hollow contracting muscular tubes that twist around one another forming a single organ, hence the concepts of the "left" and "right" heart. If these were just open-ended tubes, when they contracted they would push the blood within them both ways, which means blood would not be pumped around the body. To avoid this, the heart has one-way valves that keep the blood flowing in only a single direction. There are four valves in fact: two for the right (tricuspid and pulmonary) and two for the left (mitral and aortic). To complicate matters, each of the two tubes is subdivided for embryological reasons into smaller (atria) and larger (ventricle) chambers. In order, the blood moves from the large veins into the right atrium, from the right atrium, past the tricuspid valve, into the right ventricle, out the right ventricle (past the pulmonary valve) to the lungs, from the lungs into the left atrium, from the left atrium into the left ventricle, past the mitral valve, from the left ventricle around the body, and finally past the aortic valve.

The heart contractions are very forceful, and so the action of the valves closing is rather violent. As they snap shut, the sound is audible through a stethoscope. Cameron thought this was the first thing I needed to know to understand the heart, its sounds, and how the health and pathology of this organ can be perceived through hearing. He emphasized that it is the valves that make the sound, not blood flow, which is an important distinction since audible abnormalities in heart function typically relate to the valves.

As a pedagogical tool, this simple description of how blood flows through the heart performs three moves. Cameron connects a cognitive understanding of the body with its clinical indicators. The clinical indicators are articulated onomatopoeically, which provides a language to articulate the sounds.[9] This language then forms a bridge between the biomedical and the aural (and folk aural) understandings of the heart. When hearing this description, trainees can visualize the heart valves opening and closing. In a textbook, such descriptions of heart function are paired with diagrams, reinforcing this link.

Our conversation progressed to pathological heart sounds and then to lung, abdomen, and voice sounds. He articulated each set of sounds, mostly onomatopoeically, and in the context of his biomedical understanding of the body. He also offered me access to his library of textbooks because he saw me as a student and knew that engaging with them would be essential to gaining any clinical skill. In my field notes, I wrote, "I felt less like an interviewer and more like a student attending a lecture. Cameron commented that he sounded like a 'textbook,' indicating that he was conscious of the dynamic."

After this pseudo-lecture, I knew more about medical hearing: the kinds of sounds I might encounter, the reasons that these sounds occur, and the diagnostic significance of the sounds. My increased understanding suggests that this theoretical knowledge has a pedagogical function not only for a student's knowledge of health and disease but specifically for the configuration of their medical hearing. I was no more skilled at hearing the body, but I had gained a "feel" for why sounds happen, as Nelson, the neurologist, had described.

I asked the doctors how skilled they were at the end of their five- or six-year university studies. Most said not very, but many claimed to have been poor students and suggested that they may have developed stronger clinical skills if they had paid more attention. But it is unlikely that I had just happened to meet a number of poor students. Learning the theory is only a part of the picture. Bruce, an orthopedic surgeon, said that at the end of his training, he was little more than a glorified clerk. He then described a process that happens through which "you're assimilating all of that theoretical knowledge with the practical information that you pick up in the years after you finish to start to actually make the two mesh and work together." Angus, a general practitioner, described an undergraduate degree as "a license to experience. . . . It gave me some foundations, but really most of the learning has been experiential, on the job, doing things." These observations highlight the limits of the cognitive for hearing. But as we will see, the process of developing expert hearing is more complex than simply picking it up or learning experientially on the job.

Focusing on a Sound Within a Sequence: Supervisors' Use of Onomatopoeia to Direct Trainees' Ears During Rounds

Teaching at the bedside has long been a cornerstone of clinical education and the development of clinicians' communication skills.[10] During ward rounds, groups of medical students and junior doctors are taken to a patient by a consulting (attending) physician or surgeon (or by their registrar). They stand cramped around the patient's bed, observing the consultant's interaction with the patient and answering questions posed by the senior physician.

This is the first place that most doctors recognize their medical hearing developing. Rounds give medical students opportunities to examine aural clinical features such as a heart murmur or lung crackles. Developing this type of hearing is not simply a matter of exposure or experience, however. During rounds, supervisors use onomatopoeia to draw attention to signs within a sequence of sounds and to connect clinical observations to the biomedical knowledge gained by students earlier in seminars or lectures.

David, a general surgeon, completed his training in the 1960s and attributed his clinical skills to time spent on the wards. He told me that auscultation is not "an innate ability"; direction from supervisors during rounds, building on a foundation of biomedical knowledge, is critical. He reflected on learning to hear heart murmurs during his cardiac surgery rotation: "You would go along and listen to a patient, and the senior doctor would say, 'What do you hear?' And you would answer, and then he might say, 'Well, just listen a little more carefully to this part of the cycle.' And then you would say, 'Oh, yes,' or perhaps you wouldn't." At the time of David's training, rheumatic fever was common, a condition that often caused problems with patients' heart valves. He repeatedly encountered cases severe enough to warrant surgical intervention: "If you know what you are listening for, you are able to pick up much more subtle signs, and you tend to pick them up much more readily."

David's recollection implies that a student must first hear a cycle or sequence of sounds. With this foundation, the senior doctor then directs and redirects students' attention to sounds *within* the cycle that may indicate disease. In this teaching moment, a student may come to hear the heart of the patient through the hearing of the senior doctor.

Terrance, an ophthalmologist who also trained in the 1960s, recalled the tricky process of learning to hear heart murmurs. He told me that medical students need to work with doctors who are skilled at putting the right hearing within reach. One teaching method he found useful is the use of onomatopoeia by supervisors who vocalize heart sounds and link them to biomedical descriptions of heart function:

> They will say, "Listen to this," and they will mouth it [the sound] for you. They will say, "Lub-dub-bi-di-dub." They will give you verbally what they are hearing to try to encourage you to hear it. I can remember bullshitting because someone would tell you this and tell you that, and they'd say, "Can you hear it? Can you hear it?" And you'd say, "Yes," but I knew damn well I wasn't, and I don't think I was unusual. And there would be an explanation. "This is a bicuspid valve opening just before the other one" or something like that. They would say there is a mechanical reason for the sounds that you hear.

The supervisor does not say, "Hear the 'bi' of this heart murmur"; they say, "Lub-dub-bi-di-dub." They do not conceptualize or expect students to grasp the "bi" independently. When students are trained to hear using onomatopoeia, they do so by engaging the melody and rhythm that the "sounds like" phrase suggests. It is a way to understand the overall sequence of sounds, which first requires being told what the sequence is and then being taught variations within this sequence.

Onomatopoeic vocalizations are clearly useful, but students may feel the urge to lie when they cannot hear the sound their supervisor is describing. A student does not come to identify a heart murmur through a single hearing, though the interaction between learner and supervisor in the moment assumes the knowledge is immediate.[11] Counterproductively, putting pressure on learners to hear a significant sound quickly may shift emphasis from first grasping the sequence to rushing to hear an individual sound.

Because learning the sequence, its components, and its variations happens over an extended period, doctors need to adopt a reflective position throughout their careers. Nelson explained that when he works with students, he not only directs their aural attention toward examples of third and fourth heart sounds but also teaches them to take the role of the supervisor, comparing what they hear against what they anticipated:

I say there are two heart sounds, "boom boom," and they have their own cadence. And there is a third heart sound that you get, so it is "boom bo boom." And there is a fourth heart sound that is just before the first, so it is "bo boom boom." You hear something, you leave your stethoscope where it is, and [you] get them [the student] to put it in their ears [and] listen, and you tell them what it is. They may not hear it, and that is all right. And I will say what the things are for them to make it more easy for them to hear, and we find one for them to hear later. When you listen, you teach yourself to listen for the cadence. You say, "I am going to hear 'boom bo boom,'" and you listen for that, and then [you] go, "OK, it is not there." Hearing is often about what you're trying to find. You scan the frequencies listening.

Nelson has students hear through his stethoscope so that there is no question that they are listening to the same sound.[12] He vocalizes the cadence or sequence of the heart sounds. He highlights the signifier of pathology within the sequence (the "bo" before the "boom boom," which is heard as the "bo" before the first "boom" whether or not the second boom has sounded). He links the clinical indicators to established biomedical knowledge. He describes what a student is likely to hear to make the hearing easier.

Nelson suggested that this "preempting" (anticipating what may be heard) forms part of professional practice: "I am going to hear 'boom bo boom.' Do I? If not, I move to the next significant sound within the sequence that may be perceivable." In this way, what supervisors teach during rounds is a diagnostic process, a way of interrogating sounds. This mode of interrogation is intimately entwined with onomatopoeic vocalization. Doctors not only hear the "lub-dub-bi-di-dub" or the "boom bo boom." They form these rhythms themselves vocally. In this way, learning to hear medically is not only aural, but a matter of feeling your body move. It is the choreography of the body that places medical hearing within a student's grasp.

How Educators and Supervisors Use Metaphors to Highlight or Hide Aural Traits in New Sounds

With a lack of metalanguage with which to describe bodily sounds,[13] metaphors are a device that clinical skills educators and supervisors use to prime students' hearing in anticipation of their identification of diagnostically significant sounds in patients. The writings of René Laënnec, the inventor of the stethoscope, include a liberal use of metaphor to direct the ears of readers from his accounts of heart and lung conditions to their clinical indicators, which are audible through mediate auscultation. He compared a mucous rattle to "the idea of bubbles, such as are produced by blowing through a pipe into soapy water."[14] A dry rattle in the lungs, by contrast, is likened to snoring, friction on a bass string, or the cooing of a wood pigeon.[15] In the function of a normal heart, he described the first sound as "dull" and the second as "a noise resembling that of a valve, or a whip, or the lapping of a dog."[16]

But metaphors are not a matter of language alone. They are intimately intertwined with thought and action, and herein lies their value.[17] Laënnec hinted at this notion, writing, "I make use of these trivial expressions because they appear to me to convey better than any description, an idea of the nature of the sound in question."[18] Metaphors convey something of an embodied experience of a sound because they relate to experiences that are already shared. These correlations organize new experiences; in this way, metaphor has "the power to define reality."[19]

Despite technological advances and their implications for medical practice, medical students continue to be enthusiastic about learning to hear heart murmurs.[20] The process of learning to conceptualize, hear, and name murmurs is difficult, and metaphors are one strategy supervisors use to make hearing easier. Matthew the anesthetist recalled being introduced to various murmurs during rounds. A supervisor would take him to the bedside of a patient with an interesting murmur, and he would place his stethoscope on the patient's chest to hear a given feature. But learning to hear the murmur relied on more than placing his stethoscope in the right place. Matthew needed to be told *how* to hear it. One murmur he was introduced to is the "seagull murmur," a sound present in valve diseases such as aortic stenosis and mitral regurgitation[21]: "They would tell you what you were supposed to be hearing. They would say, 'This patient has what you would call a 'seagull' murmur. It is high pitched and sounds exactly like a seagull flying along in a high wind. See if you can pick it [out].' And sure enough, after some time, you could believe that it did possibly sound like a seagull. You would gradually get the terminology and listen for it another time." Metaphors provide a language with which the supervisor and student can talk about a sound.

They are particularly useful because they are based on sounds with which the student is already familiar.[22]

Curious about the role of metaphor in learning to hear the seagull murmur, I thought about the short, high-pitched chirps a seagull makes. I could not imagine that the heart could make this sound. The first time I heard a recording of a seagull murmur, I immediately noticed that there were short, higher tones above the first and second heart sounds. While I was not completely convinced that what I had heard sounded like a seagull, the metaphor helped me identify the short, high-pitched tones among the surrounding noise. The next day, I found a recording of a seagull's call and then returned to the recording of the seagull murmur. Like Matthew, on this second hearing, I was more convinced of the similarity and immediately recognized the murmur when I heard it. While the two sounds are never exactly the same, over time the perceptual experience of the seagull's call and the seagull murmur become similar.[23]

The use of metaphor to convey an aural trait is effective only when supervisor and student share a conception of a particular sound, in this case a seagull's call. While metaphors reference a more "basic" concept or sound, they are also the product of learned perceptual experience; thus, this way of building aural knowledge relates to a person's surroundings. We see the need for students to first learn the metaphorical sound in the case of learning to hear the so-called mill wheel murmur. This is a mercifully rare type of murmur that is an indicator of a life-threatening intracardiac air embolism in which the heart fills with air (or other gases) and is unable to pump blood. In Australia, mill wheels are uncommon, and Matthew had not encountered them when this murmur was presented to him by a clinical skills educator. Thus, he first needed to hear a recording of a mill wheel before hearing for the murmur in a patient. In the mill wheel murmur, the presence of air creates a churning of air and blood and can be heard as a "swooshing" or "splashing," hence the link to the sound of a mill wheel. Given the rarity of this murmur, Matthew was not exposed to

it again until after having practiced for thirty years. During an operation, the patient's condition started to deteriorate. Among his other
investigations, he auscultated the patient's heart and heard the telltale
"swooshing" and understood its significance instantly.

Synergies exist between biomedical appreciations of the body
and metaphors for hearing diagnostically significant sounds. In the
case of the mill wheel murmur, it helps that the sounds of a mill
wheel and the mill wheel murmur arise simply from the churning of
liquid and air. In the case of the fourth heart sound, we see a similar
pattern. The fourth heart sound is caused by reduced blood flow
through the coronary arteries, which affects late diastolic relaxation.
In nontechnical terms, this means that the larger chambers of the
heart are abnormally stiff, meaning the smaller chambers have to
contract more forcefully to move blood through, causing an audible
reverberation. The metaphors supervisors use to direct students'
ears to the fourth heart sound echo this biomedical understanding.
Nelson shared the following description with me, as he did with
his registrars and medical students: "If you have got a thickened-
up heart, it is like directing a hose directly against a bucket, and
it makes a 'ding' noise as it hits the wall. But if you [stick] a hose
into a balloon, it is [pliant] enough that it stretches so you don't get
the reverberation. With high blood pressure, the heart wall doesn't
stretch properly, so you get the 'donk' like a hose in a bucket rather
than a hose in a balloon."

The fourth heart sound is heard as a low frequency before the first
heart sound. While it evokes a common aural experience, it does not
sound like water from a hose hitting a bucket. The value of this metaphor is in the concepts of the stiffness of the bucket and the pliability
of the balloon, which allows for an appreciation of normal (pliable)
and pathological (stiff) heart function.

Metaphors are not just about knowing one sound and then
coming to know another through its aural similarity to the previously known sound. They also recruit other sensual modalities. The

metaphors of the mill wheel and the bucket or balloon are both visual. We can see the churning of a mill wheel, the stiffness of a bucket, and the stretchiness of a balloon. These images mirror what is happening in the body, allowing us to see a heart's stiffness, pliability, or churning as well.

Metaphors also rely on culturally situated concepts of movement. Doctors must appreciate the potential significance of a perceived sound; for example, the third heart sound can be innocent or cause for concern. Asked how he could tell whether the third heart sound was an indicator of pathology, Nelson said, "It is like the spinnaker on a yacht. . . . A young, healthy person can snap out the heart like a spinnaker. If you have had a heart attack and you have a floppy piece of heart muscle, it is like my mother's breasts: they flop down like a tennis ball in a sock. So when you listen to a person's heart that is weak, they do not look like you [young and healthy]. You might have a third heart sound because you're a great tennis player, and your heart dynamically throws it out."

This metaphorical appreciation of heart function evokes levels of fitness for medical students (the yacht or the less sporting tennis ball in a sock). The heart can move dynamically or energetically as a great tennis player might. Supervisors use this metaphor so students can transfer their sense of the sporting body's motility to their hearing of the third heart sound as normal. In contrast, the movement of the body of an older woman is treated in derogatory terms and so evokes a pattern of movement heard as pathological. These metaphors also evoke images of these bodies.

At one level, the metaphors that Nelson uses for the third and fourth heart sounds are more instructive regarding the sources of the sounds than the sounds themselves, so it would be reasonable to assume that they do not directly aid students' hearing. Nelson did not make this distinction. When he shared these metaphors with me, he gave me the impression he was describing the sounds. Until I heard recordings of them, I thought that the fourth heart sound sounded something like water from a hose hitting a bucket and that the third heart sound sounded a bit like a spinnaker catching the wind.

This discovery caused me to question whether metaphors are only another way to articulate a cognitive appreciation of heart function, which then structures understanding for the hearing of the sound that follows. While this understanding may be useful, it does not explain why such metaphors are given as descriptions of actual sounds. One explanation is that the movement they refer to is not only conceptual; a sense of movement conjured through metaphor can then translate into a hearing of movement as well. Both the third and fourth heart sounds are characterized by a rhythmic irregularity more than a difference in timbre. We can see, then, how supervisors may use metaphors to emphasize patterns of movement as prosodic cues, thus drawing trainees' attention toward this aural trait.[24]

How Educators and Supervisors Teach Students to Use Their Own Bodies to Simulate Pathological Sounds

The process of learning to hear pathologies in patients' bodies is often protracted. Medical students must encounter sounds many times before they are rendered audible, but exposure alone does not mean that sounds will be heard. In a creative response to this problem, which also has the benefit of not requiring patients, clinical skills educators and supervisors guide students to discover the sounds of their own bodies and to use their bodies to simulate diagnostically significant sounds.[25] They also refer students to aural knowledge and practices outside the medical context that work as proxies for pathological sounds and techniques for revealing them.

The doctors I spoke with recalled auscultating and percussing their own bodies as students and now encourage their students to do the same. The body should sound particular ways in particular places, and changes to those sounds draw attention to a potential problem. For example, Cameron explained to me that when someone has emphysema (a condition most often caused by smoking in which the inner walls of the air sacs in the lungs break down and rupture), the lungs expand, resulting in breath sounds and vocal tone that are "hyper-resonant" or "very hollow-sounding," rather than vesicular, or low pitched, as in normal breath sounds. While healthy lungs do not sound resonant, air moving through the trachea sounds "a bit like a resonant lung, where all the air spaces have broken down into a big cavity, and the air is moving through a large airway." By placing a stethoscope over their own tracheas, medical students can accustom themselves to the hyper-resonance heard in the lungs of a person with emphysema. Cameron says to his students, "Listen to the sound of your trachea, and if you can hear that sound in the bottom of your lung, then it could indicate emphysema." In this way, students learn to hear the sounds of one part of the body by comparing them with those in another.[26]

Other sounds can be simulated. Pulmonary edema is a condition in which an abnormal buildup of fluid develops in the alveoli (air sacs) of the lungs. The presence of this fluid means that when air moves through the alveoli, they pop open. Through a stethoscope, a doctor can hear "crackles" or "pops." These sounds are not immediately audible and understandable, as readers untrained in auscultation will be aware. Working with me as if I were a medical student, Cameron guided me to replicate a sound close to what I should hear through a stethoscope. He explained that I could generate the sound by wetting my fingers with a bit of saliva, putting them to my ear, and pulling my fingers apart. He demonstrated this for me, and as he pulled his fingers apart he said, "You hear a little popping noise as they open up like that." Through this process, Cameron directed my hearing and drew me into his aural standpoint. When I copied him, I was excited by the sound I produced and heard and felt that I had taken a step toward the right hearing.

I was taught to hear pericarditis next, a condition in which the two membrane layers that encase the heart become inflamed. For patients with pericarditis, when the heart beats, the layers "grate" against each other rather than moving without friction as would be the case with a healthy heart. As Cameron explained the normal movement of these layers, he gently rubbed his palms together. After demonstrating the normal movement and explaining the pathology biomedically, he simulated the sound of pericarditis with his own body to direct my hearing. "We call it a 'rub,'" he said while rubbing his palms together more harshly. "Not a particularly technical term, but that is the term we use. It sounds like a scratchy sort of sound." As he continued to imitate the sound with his hands, I joined in. These ways of hearing through sound simulations rely on sensory translations. As Maurice Merleau-Ponty put it, "Every perceptual habit is still a motor habit and here equally the process of grasping a meaning is performed by the body."[27]

Similarly, the sound of excessive fluid in the lungs can be simulated by rubbing one's hair. When listening to a patient's chest to assess a lung condition, Phillip, a general practitioner, is listening for the presence of fluid, either inside or outside the lungs. Does he hear normal breath sounds or crackling? If there is thick fluid like mucus or thin fluid as in pulmonary edema, he will hear crackles. He explained that you can mimic this sound by moving one's body to produce a similar sound: "If it is just extra fluid and there [are] not reduced airways, then the tissues of the lungs will stick together, so it is a bit like getting . . . hair between your wet fingers and rubbing it, and you will get a crackly sound as the surfaces come together and then come apart; there is a light crackly sound. We can hear that in the lungs when there is just a bit of excess fluid." Phillip's ability to hear crackles relied on an exploration of his own body, and he encourages his students to learn the same way. As we sat together, repeatedly wetting our fingers and rubbing our hair, I began to aurally appreciate what is meant medically by the term *crackle*.

I asked Phillip what *dull* and *resonant* sound like in the context of lung health. He said, "A dull sound is a very short sound. A resonant sound tends to start off loud and then tails off, gets quieter and quieter, over a longer period of time." To help me understand this aurally, he first used metaphor to approximate the experience. He compared the dullness or resonance aurally perceptible in the lungs to the sounds transmitted in different kinds of physical space: "If you go outside and talk to the sky, your voice will not resonate. If you go into a cathedral with brick walls and speak or clap your hands, you will get a sense of resonance because that sound will stay there for a long time after you stop talking."

On that foundation, my lesson in hearing resonance moved to an example in the body. When one percusses the abdomen, Phillip explained that it is "easy to hear the change from resonant to dull." He then tapped his torso in two places. I imitated. He asked if I could tell if the resulting sound was resonant or dull, and I was embarrassed to say that I could not. In response, he tapped his torso in a different place. "That one is dull," he told me, and I could hear the difference. Only after hearing the comparison could I distinguish between dull and resonant.

Students are also guided to experiment with inanimate objects or draw on established aural, embodied knowledge of such objects. The practice of tapping on a water tank in several locations vertically to establish the water level is commonly referred to in the context of percussing the chest. In percussion, the doctor's nondominant hand is placed against the chest wall, and with the index and middle fingers of the dominant hand, the doctor taps in a hammer-like fashion against the hand placed on the chest wall to produce (and feel) the sound of a water tank.

Nelson was trying to teach me to auscultate the lungs. He started by asking, "Have you ever tapped on a water tank?" I had, so he continued that hearing the lungs involves percussing the chest to feel and hear the sound produced. He explained, "When someone has a dense effusion [a buildup of fluid in the pleural cavity, the space separating the lungs from the surrounding structures], it is really easy. It really is 'hollow, hollow, hollow, bomp!' A big change." In this context, it is a *change* in sound that matters.

HOW DOCTORS REFINE THEIR HEARING FROM ONE CASE TO THE NEXT

"Hear That Change?" How Supervisors and Patients Guide Hearing During Medical Procedures

The medical education model is such that medical students consult with patients and perform medical procedures under supervision. In this context, supervisors continue to play a role in guiding their students' clinical hearing well into the doing of medical and surgical work.

Bruce, the orthopedic surgeon, told me that learning to perform a surgical procedure like a knee replacement involves learning the sounds of the tools used as they pass through different types of tissue. Missing these aural cues can cause a lot of damage, particularly to nerves and blood vessels. He explained, "When you drill a hole to put a screw in, you can actually hear the pitch change as you're drilling through the bone. And just before the drill is about to emerge from the end of the bone, the sound changes." The same is true with cutting through bone with a blade, when "you can hear the pitch change just before you get to the end." In both cases, the change in sound tells Bruce that "you have to back off; otherwise, you're going to cut other stuff apart from the bone" (figure 1.2).

A senior surgeon supervising an orthopedic registrar must draw attention to these types of sounds and their meaning to both prevent errors and shape the registrar's hearing.[28] Bruce recalled that the surgeons he worked with early in his career would often say to

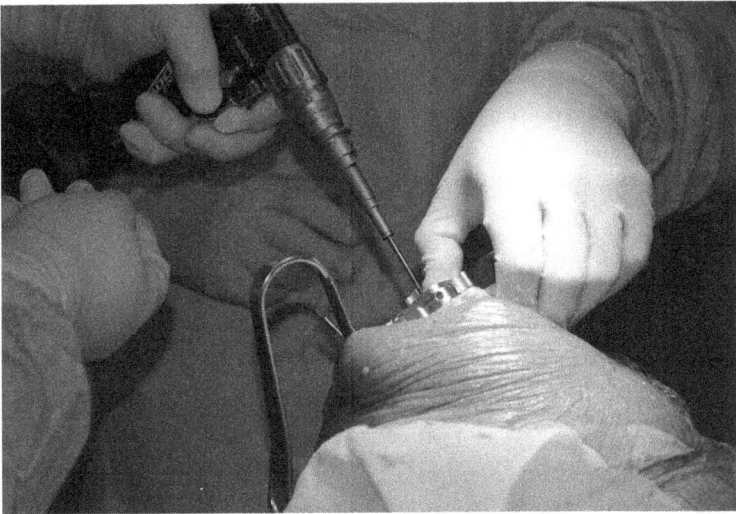

FIGURE 1.2 Two sets of hands and ears are involved when operating the drill during a knee replacement surgery.

him, "Listen for that auditory cue." Now he is a supervising surgeon. He explained that when he works with his registrars in the operating room, "I will say, 'Listen for this drill; you can hear it coming through. Listen, listen, listen—hear that change?' . . . And they will go, 'Ah!' That way, they can be careful the next time around. Hopefully they only plunge through three or four times before they work out exactly what they're doing. That is the way we all learn." The senior surgeon provides a running commentary throughout the operation. In a registrar's first few surgeries, Bruce, as the supervisor and the surgeon ultimately responsible for the surgical outcome, does the important hearing on behalf of his registrar to ensure the procedure progresses safely. By directing the registrar's aural attention to what he hears, he shapes his registrar's hearing as a replica of his own.

The development of students' perception relies on their supervisors pointing out the transitions from one sound to another, but this is not only a matter of aural contrast. Hearing the change in the sound of a drill or blade moving through bone also involves moving and feeling throughout the surgery. Bone comprises two types of tissue, each with its own density. A drill passes more slowly through cortical bone, the hard outer layer. When it reaches cancellous bone, the inner layer, which is softer and spongy, a drill moves faster because there is less resistance.

Attending to changes in sound also happens in conversations with patients. Robert, a general surgeon, explained that the quality of the patient's voice can be pivotal diagnostic evidence; as such, the patient can be called on to guide the doctor's hearing of "normal" vocal tone. He described the case of a patient with a condition affecting the thyroid gland. The thyroid is situated in the throat, with a lobe on either side of the windpipe. Thyroid cancer can paralyze the vocal cords because of the proximity of the gland to the vocal cords, resulting in a hoarse voice. As Robert had specialized in this area, he was attentive to this vocal quality when taking a patient's history.

Unlike with heart sounds, the diagnostic significance of vocal quality is not typically addressed by clinical skills educators and supervisors. Building an aural appreciation of vocal tone happens "on the job." Robert explained that a hoarse voice is distinguishable from a normal vocal tone through aural contrast. As it is the change in vocal tone that is critical in diagnosing thyroid cancer, he cannot form an aural judgment of voice disturbance independent of the patient's aural knowledge of their voice. He must ask his patients if they have noticed a change in their voice. He explained, "Suppose you saw the person beforehand and spoke to them, and then [you] speak to them after and think there is a change. You ask them, 'Is that quite right?' And they say, 'No, it doesn't feel quite right.'" The patient's aural knowledge thus directs Robert's hearing of normal and abnormal sounds and contributes to his decision of whether to send the patient for further tests.

How Doctors Exploit Synesthesia to Hear Normal and Pathological Sounds in Patients' Bodies

Most of the doctors I interviewed talked about the importance of coming to appreciate "normal" first. David, the general surgeon discussed earlier, told me that learning to hear normal sounds gives medical students "a basis to work upon." Patrick, an gynecologist/obstetrician, told me that "you have to have a yardstick" to assess health and disease, and learning what normal sounds like delivers this. But health and pathology are not absolute categories. Physiological diversity means that performing diagnostic work requires doctors to engage with signifiers of various conditions as they manifest in different bodies.[29] The embodied knowledge required for diagnosis is an ongoing project that doctors engage in with each new patient, attentive to aural contrast and other cues.

When Phillip places his stethoscope on a patient's chest, he hears for the different ways that air moves in and out of their lungs. In the case of a pneumothorax (a condition in which air leaks into the pleural space, causing the lung to collapse, commonly known as a collapsed lung), the unaffected lung will produce normal breath sounds, and the affected lung will be much quieter. In a normal chest, the lungs are stuck to the chest wall, and when auscultated, a doctor will hear air quietly moving in and out of the airways. In contrast, when a patient has a pneumothorax, "There is an airspace between the lung and the chest wall, a completely hollow space, and there is not much transmission through that, and that is going to be even quieter still, so you get very low or very quiet breath sounds on that side."

Hearing comparatively supports Phillip's diagnosis of a pneumothorax when the lung sounds are abnormally quiet on one side. He explained, "Those are the kinds of sounds we're looking for . . . you take the breath sound as the basis for comparing one lung with the other." Each diagnosis requires hearing the relative character of sounds in a patient's body, which is achieved partly through contrasting hearings.[30]

In Phillip's chest examinations, he also percusses the chest wall at different points to hear the nature of the tissue that lies beneath. The relative character of what he hears informs his diagnosis: "When you tap on the chest wall like that [he demonstrates by tapping on the table with two fingers six times], on the normal side you will get normal, resonant transmission. On the other side, you will get a really loud, resonant transmission because there is a bigger empty air space there." He can both hear and feel resonance by asking the patient to say "ninety-nine" while his palms are positioned on the chest wall: "On the normal side, the sound gets transmitted best through solid or liquid, so you will get some sound transmission with some resonance because there is both air and lung tissue there. On the side where the lung has collapsed, you'll probably get very little transmission of the 'ninety-nine'; it will be diminished because there is only the air, not the solid, to carry it through."

Sounds must ultimately be elicited, so hearing through contrast is also a matter of moving and feeling and so in this way his hearing is synesthetic. Phillip comes to hear by moving his body to percuss and palpate the patient's chest. Aware of the embodied nature of the sounds themselves, he manipulates what he can perceive by asking patients to move their bodies. His hearing relies on patients performing specific actions to animate signs that would otherwise be imperceptible.[31]

Bruce, the orthopedic surgeon, is particularly sensitive to the sounds of the body's frame. Joints can wear away the layer of cartilage that allows for frictionless movement. In cases of arthritis, the patient "creaks" and "grates" as they move. He explained, "That is basically the auditory manifestation of the fact that the joint has lost its lining layer of cartilage. As soon as I hear or feel that, I know that the person has a problem."

Learning to hear arthritis was not part of Bruce's medical training. He learned to hear arthritis by first seeing and feeling normal and abnormal presentations in his patients. His assessment begins in the waiting room. He watches patients' faces as they stand up from their chairs to see if they are in pain, and he observes their gait as they walk into his office.[32] By paying attention to these other sensory channels across a series of patients, he further developed his hearing: "I think I just picked it up. And I realized that when people's knees felt like that [i.e., were arthritic], it was actually making a noise. And then with some people you can actually hear it as they walk. It sounds like wheels that need oil."

Again we see here how hearing is synesthetic in practice, rather than specific to the ear. To reinforce the connection between feeling and hearing bodies, Bruce had me place my hand on his knee as he moved the joint to extend his leg. He asked me not whether I could feel the grates or grinds but, "Can you hear that?" On my first attempt, I could not. We repeated the exercise. "OK, I can hear that," I said. Each of the senses "spontaneously overflows towards all the rest."[33]

How Doctors Hear with Diagnostic Instruments

Since the early twentieth century, much effort has been put into making clinical decision-making scientific.[34] As in other domains, visual evidence is often privileged over other ways of knowing.[35] Echocardiography translates circulatory system function that would otherwise be heard into a visual output (e.g., data, graphs). Medical imaging technologies from x-ray to sonography allow the body to be seen beyond the possibilities of human sight.[36] Experienced doctors express a tension between clinical ways of knowing a patient and a mode in which the patient is scanned, tested, and diagnosed before they are seen.[37]

However, ethnographies of medical work reveal that contemporary practice continues to be sensory as much as datafied.[38] In thinking about diagnostic technologies as a potential replacement for clinical skills,[39] it often goes unnoticed that doctors can use technologies like echocardiography to refine auscultatory technique. Before the widespread use of echocardiography, cardiologists would assess patients via auscultation and would report their findings on a patient's chart in a hand-drawn diagram to represent the perceived sounds, presenting an opportunity for a medical student to hear and re-hear a patient's chest in conversation with their graphic depiction. A back-and-forth would take place between the drawing and the patient, with the visual directing the student's aural attention.

With the pervasive use of echocardiography, such drawings typically no longer feature in patient charts, a change lamented on pedagogical grounds by doctors like physician and clinical skills educator Cameron. However, senior doctors and medical students alike similarly hear with echocardiograms. Nelson, the neurologist, described working with both auscultation and echocardiography: "You will get feedback through listening to a lot of heart sounds, from other people telling you what you are listening to, and then also from seeing changes on a cardiograph that correlate with the sound. That sound is that thing that I can see there [on the echocardiogram]." Samuel, the cardiologist, also described this practice: "Repetition is the key. One way is to use an echocardiogram and have input from the machine. Then you can see the heart valves opening and closing and correlate them in your mind." These practices point to how Cultivating and "doing" hearing is involved in the material arrangement of the stethoscope and echocardiography.[40]

Refining one's hearing with echocardiography is an ongoing process rather than a technique used only by students. Samuel explained that each new patient presents an opportunity to test and extend his hearing in conversation with the echocardiogram: "Echo gives you an amazing amount of information about the structure and function of the heart. The noises that you auscultate are sometimes very indefinite, and when you see the echo you think, 'Shit, how could I have missed that?' . . . [But] I am a clinical cardiologist, and I think that the stethoscope is absolutely essential. It gives you a clue of what you should be looking for. Tests are just confirmatory, and if they [what was heard on auscultation versus seen in an echocardiogram] are conflicting, you may have to change your view."

Samuel's identity as a cardiologist is closely bound to his specialized auscultatory skills, yet he can both hear and see more with echocardiography. Rather than disregarding the practice of auscultation, he uses the echocardiogram to refine his hearing. After reviewing a patient's echocardiogram, he re-examines them, hearing in light of what he has seen, translating the visual back to the aural.

Such a practice would be an indulgence at Samuel's level if learning was its only purpose. However, the combined use of auscultation and echocardiography also demonstrates the embodied, interpretive work of decision-making. Rehearing is a way of recontextualizing and reinterpreting a patient in light of the data.[41] It is a way of understanding not only to narrow down possible diagnoses during the initial patient examination but also later to assign meaning to the echocardiography results.

WHAT WE LEARN FROM DOCTORS ABOUT HEARING

The case of doctors shows us how hearing comes in and out of consciousness. Parts of hearing occupy the conscious domain, as in auscultatory listening when a doctor pauses other parts of the interaction to focus only on bodily sounds perceptible via a stethoscope. Rendering hearing conscious requires disattending those other parts of the interaction that would occupy attention, as in listening to the patient's account of their condition. The stethoscope indicates a need for silence, signaling to the patient that the doctor is doing this auscultatory listening, so the patient animates the clinical signs as requested and otherwise limits distractions.

Hearing in a way that suspends other aspects of the ongoing interaction between doctor and patient is a luxury. Most often, doctors do their hearing unconsciously. Medical hearing typically must occur in the background because consciously attending to the nuances of bodily sounds would prevent a doctor from hearing what their patient is saying, and so they might fumble the greeting, or they might miss important information. In an operating room, a surgeon who has turned their conscious attention toward a single set of beeps is directing their focus away from members of the surgical team, as well as the task at hand. There is always too much information around us. Our capacity for conscious attention is orders of magnitude less than what our unconscious mind can attend to, a concept referred to as the "capacity principle."[42]

The doctors I interviewed claimed that their unconscious hearing is brought to the fore in times of trouble. They rely on the movement between the unconscious and the conscious. When their unconscious evaluation of evidence hits on things going wrong, they become aware that they need to give their complete, conscious attention to the problem at hand. They trust both their unconscious monitoring and their ability to bring about their conscious attention at the right time, as in the example of anesthetic monitoring. The need for the transition from unconscious to conscious attention is likely accounted for by the greater level of precision achievable with conscious attention. While our unconscious can process and assess vast amounts of evidence,[43] it is less well suited to making decisions that require work with rules and logic like the doing of arithmetic. Consciousness also allows for more focused thoughts.[44]

Those mostly unconscious aspects of medical hearing also come to the fore in training programs. Despite how important this mostly unconscious knowledge is, the profession and medical education institutions know that it is not innate, or beyond deliberate transformation as Pierre Bourdieu would have it.[45] This is more than assigning meaning to an audible cue that can already be heard. The study of hearing as lived and developed by doctors reveals how hearing is, by its nature, ontologically and socially constructed. From the early years of medical school through each consultation and procedure performed, doctors' hearing emerges through the collective effort of the medical community and their patients.

Certain aspects of hearing are displayed for patients, while other aspects are hidden. However, displayed and hidden hearing are not directly correlated to consciousness or unconsciousness; that is, conscious hearing is not necessarily displayed, and unconscious hearing is not necessarily concealed. Displaying hearing means that doctors look like they are listening. In auscultation, the stethoscope is an aid for the display of hearing. Patients know what the device is for and so see auscultation as a moment in which their body is heard.

The vast majority of medical hearing is hidden. The nature of hidden hearing relates to perceptions about clinical work and diagnostic evidence. Increasingly, there are medico-legal reasons that doctors need to provide test-based evidence to support their judgments. They do not typically tell patients that they are recommending a particular course of action based on the creak of their joints or the quality of their voice. Hidden hearing is something that doctors do in combination with other ways of knowing, with the aural cues they have perceived being less evident in the final rationale for a particular treatment decision.

Developing medical hearing is an ongoing process. Doctors' accounts moved quickly from experiences in medical school to descriptions of how their sense of the human body had developed over the course of their clinical practice. Studies of clinical education are typically limited to skills labs or the type of learning that happens on rounds.[46] Senior doctors showed me how doctors continue to refine their hearing well after their early medical school training. Each patient presents an opportunity to expand their appreciation of normal and abnormal aural presentations of the body. In addition to aural cues perceived in a physical examination, patients can also comment on whether they have heard a change. The refinement of hearing also happens in relation to devices, which introduce their own forms of sensory work and provide opportunities to refine doctors' aural skills by showing—via data—what might be heard.

What expands the concept of hearing the most is the realization that hearing relates not only to the ear. The case of doctors shows that hearing can be done via touch, as in percussion and the feeling of arthritis.[47] Hearing also involves seeing, as in the case of hearing heart function with an echocardiogram or hearing emphysema in relation to seeing a pack of cigarettes. The synesthetic quality of hearing reflects the reality of being in the world. We almost never sense the world through the isolated channels that we account for in our language; that is, seeing with eyes, hearing with ears, and so on. Synesthesia is exploited in the development of hearing, as in the pedagogical techniques that train medical students to use their own bodies to generate and find sounds. This is an observation common to each case addressed in this book.

2

HOW MUSICIANS HEAR

Musicians face different challenges from those of doctors when it comes to mastering hearing. First, they encounter the challenges of hearing from different positions in social interaction. Singers and instrumentalists principally manipulate their bodies and instruments to make sounds for the hearing of others. In some of their actions, doctors perform like conductors, as when they guide patients in how to produce sounds (e.g., "Cough"). But for the most part, when they make a diagnosis, they act more like a member of an audience: they listen to the sounds that are, in effect, played by someone else's body. Musicians also understand that the standard of evaluation is primarily based on what others hear, so they develop their musicality with this in mind. Doctors, on the other hand, work mostly with the sounds made by patients' bodies and pay little attention to how patients audibly register the process of physical examination.

Musicians and doctors both use instruments but in different ways. For doctors, tools like the stethoscope aid the ear, not only by amplifying the body's sounds but also by producing uniquely diagnostic sounds. For musicians, playing their instrument produces music, but in terms of listening, their instrument is also their nemesis. Their instrument creates obstacles to good hearing in that they often introduce "noise" that the musicians would prefer to hide from audiences, like saliva traveling through a French horn or screeching sounds produced as fingers brush guitar strings.

A further problem of instrumentation for musicians, but not doctors, derives from the collective nature of much musical production. Doctors often collaborate with one another and may work in teams, as in complex surgeries, but in animating many musical forms, like orchestral and chamber music, players participate in a collective project. Musicians performing with others find that the sounds from their own instruments can get in the way of their hearing of the sounds their fellow musicians are producing.

The "ongoingness" of music is a problem unique to musicians. Whereas doctors can often pause or have a patient "replay" a clinical sign, in live musical performance there is no "time-out," no possibility of stopping and redoing. Players have to "hear" a note before it sounds, so they can organize their bodies to produce the music that will be heard if they move in a particular way. When playing with others, they need ways to "hear" ahead to coordinate and keep the music going. The unique temporal challenges of making music reflect that what we think of as hearing is synesthetic. Players listen via gestures from conductors and section or band leaders that signify what should be heard and played.[1] Conductors and leaders must "hear" even more into the future than musicians: they must "hear" the notes as they expect them to sound in their minds, so they can move to direct the players accordingly.[2] Musical synchrony also owes a lot to a collective hearing and feeling of the rhythmic pulse.[3]

With these challenges in mind, the following analysis examines the distinctive strategies that musicians use to develop their musical hearing. I interviewed twenty-seven musicians working in different areas of musical life. All were or had been working musicians in various social contexts: playing for audiences in recital halls, for dancers at clubs, and to patrons of pubs. Some were also teachers, artistic directors, composers, and producers. They played in a variety of musical traditions, including classical, jazz, rock, metal, Latin, and electronic. This diversity allows us to discover aspects of hearing that apply broadly to playing music, rather than those that are unique to a specific type of music, such as improvisational jazz.

While imperfect as a research method, interviews provided an important pathway into musicians' biographies and their accounts of their embodied experiences and interpretations. Listening in music-making has tended to be an aspect of practice that has escaped attention in studies of music performance and rehearsals that have adopted observational approaches.[4] We can't see how musicians "do" hearing, or even what they are hearing, so we need them to tell us.

To make up for some of the shortcomings of interviewing as a method, I observed practice sessions and concerts, which acted as an extension of the interviews. Participants invited me over when other players were joining them for a rehearsal, or said I could stay on after an interview when a rehearsal was taking place, or took me to a gig they were playing later that night, or let me watch their solo practice. I went to some concerts alone, mainly classical recitals but also a few rock and metal gigs. I observed the spatial organization of players and leaders, the gestures that coordinate playing, the use of scores, how players relate to audiences, and efforts to construct listening among audiences as in the use of performance notes in classical recitals.

My analysis is also informed by my experiences as a musician. I have played classical piano and flute since the early nineties, mostly solo but also in chamber ensembles, orchestras, bands, and choirs. I also draw on accounts from musicians' autobiographies.

I begin by looking at strategies to develop hearing in practice phases. Musicians in training need aids to reach into how they are hearing so that they can critically reflect on and change their understanding of musical sound. The first aids that I address come from lesson environments, where a teacher can share tricks and tips to identify musical elements and can develop students' hearing via proprioception: their neuromuscular sense of body position and movement. Proprioception responds to one of the challenges of hearing.

Musicians know they need to take the position of the other to adjust their performance, but their interpretations of their musical gestures are not what the other will hear. In developing their hearing via proprioception, they circumvent this problem.

The second group of aids comes from engaging with recorded music played by working musicians. Teachers can encourage students to engage in such activities, but the development of hearing comes from the student's analysis of the recording, their embodied translations of what they heard into their playing, or in the act of writing down what they heard. The latter includes the practice of transcription particularly adopted by jazz musicians and the practice of playing along with recordings adopted mainly by rock musicians to improve both their playing and hearing.

The third group of aids speaks to how players do hearing when the music is ongoing. Hearing is mostly unconscious, but players, conductors, and band and section leaders use various strategies to bring momentary conscious attention to how players are doing hearing. This hearing cannot be an exclusively aural exercise. Observing the gestures of a subset of coplayers or the conductor means that hearing alone does not have to be responsible for all aspects of musical coordination. Players also "hear" through the feel of the music as they produce it, including through their shared sense of the rhythmic pulse. Particularly in larger groups, musicians hear collaboratively, each focusing their hearing on a subset of players or leaders.

AIDS TO MUSICAL HEARING IN LESSON ENVIRONMENTS

Hearing for Testing Purposes

Most of the musicians with whom I spoke had extensive formal training, typically in the form of private weekly lessons with an instrumental teacher. Some had begun with small group lessons, a common approach for young brass and guitar students learning at school. In these lessons, teachers adopt various strategies to help students learn how to hear music. Because such lessons are time bound (typically 30 to 60 minutes per week), teachers often use methods that can rapidly develop students' ability to understand what they should be hearing.

In Australia, teachers of pre-tertiary classical students often use the syllabus of an examining body such as the Australian Music Examinations Board as their curriculum. The syllabus gives teachers a structure to follow and a set of benchmarks to assess students' progress at each level. Instrumental lessons center on learning repertoire, often on an annual cycle, which culminates in various concerts, competitions, and finally an exam that serves as a display and evaluation of the student's progress. Students are also required to take dedicated studies in theory, sometimes called "musicianship," which covers matters of structure and harmony as separate from a student's playing.

Both performance and musicianship exams contain an aural component, though it has a relatively minor weighting and so is commonly given commensurately little space in lessons. Teachers following an examining body's syllabus typically use practice tests developed by the examining body as their teaching materials. These tests can be routinely implemented and provide a way to break lessons down into discrete, tangible, assessable tasks. Practice tests are the explicit work on hearing that supports students in identifying and naming the building blocks of music in Western traditions. Students must be able to hear harmonic relationships and tonality. While absolute or perfect pitch is prized, it is typically only relative pitch that is tested for. Composers also adopt a certain rhythmic pulse in the music. Students work on being able to hear note length and groupings of rhythm, or the time signature.

As teachers work through practice tests, they commonly give students devices to help them find the right answer. For tests of hearing harmonic intervals, teachers guide students to hear the intervals with their memory of the first interval in a well-known song. A classical cellist named Emily explained, "At the conservatorium, you have to be able to identify all intervals, and you have to be able to recall them instantly. The way a lot of people, even people with great musical ears, still hear the intervals is by drawing on knowledge of [the first interval of] 'Somewhere Over the Rainbow,' which is an octave; 'Advance Australia Fair' [the national anthem of Australia], which is a perfect fourth; or 'My Bonny Lies Over the Ocean,' which is a sixth. So much of it is about memory and recognition." Within this system, the first interval of the well-known song is associated with the interval name (for instance, "Happy Birthday" starts with a major second). Interval "cheat sheets" are broadly available as resources for students hoping to improve their interval recognition (table 2.1).[5]

In practice tests, the teacher plays the student two pitches separate from any other pitches that would ordinarily surround them in a musical phrase. The student checks which song matches the played interval in their mind (e.g., "It sounds like 'When the Saints Go Marching In,' so it is a major third"). This technique is oriented toward an interactional context in which a teacher or examiner will assess a student's hearing as separate from their playing. Students meet this artificial challenge by using another artifice: analogy to a known song (and one without prestige, like "Happy Birthday").

This type of hearing is not directly related to the hearing that musicians do when playing for an audience. If a player needed to hear an interval in a performance, the music would not stop for them to think of an analogy! Singing one song to hear another that continues to play on is a fool's errand. Musicians I interviewed who learned to play by ear did not mention refining their hearing through this technique.

Teachers use similar devices for hearing other elements of music, too. For the test that requires students to identify whether a passage is in triple or quadruple time, teachers coach students to try marching or swaying to the musical fragment. We march to quadruple time (i.e., 4/4 time), and we sway to triple time (i.e., 3/4 time), as in a waltz.

TABLE 2.1 INTERVAL "CHEAT SHEET"

Interval	Ascending	Descending
Minor second	*Jaws* theme	"Joy to the World"
	The Pink Panther theme	"Für Elise"
Major second	"Happy Birthday"	"Mary Had a Little Lamb"
	"Frère Jacques"	"Deck the Halls"
	"Rudolf the Red-Nosed Reindeer"	"Three Blind Mice"
Minor third	"Greensleeves"	"The Star-Spangled Banner"
		"This Old Man"
		"Frosty the Snowman"
Major third	"When the Saints Go Marching In"	Beethoven's Fifth Symphony
	"Kum Ba Yah"	"Summertime" by George Gershwin
Perfect fourth	"Advance Australia Fair"	"O Come, All Ye Faithful"
	"Amazing Grace"	
	"Hark! The Herald Angels Sing"	
Tritone	*The Simpsons* theme	
Perfect fifth	"Twinkle, Twinkle, Little Star"	
Minor sixth	"The Entertainer"	
Major sixth	"My Bonny Lies Over the Ocean"	"Nobody Knows the Trouble I've Seen"
Minor seventh	"Somewhere" from *West Side Story*	
Major seventh	"Take On Me" by A-ha	
Octave	"Somewhere Over the Rainbow"	

In a lesson, the student can move their body to march or sway, sometimes testing both to see which feels right. Another device is to try counting with the music (e.g., "Do you get to three or four before you feel the rhythmic pulse that starts a new bar?"). In exams, students imagine moving or counting to hide the artifice.[6]

These devices are great teaching techniques for the problem that teachers face of finding conventions that they can repeat from one student to the next. By teaching students to associate intervals or to imagine moving this way or that to the music, teachers provide students with straightforward, valuable techniques that work more or less immediately to change how they hear music.

However, some musicians, like Hannah, a classical pianist, felt that working on hearing independently of playing means that students learn to hear musically only for testing purposes.[7] Hannah recounted her experience of matriculating through an exam-based system, the common process of completing a grade each year from the age of seven. Despite being a strong student in the context of this system, when she got to university, a time during which the demands placed on professional players often become apparent, she realized that she was "very narrowly skilled" and increasingly limited by her aural skills: "I found I could play, but I wasn't a functional musician at all. I could learn a program, but I wasn't used to doing it quickly; I wasn't used to learning a lot of music. We did four hours of aural training a week at university, and I was terrible at it! I had no idea! I really struggled with that side of things." She thought back to her pre-tertiary aural training:

> It is seen as something that is just a little corner of the exam form. You cram the ear tests in [a few weeks before the exam], and it is nothing but luck. I think that teachers tended to think that you could do these things or you couldn't. They would hammer out a few chords, and you were supposed to sing the top note. And if you couldn't, they wouldn't really do anything about it, and you didn't do well in your aural component [of the exam]. It was really seen as quite separate and treated separately from your playing, which is crazy.

In a way, listening is a soft skill for music students, in curricula but out of focus, developed so that students can meet formal educational milestones that will allow them to advance—but without complete mastery.[8] The university-level aural training Hannah described is closely tied to harmony lessons, which develop and test hearing by requiring students to sight-sing atonal, twelve-tone music with a strong focus on rhythm. While the method adopted by Hannah's university went some way to developing her hearing—she said that she can now sight-sing most things—it also developed a particular aural skill set isolated from her playing.

Formal training plays an important role in developing musicians' technical excellence and provides an analytical framework with which to listen to music. That said, the musicians I spoke with largely agreed that there is a difference between learning to hear as isolated in an aural test and an embodied sense of hearing necessary to the work of playing. Michael, a university-educated pianist who started lessons at age four, described his nearly two decades of formal training as "like primary school," particularly for his ear. He said that it set him up but stopped short of giving him the aural skills he needed to play professionally. Lachlan, a violinist, who began lessons at age seven and completed university studies in music said that "a course is only really a very small part of being a musician."[9] Hannah abandoned her degree program, as did cellist Emily, composers Edward and Todd, and jazz pianist Michael.[10] Each believed that they needed to develop their hearing in connection to their playing, which took more time and space than typically available in lesson environments.

How Teachers Develop Students' Hearing Through Their Proprioceptive Sense of Their Sound

Musicians' training often involves body exercises: learning how to shape and hold tension in the lips to play certain sounds on a flute or trumpet; learning how to move one's hands in relation to each other on the piano or how to get a pinky here and a thumb there; and for singers, learning to manipulate the vocal cords and diaphragm. Some musicians, such as the internationally renowned pianist and conductor Daniel Barenboim, have suggested that the hearing aspect of playing is "impossible to teach" in comparison to placing the hands on the keyboard and balancing the weight of each finger. He wrote:

> No matter what instrument you play, or whether you conduct or sing, you will only produce the sound you want if you hear it in your head a fraction of a second beforehand. This is the part of the music that is impossible to teach. I could teach people how to put down their hands, how to balance the two Ds, the three Gs and the three Bs in the opening chord of Beethoven's G Major Concerto, that there is a register where the note has a tendency to be louder, and that the thumb has more weight than the little finger. But if a student is unable to imagine the sound before he starts to play—even if it differs from what I am trying to explain to him—he will never produce the sound he wants. This ability to hear the sound and the phrasing you want in the inner ear is one of the most essential qualities.[11]

An essential part of playing is a kind of pre-hearing, forming a sense of what the sound needs to be before moving to make it. What we ordinarily think of as hearing music is a retrospective activity; we hear what was already played. But this is just the tip of the iceberg. Players must also work on developing a sense of what the sound *will* be if they move their body this way or that.

While getting at this is difficult—some say impossible—teachers can work with students to develop a proprioceptive sense of the sounds that they will form, attending to hearing through an internal sense of body position and movement. Having heard the sound that a student has produced, a teacher can deconstruct it and suggest embodied cues within the student's reach to produce a different sound the next time. The student acknowledges that the teacher understands how to move their body to produce the "right" sound, so they must make themselves an appendage to the body of the teacher to appreciate how to create that sound. They feel with, and off, the already skilled body of the teacher.

Various pedagogical approaches recognize the significance of movement in learning to hear music, including the Kodály, Orff, and Dalcroze methods.[12] Curwen hand signs from the Kodály method are commonly used in the American choral tradition to develop absolute or functional pitch recognition.[13] Each pitch within the seven-note scale has both a solfège syllable and an associated shape that the musician can form with their hands. When vocalizing a given pitch, the musician sings a syllable and moves their hand to make the sign (e.g., a fist with the palm facing down for "Do," a flat palm parallel to the ground for "Mi"). Thus, solfège is reinforced both visually and kinesthetically (figure 2.1).

Cellist Emily learned from a teacher who used elements of the Kodály method in advanced instrumental teaching. A string instrument like the cello is tuned to concert pitch through adjustment to the fine tuners and pegs, with further adjustments made through finger placement in the formation of each note. To work on intonation, Emily's teacher taught her to sight-sing in rhythm syllables and solfège with Curwen hand signs. When presented with a new piece of music, Emily and her teacher would sing and sign each musical line together as a first step in preparing Emily's body and ear to form the notes. Emily worked from her teacher's vocalization and hand movements to sing and sign the pitches herself.[14] Seeing and feeling the vocalization required her to pay attention; it forced her to think, How far away physically is that interval? Her playing followed the vocalization: "Trying to hit the high notes in 'The Swan' [a composition by Camille Saint-Saëns], if you are singing the next note in your head, it makes you stop because it is a long way away. When you sing a high note, you have to prepare your body. The same preparation is required to play a high note on the cello. Then, when you play, your whole arm moves to point towards the note."

NOTE.—*The diagrams shew the hand as seen by pupils sitting in front of the teacher toward his left hand. The teacher makes his signs in front of his ribs, chest, face and head, rising a little as the tones go up, and falling as they go down.*

FIRST STEP. SECOND STEP. THIRD STEP.

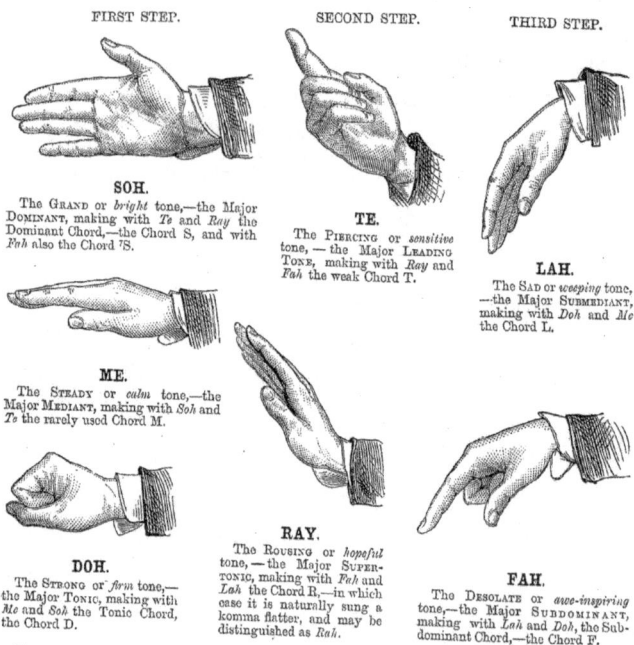

SOH.

The GRAND or *bright* tone,—the Major DOMINANT, making with *Te* and *Ray* the Dominant Chord,—the Chord S, and with *Fah* also the Chord 7S.

TE.

The PIERCING or *sensitive* tone, — the Major LEADING TONE, making with *Ray* and *Fah* the weak Chord T.

LAH.

The SAD or *weeping* tone, —the Major SUBMEDIANT, making with *Doh* and *Me* the Chord L.

ME.

The STEADY or *calm* tone,—the Major MEDIANT, making with *Soh* and *Te* the rarely used Chord M.

RAY.

The ROUSING or *hopeful* tone,—the Major SUPER-TONIC, making with *Fah* and *Lah* the Chord R,—in which case it is naturally sung a komma flatter, and may be distinguished as *Rah.*

DOH.

The STRONG or *firm* tone,— the Major TONIC, making with *Me* and *Soh* the Tonic Chord, the Chord D.

FAH.

The DESOLATE or *awe-inspiring* tone,—the Major SUBDOMINANT, making with *Lah* and *Doh*, the Sub-dominant Chord,—the Chord F.

NOTE.—*These proximate verbal descriptions of mental effect are only true of the tones of the scale when sung slowly—when the ear is filled with the key, and when the effect is not modified by harmony.*

FIGURE 2.1 Hand signs from John Curwen's *The Standard Course of Lessons and Exercises in the Tonic Sol-fa Method of Teaching Music* (1882).

This vocalization device uses the changes that occur inside the body in vocal placement to instruct the player on how to move their arm to produce a given pitch on the cello. As one's body moves to sing a note, one experiences an aural embodied sense of how far to move as one reaches toward the note on the cello. While in Emily's recollection, the vocal cue readily translated into the movement of finding the note, a cognitive embodied leap occurs between the two. The sung cue is abstracted from the movement of forming the cello sound.

In his account of learning to play the cello as an adult, John Holt described a similar technique for working on timbre or the particular tonal quality of the sound: "Bill [Holt's teacher] used to tell me to open my throat, as if I were singing. Sometimes, when my high notes sounded too thin and shrill, he would say, 'Put a bubble in it.' I half knew what he meant, though I didn't quite know how to do it."[15] As in the training of medical students, music teachers can use metaphors to isolate and direct students' attention toward an element of the sound that they need to create. In being told to open your throat, or put a bubble in it, the student experiences a feeling in the inner lining of their body of additional space around the note or richness of tone. They are working on creating the right sound without focusing on how to play or what is heard; rather, they are developing a proprioceptive sense of what the sound needs to be. The hope is that this will teach the student how to adjust their movement when playing in the preferred direction, based on the new "pre-hearing."

Emily spent hours every day, with her teacher and alone, working on intonation in scales and pieces using this strategy. The specifics of the pedagogical relationship are significant. Whereas for many classical music students, the teacher principally hears on behalf of the student, Emily's experience was one in which trust in her teacher's ear was always considered an intermediary stage; she knew that another self-sensing way of knowing needed to take over:

A lot of hard work and a lot of trust of my hands [was involved]. It was a physical thing. And I had to trust other people like my teacher. And I learned to hear the sounds, too . . . the way that my teacher taught me and the way she helped fix my intonation, this is what I was talking about with my trust of her . . . when I was playing my scales, she always taught me to sing the next note. So, what I would do was I would play one note, and I would do this out loud for years and years, every practice, and I would do an hour and a half of scales before any practice. I'd sing the next note before I'd play it because quite often, it was easier for me to visualize the sound in my head, make it vocally, and then play it than [to] just [play] it before focusing on the sound I was aiming for.

In her practice, Emily would sing and play pitches, and this would continue as long as she heard herself being in tune. She recalled that years before when there was an error in tuning, her teacher would have stopped her—"OK, that's not right. Is it flat or is it sharp?"—and by doing so, she invited Emily to reflect on and correct her tuning.

Since Emily stopped taking lessons, her teacher's hearing and correction have lingered in her mind. She continues the same pattern of vocalization, moving to play, and hearing the sound, making a physical correction in cases of error. She questions each note physically and aurally—"Is that one right? Hear and feel. Is that one right? Hear and feel." The physical adjustments she makes in response to her hearing and feeling are directional. If she hears and feels a flat pitch, she moves toward the bridge of the cello; if she hears and feels a sharp pitch, she moves toward the pegs. She practices constant embodied checking in the shadow of her teacher's hearing of sharp and flat.

How tuning operates varies by instrument. On a woodwind instrument such as a flute, the head joint can be pushed in slightly or pulled out a bit, and the player makes continuous adjustments to their embouchure, air speed, and air direction to remain in tune over the instrument's range. Alex, a classical flautist, explained how students can be coached to experiment with how slight adjustments to their body change the produced sound, serving to refine their hearing in the process. He said, "We might just sit there playing a note, and then you encourage them to move either side of the note, and just hear the effect of it, and get them to find where it sounds 'pure'; [that] is the word that I would use. . . . In teaching, it would be more, 'Move one way. Does it make it sound better or worse?'"

This teaching strategy develops students' hearing by encouraging them to pay aural attention to changes in the sound related to movement around the note, rather than by the teacher providing direct feedback based on their hearing of sharp and flat. With this technique, Alex can play a given pitch simultaneously with a student, allowing them to experiment with pitch in a relative sense: "When you use two instruments of continuous matching tone, like flutes, then you can actually hear the beating, which is faster when it is out of tune and slows down as it gets closer [to being in tune]. You can hear clashing overtones, which cause this extra vibration, which is what we hear as being out of tune, and it is just another thing to listen for. But the beating is the same whether you're too sharp or too flat."

The "beating" that Alex referred to is the perceptible interference pattern between two sine waves that occurs when players form the same note in unison but not identically. The interference is heard as a "wah wah wah" sound, with pulsations in loudness within the flute's tone. As the players approach the same pitching of a given note, the waves move closer together, and the beating slows down to the point of being imperceptible. As they diverge, the beating speeds up. Some music traditions exploit this beating as a compositional or expressive device, but in Western musical traditions, beating is typically heard as dissonance.[16] With this knowledge, players use their hearing of beating as a cue to adjust their pitch toward consonance.

How Teachers Act as an Audience, Choreographing the Musical Body

A sticking point in forming the right sounds is getting a grasp on how others hear produced sounds. This problem is nowhere more acute than in the case of singing, in which the instrument is the musician's body. Singers can hear their pitch but not accurately perceive their vocal quality. The singer's mouth, throat, and head create resonance; the audience does not have that same "noise" or filter. Vocal tone as perceived in a singer's own body can thus differ dramatically from what an audience hears. This difference explains the surprise, even horror, that we often experience when we hear our voice in a recording ("Is that really what I sound like?"). The resonance created by the singer's body means that singers cannot rely on what they hear as they sing in order to perfect what the audience will hear. They know that they must take the position of the other to adjust their performance, but their interpretations of their musical gestures are not those of the other.[17]

Madeleine, a classical singer, explained that unlike musicians who play instruments, singers often sing for a long time before beginning lessons. They come to lessons with "preconceived ideas" about how they sound and "muscle memories" for the production of those sounds. One of the first tasks for teachers, then, is alienating singers from their hearing of their sound. Teachers must tell them and show them that their hearing and muscle memories are not serving them. Madeleine sometimes provides feedback to her students based on her hearing: "That sounds bad" or "That sounds better." However, she finds that it can be tricky to get students to accept this feedback. Recalling relearning her own hearing and singing, she observed, "It took quite a while, and there was a lot of questioning— 'Are you sure this is acceptable?' Then having confirmation that the sound was acceptable gives you permission to accept the sensation and make the sound."

When teaching students, Madeleine adopts other strategies to get the message through. Recordings are a way to get a singer outside their body, to appreciate the qualities of their voice from the perspective of an audience:

> It is such a hard thing to get through to a student. I record every lesson so they can go home and listen to it. Whether they listen to it is another story! Getting instant feedback on their aural [perception of their sound] is important, but still, it takes a long time for them to relate the aural to the sensation. Once they have heard a few of those recordings, they understand, for example, that while forward sensation sounds awful in your head, it sounds quite fantastic to everybody else. For the student to be confident that the sound that they are outputting is acceptable takes a while.

"Forward sensation," also known as "forward placement," calls for a concentration of resonance at the front of the face through a singer's tongue position and the shape of their mouth and throat. But because the tone produced this way sounds "awful" to the singer, they are unlikely to adopt the technique if they hear it only in the moment they produce it.

Once the student is convinced to change their sound, Madeleine works on vocal tone via body positions and movements, and the sensations created in the process of sound production, such as lip vibration. As in vocalization devices used by cello players, the singer's strategy is to bypass hearing and focus on proprioceptive awareness: understanding how the body is used in producing sound. This strategy has resonance with Maurice Merleau-Ponty's description, "I hear myself with my throat."[18] The student's hearing is improved by being disattended as the teacher shifts the student's focus from their sound to self-awareness of their body position and movement. In the context of teaching singing, Madeleine explained, "You have to go to the sensation first because what they're hearing is not what everyone else is hearing. . . . I can hear things like whether someone's pelvis is locked when they're singing. You can hear that there is a constriction; the airflow is not as efficient as it should be. You're constantly listening and looking to understand what is affecting the sound, so things like whether the pelvis is locked, if there is constriction around the larynx, if there are postural issues, and then issues to do with air pressure."

In hearing these constrictions, Madeleine can work with the student to change the sensation to get a different sound. Teachers are necessary because audiences will not, cannot, or do not care to correct a singer; they either approve of the singer or not. A dedicated teacher plays a different role. They do not simply hear as "an other" or explain how an audience will hear. They dwell in the student's body to show where, in regions accessible to the student, changes can be made and felt. They choreograph the production of sound, directing attention to how the student's body parts work together to produce one sound or another.

Tom, a pianist and vocal coach, similarly articulated his role as offering proprioceptive corrections in response to his hearing of the student's sound and appreciation of embodied sound production. In a lesson environment, he stops students when he identifies a point in the singing that needs work: "Could you raise your soft palate more?" "Could you retract the false vocal folds more?" "Could you add laryngeal tilt?"

As readers unfamiliar with these terms will be acutely aware, students' adjustments based on these proprioceptive corrections require an appreciation of what the cues mean. Training programs, such as Estill Voice Training, have been designed to give a language for the development of singers' proprioception so that they can change the sounds they produce by paying attention to their body rather than the sounds themselves. Students learn about vocal physiology through kinesthetic exercises and by seeing inside the body through diagrams and video endoscopy of the vocal folds. Singers' control of their sound follows.

WORKING ON HEARING IN INTERACTION WITH RECORDED MUSICAL OTHERS

Transcription as a Technique to Develop an Analytical Orientation Toward Music

The second set of aids used to refine musicians' hearing focuses on applying conscious attention to hearing through the use of recordings. Transcribing recordings is one of the most effective approaches to refining musical hearing apart from playing. In this context, *transcription* means musicians' notation and involves writing out the notes to represent what they have heard in a musical passage. Jazz musicians often do this type of transcription to work out what is being played in recordings of improvised solos. In the words of Lonnie Hillyer, a trumpeter, "All of the great jazz musicians have also been great teachers. Their lessons are preserved for students on every recording they made."[19]

By transcribing what they hear in a recording, musicians can create a score for an improvised solo, but this is a secondary function of transcription. Musicians primarily transcribe scores from recordings as a resource to build their musical vocabulary; it helps them learn how to think about music.[20] As Mark, an orchestral trombonist, put it, "You need to listen to recordings. A lot. A lot. . . . It is the formation of what goes on in your head."

Players also transcribe to improve their hearing. When they try to give visual expression to what they hear through transcription, they are encouraged to listen "better." Pianist Michael described seeking out a teacher who encouraged him to work on his hearing through transcription, not in anticipation of a test but to develop his aural skills for professional work. In the end, he studied under a jazz trombone teacher who pointed out where his hearing was falling short and encouraged him to write down what he heard until he could get it right. Michael contrasted this pedagogical approach with the more repertoire-focused lessons he had had with his classical and jazz piano teachers:

At that high [a] level, I don't need someone to tell me how to move my fingers on the keyboard. I could go back and get a classical piano lesson, or after you've been doing it for a while you . . . just sit there at the keyboard and figure out how it works for your hand. But the opportunity to just discuss things and to have someone say, "You can't hear chords with more than six notes in them. You're messing up these voicings; go back, spend fifty hours, transcribe them properly, and then come back and see me"—that had a huge impact on my ability to perform, much more than anything I learned from my jazz piano teacher. . . . It's a wake-up call from somebody with professional standards, which is very different to university standards. . . . Many people can play a Rachmaninov concerto, but very few people can hear all of those parts and have an emotional attachment to them and really understand that, while they are playing this, the second violin over there is playing this harmony, and that's why it works. . . . Reading a Rachmaninov concerto is not an easy thing to do, but if you compare that to hearing all of the parts in the orchestra, it's a walk in the park.

When transcribing, musicians shift their position from audience to analyst. They work not on what they have heard but on their hearing. Audiences hear in a single pass. They grasp the overall shape of a line, the feel of the rhythm, a sense of harmony and texture. David Sudnow reflected that when he first attempted solo copying, he found he only vaguely understood a melody he thought he knew: "I had been glossing the particularities of the notes in many of my hummings, grasping their essential shape perhaps but not singing them with refined pitch sensitivity."[21]

In transcription, musicians pour over a recording, starting, stopping, notating, and replaying the music in artificial divisions. They use their hearing to perfect their writing of the transcript. In each pass, transcribers hear what they have not yet transcribed, so they continue listening and transcribing until they have captured all of it. The transcript becomes a resource to rehear the recording.

Various tools are available to make transcribing easier, but these are useful primarily when students will be assessed on their transcription skills. Contemporary music notation software can slow a recording, provide space to capture the transcriber's analysis of the notes, and play back the notation so the transcriber can aurally check their score against the recording. While such technologies make transcription faster, they reduce the extent to which the transcriber moves from audience to analyst and thus limit the development of musicians' hearing. Michael reflected critically on the use of such software:

> All the kids now use this software, and when transcribing, you can just slow down the music, which means that where transcribing a really hard saxophone solo would take me weeks of listening back to it [transcribing by hand], it is fast. Now they [can] do it in a tenth of the time because they can just slow it down. But you have to wonder where their aural skills are at. In a gig when [someone would play] the same thing at speed, they would have no idea because they can only listen to things really slowly. . . . You don't really earn the same results as you do when you just turn the record player back. You really want to get that line right because you're sick of going back, so you really listen closely.

Michael qualified that, while notation software may be an effective learning aid, "most people are lazy." He claimed that students who use software for transcription misunderstand the function of the activity.

The ability to transcribe music effectively should have meaning for students beyond simply passing a test; it is a crucial skill because it develops musicians' hearing. Transcription takes the musical line as heard outside the musician's body, configuring what will be experienced inside as the transcriber writes down the notes they hear and finds those notes on an instrument. This transcendence from outside to inside must then be reversed in playing as players imagine the sound they want to produce, know how it will be heard by others, and then move their body to make that sound.

A trombonist named Scott described how the transcriber's shift from audience to analyst is aided by playing notes as heard. Scott explained that he would put on a recording and listen to a short passage or just a single note. After listening to the passage or note, he would pause the recording and sing back his memory of it. He would then try to find the note on his guitar before writing it down. The trombone, his primary instrument, was too loud for this, especially because he sometimes needed to work to find the notes on his guitar while the recording played. I asked whether using a different instrument affected his hearing of the notes owing to the differences in timbre and his relative fluency on the two instruments. He said, "No, not at all. It may not even be in the same octave or pitch or anything, but just hearing the note is enough, even if I'm playing an octave or two higher. I generally play it at the same pitch because it just makes it easier. You just lock in, and it sounds the same, but it is enough to just hear the pitch, the intervals, and the melody line right."

After he has written down his heard and played passage or note, he can then play back the transcript to check its accuracy. The phases of finding and copying the passage or note and then checking the passage or note as written by playing it back create contrast pairs, with the recorded other as the "preferred" and the transcriber's playing as potentially "faulted."[22] Scott said that his ear could sometimes play tricks on him, particularly when he was transcribing multiple parts of a brass section. Playing from his transcript and replaying the recording are ways for him to check whether his hearing was right. After another, more focused hearing of the recording, he can hear more and more: "You think you're hearing something, and then you go back to it a few months later and listen to it and realize you were wrong."[23]

Feeling for the notes of the recorded player moves Scott, as the transcriber, further into his hearing of the piece. This is not a matter of accounting for what was heard; a transcript is not just a retrospective description. Rather, it is the beginning of retrospective anticipation, of "hearing," in an embodied sense what a player's body movements will produce. By engaging in this process, the musician is developing their ability to "hear ahead" cultivating a proprioceptive sense of the sound that will follow. Scott confirms whether he has heard correctly not by looking at the transcript he has produced but by hearing if his playing aligns with what he has written down.

How Students Make Themselves an Appendage to Recorded Exemplars

A few musicians I spoke with had developed their technique and hearing largely or completely outside formal learning environments. These musicians mostly played popular music styles. Jack was a guitarist and singer in metal and rock bands. Cooper and Nathan were both metal guitarists. Andy and Peter were rock guitarists. Amy was the odd one out, playing many instruments in many genres: she was a singer and composer of electronic music, a violist in an early music ensemble, and a lover of rock guitar, opera, and folk.

All these musicians had adopted one common learning strategy: they all "played along" with recordings. In playing along, musicians sit facing their music player (a device that plays digital audio files or a record player) with their instrument and related equipment like an amplifier. The recordings they hear and play along with are standard releases, not versions of songs with parts taken out for practice, as may be used by classical instrumentalists when preparing for an accompanied recital. Musicians playing along do not use sheet music as they play, though they may review the tablature or score in advance.

This is a method that helps a player with the challenge of getting the flow of the music. It works on hearing via playing. A player's hearing of a recording acts as a guide to proprioception, or how they need to move their body to make the sounds they hear in the recording. They work on hearing better to improve how they play along. Transcription does this in a way, too, but involves the additional phase of writing down what one has heard before playing it. Playing along is thus more direct and solves a problem for those players who do not read music. By playing along, such musicians can skip the writing down and move straight to playing a riff.

Amy, who had been playing for thirty-five years when we spoke, taught herself to play about twenty instruments by playing along. The approach was a practical response to her learning environment, where she had no other resources at her disposal beyond seeing and hearing the music of others.[24]

> For me, a large portion of how I learn has been to look at how other people look and listen to how other people sound and to imitate that to a point, to the point where you get the tone or the phrasing that you're after. . . . I would listen to music and discern pitch, phrasing, note length, and tone. If it was an electric guitar solo by Pink Floyd, for example, one of the first things I would do would be to put on a record and get my guitar to sound like that, and then think about where else I could use that thing. So in learning to play a guitar solo, I would be learning how to play the guitar. I didn't know what I was playing; I couldn't tell you what notes they were. It was mainly imitating the phrases that gave me technique and also learning about the tone, as well, and thinking about how to make my sound like that.

As in transcription, working with a recording in this way creates a contrast pair.[25] The juxtaposition of Amy's sound and the sound produced by the recorded player either confirms that she has been hearing and playing right or highlights where she is falling short. Hearing the gap between her playing and the recording becomes a resource for her to hear and move differently the next time. She described comparing her sound with the recorded sound and working to close the gap, stopping herself and making corrections where needed to please the ear of the other she imagined playing for. She explained, "You listen to the differences, really. That is, you listen not so much to what it is but to the difference between what it is and what you're doing. It's like a ruler: here are three centimeters, here are five, and I want you to feel those two centimeters [in between]."

Amy said that this learning process was one of a "masterclass by approximation." The practice is not really about hearing to identify the notes, as in the case of students preparing for a test. Rather, she is hearing to learn how the player on the recording worked their body to understand how to work hers. Playing along with David Gilmour of Pink Floyd, Amy is *being* David Gilmour as he played in the recorded moment. She uses hearing to understand the movements she must make to produce the desired sound.

This anchoring of one player to the body of another was also evident in the practice of Jack, a guitarist and singer. Jack had been playing guitar, mainly metal, for about twelve years when I observed his practice methods. In playing along, his performance of his chosen part was imperfect, to an outsider almost frustratingly so. But for Jack, this practice was about getting a song under his belt rather than performing per se. As the track started playing, he would often take on the challenge of the lead, sometimes coming in straight away, sometimes a few bars behind. When the recording reached a section he was yet to master, he would drop out for a few bars, jumping back in when he heard a cue for a part he was more confident in playing. I asked him what he thought he was learning from this:

Most people, I suppose, pick up a guitar as a kid, they get lessons, they learn scales, and they learn their chords, and they slowly build up from there. I was not interested in that at all. I wanted to just play the riffs and play the solos, in fact, straight away. I started . . . teaching myself some scales and developed an awareness of chords, but they don't feature very prominently, at least in the music I was listening to at the time.[26] I just started learning songs, basically, mostly Metallica and Megadeth because they're very guitar-focused styles of music. The guitars are very prominent in the mix, and you can easily follow it and play along to it. I developed most of my skills by playing those songs, and also by playing solos where I could, but not very successfully. There was no attempt to play independently of the recordings because I wanted to play along with the drums and the bass and the vocals. That would also force me to keep up with the music, and some of the music was extremely technical. I had a style of learning where I would learn a technical riff, say, fairly loosely—my timing wouldn't be very good or anything—but then I would just keep playing along to the record until I sounded exactly the same. I would just massage it, basically.

By playing along, Jack makes himself an appendage to others' playing.[27] The recording offers an exemplar that he works toward as he compares his sound with the recorded players. Some riffs are easier than others, and these are mastered first. In harder parts, he is challenged with "keeping up." His timing is carried along by the recorded players, who already know the individual lines, the entry and exit of those lines, and the rhythmic pulse. Jack said that he uses his ear to "massage" his sound until it sounds the same as the recording.

At one level, this imitation brings to mind George Herbert Mead's notion of "taking the role of the other" to develop self-consciousness and comprehend the appropriate conduct.[28] When playing along, Jack "plays at" being the recorded musician, creating what an audience would hear as a recognizable version of the musical other. But this is not taking the role of the other in a purely interactional sense. Rather, this is a form of embodied self-reflexivity in which Jack uses what he imagines of the movement of the other as an anchor for his work on the inner lining of his body.[29] Multiple sensual graspings make up what Mead expressed as a process of "internalization."[30]

DOING HEARING WHILE PLAYING

Hearing to Blend In with Other Players

Struggling to learn the sheer volume of music that professionals must is one way that musicians articulated feeling ill prepared for professional work. The musicians I spoke with described various folk theories about how to overcome this challenge, with the pressure of having to do better chief among them. In Michael's words, "There is just no substitute for working. Being forced to perform in challenging situations. Having people tell you, 'Learn forty songs. You've got a week, you'll be up on the bandstand, [and there will] be an audience.'" Such folk explanations suggest that the problem is principally one of motivation.

Studies of expert practice in diverse work domains highlight a marked difference between the rule-driven processes of the novice and the fluid, continuous action of experts.[31] From this perspective, we may see the problem as not entirely one of the speed of learning a piece. What distinguishes professional players is their ability to play music that is not totally locked down. For classically trained students who need to learn six to eight pieces over the course of a year in preparation for competitions and exams, learning to play those pieces is a function of repetition and memory.

Professional performance is a different beast. It is much more about the creation of music one unique time through. Robert Faulkner and Howard Becker pointed out that jazz musicians arrive at a gig to make music with other players whom they might never have met before.[32] Because the jazz repertoire is only a "useful fiction," jazz musicians must form a temporary agreement among themselves to produce a night's performance.[33] This requires negotiations and continuous mutual adjustment to arrive at a shared sense of jazz (i.e., tunes and the keys they are to be played in). Even after a version of a piece is selected, players take "minor liberties."[34] As Paul Berliner explained, "They [jazz musicians] vary such subtleties as accentuation, vibrato, dynamics, rhythmic phrasing, and articulation or tonguing, 'striving to interpret the melody freshly, as if performing it for the first time.'"[35]

In highly prescribed traditions like classical music, there is also an element of interpretation that conductors and players work through as the music is being played.[36] Fundamental elements of musical sound, such as the precise pitch of concert A and the harmonic relations between notes, vary significantly enough to present a problem for players.[37] Violinist Lachlan explained, "People need to develop concepts that agree, and that is what you do when you play with people. You agree that 'A' is going to be 'X' for the evening."

Hearing is a resource for playing in this context, what Harold Garfinkel might have called hearing for "all practical purposes."[38] Musicians hear not for some ideal notion of what the sound should be but as a means by which they can render a "good enough" performance. Michael explained that he needed to transcribe for hundreds of hours so that on the bandstand, he could hear the music as played by others and adjust his playing to match:

> What we're dealing with is sound: our ability to hear sound, produce sound, hear our own sound, hear other people's sound, and mix our own sound with other people's. Or we arrive at our own sound through listening to so many other people's, absorbing it and mixing it. I did a lot of intensive ear training in order to get to my point now . . . because in a gig, someone is just going to pick up a guitar, look at you, and go [here, Michael vocalized a strummed guitar sound], and you have to know what that is and work around it. If you don't do those umpteen years of learning to hear complex harmonies, in real time, you can't really perform because you don't know what they're doing.

Using the language of "blending" a player's sound with those of the rest of a group is how musicians expressed this type of aural work. They said that this is something that good players do continually. They work to hear themselves in relation to what other players have just played—in this key or that, more or less sharp or flat, a more rounded or piercing tone—to create a blended sound in real time.

Orchestral trombonist Mark emphasized these hearings as being central to understanding the sound that he will need to form. He said that group performance requires musicians to "adjust to what other people are doing" to the extent that, for professional players, the movement of playing becomes insignificant. To this end, he described spending most of his time hearing how other ensemble players were treating the music to apply it to his own playing:

> I am constantly listening. Constantly. It is all I do because we have a lot of bars [of] rest. I am constantly listening to the orchestra, how they play. . . . You're listening because somewhere along the line, you will have to play something that the violins or the woodwinds have just played, and you will have to play it the same way. You can't just go off on a tangent and play it a different way. You have to play in the same style, so if you're not listening, you're not doing your job. . . . You have to know your instrument so well that playing your instrument is not a concern; the concern is, How do you fit in with what is happening?

Mark hears so that when he plays, his sound will be heard by the conductor, the other players, and the audience as being related to what he has heard the other instrumentalists play. For professionals playing in a performance, attending to how others are treating the music becomes the main focus. This hearing work involves musicians discerning the distinct quality of each performance "this time through," as Garfinkel might say, taking cues for their playing from the sounds around them.

This type of hearing is vitally important to professional ensemble musicians, but for various reasons it cannot be the only way that musicians do their hearing when playing. First, amateurs focus more on playing their instruments and thus are more distracted from hearing than are experts. As Mark pointed out, to hear in order to blend in, a player must be past the point that the bodily movements involved in playing an instrument are a main concern. Max, a jazz trumpeter, observed a development in his practice along these lines: "I found I had to get to a point where I could slowly concentrate, like stop worrying about what I was doing physically onstage, and could commit concentration to observing what other people were doing. I realized that I

[was] not listening as much as I [could] be to other people and responding; I was more just thinking of things and doing them on my own."

Second, producing sound can get in the way of less experienced musicians' ability to hear and respond to others. Musicians must hear how other players in their section are treating the music as they play along with them. Trombonists use their tongues coupled with their airflow to give notes different articulations or shapes, from legato ("connected") tonguing, in which the tongue is almost flapping in the breath, to staccato ("separated") tonguing, which places a heavier accent on each note.[39] The tongue movements that contribute to players' articulations happen inside the body, meaning that following players (e.g., those auditioning to join an ensemble) cannot see the tongue movements of the principal that they must imitate. They have to hear their fellow players' articulations to match the movements of their tongues. Mark said that in the orchestra he plays in, the success of auditioning musicians hinges on this ability:

> If you get someone in who you're trying out, if they don't succeed, it will be for a whole variety of reasons. One is that they don't listen. . . . They might tongue in a different manner, which means that they won't fit into the way the section starts a note. If they're tonguing in a completely different manner to the way you are, then it is not going to blend. So the main thing is about blending. Blending with the tuba, blending with the trombones, blending with the double basses, blending with the contrabassoon, the bass clarinet, and the timpani, and just fitting in with the orchestra.

Matching one's sound to the sound of adjacent players is far from straightforward. Mark's account of hearing how the violins or woodwinds treat a line to play a related version of that line is an ideal scenario because there is a time delay. He has the time to hear others first, so he can use the information he collects from that hearing to inform how he will play his line.

To blend in with one's section, players must relate their own sound to those of others *as they play*. Flautist Alex explained, "The time constraint is one of the things that makes music challenging. It is not that you have to play it but that you have to play it *right now*. If you pause when you speak to think or take a breath, your speech still makes sense. But if you pause in music, it loses its coherency and its meaning."

Third, even when all players are involved in a sequence of action, not all can be equally aware of how they relate to one another. The sheer complexity of the music, particularly in larger ensembles, means that it is difficult, if not impossible, for players to hear and adjust to all the sounds all the time. Mark directs his attention in various ways. For example, when not playing, he attends to how a section carrying the melody is treating the music in terms of the shape of the line. When he is playing, he narrows his focus to how adjacent players are subtly adjusting their articulation and timbre.

Hearing to blend in is thus a critical performance strategy but one that presents dilemmas. Ensemble players must find ways to do hearing among the cacophony of others' sounds, ahead of what will be heard when they, and others, move to play. The following analysis looks at some strategies that performing musicians use to make it easier to hear.

The Organization of an Ensemble Guides the Stratification of Hearing Responsibilities

Efforts to blend in are mostly partial. Once an ensemble reaches more than about four players, players do hearing by narrowing the scope of the sounds they focus on to guide their own playing. That is, they attend to how a smaller number of players are treating the music and disattend what others are doing. Composer and artistic director Edward observed the relative attention players may pay to one another depending on the size of the group: "It is impossible with an orchestra to say, 'How is the sixth violin from the front relating to the trombone player?' because they're not. But in a string quartet, everybody has a relationship all the time."

That ensemble musicians can play out of relation, at least directly, forces us to consider how ensembles hear together and play cohesively. Different music traditions, and groups with different combinations of instruments, have their own arrangements of hearing tasks. While the particularities differ, they have in common that players typically subordinate their hearing to that of another.

In larger ensembles, achieving cohesion typically involves a conductor tasked with hearing the whole while simultaneously hearing its parts in almost inconceivably fine degrees of detail.[40] In the words of the conductor Gunther Schuller, musical interpretation has a certain "aesthetic morality."[41] Conductors are the guardians of musical interpretation.[42] They create a division of labor by "hearing for" players as an aid. Schuller described seven "kinds of ear" in conducting. These "ears" include hearing for harmony, pitch and intonation, dynamics, timbre, rhythm and articulation, balance and orchestration, and line and continuity.[43] The conductor's role is to analyze the score and use their aural imagination to determine how it might be rendered in performance. They direct the players based on their hearing of how the music has just been played, and they anticipate how the music will be played following their gestures.

Musicians who play in ensembles with a conductor subordinate their hearing to the conductor to a significant degree. However much they grumble, players seldom question the conductor's right to tell them how to play.[44] That said, even for the most skilled conductors, hearing everything is incredibly difficult; while conductors aim to develop their aural skills and render themselves "aurally/mentally free enough to hear precisely," the scale of the task is such that when conducting, "it is not always possible, even for the best ears (and minds), to hear everything."[45] For example, the conductor, engrossed in the overall expression of a passage, may miss small intonation or rhythmic errors by individual players. Both the conductor and players understand that the players retain some artistic license and some responsibility for precisely how a direction from the conductor is translated into the playing of a passage.[46]

Players attend to their sound not only in relation to the conductor and their own sense of their sound but also to the "subsets" of action happening all the time. Similar to Mark, Latin and jazz trombonist Scott described how players alter their sound production in relation to other section players hierarchically. Section players typically focus their hearing on how the section principal is forming a line. If Scott is playing the second or third part, he continuously listens to the musician playing the first part to subtly adjust his pitching to align with theirs. Tutti ("together") playing shows up whenever this type of hearing is happening:

If you're not locked in together and you're a bit loose, it just sounds crap; it's terrible. . . . But if you hear a band that is really just there, yeah, grooving together, it is an amazing sound. So I think that's important: that everyone is listening to each other and playing together. . . . I guess I listen to their tone, and especially on trombone everything is tuned as you're playing; you've got to have your ears open all the time. . . . You can very easily just play where your set positions are and not be right. You've got to listen. So if I am playing underneath someone, I am listening all the time to their sound, their tuning. Especially when you're playing in octaves, you just have to make sure that the octaves are ringing and the octaves sound perfect together. If you're a little bit sharp underneath them, it is going to sound crap, or if you're a bit flat, it is just not going to have the same effect. So just listening in and when I am melding my sound to them, I will also listen to their tone and the way they are phrasing things, and I guess I try and make my sound wider and my timbre as big and broad and sweet as I can. You can make so many different sounds on a brass instrument, and you sort of—I can't put it into words. It is about the air and your lips.

In the bands that Scott plays in, a band leader takes on some of the aural work of cohesion, particularly when the group transitions from one section of a piece to the next. Scott also needs to hear and play off adjacent players, following the first desk (i.e., the player playing the first part), to form the right pitch, articulation, and timbre.

Players specialize in hearing for certain things depending on their instrument and role, and they cooperate on that basis. In jazz, the drummer typically sets the rhythmic pulse, alongside the string bass player, who is responsible for the harmonic and rhythmic structure. The piano shares these rhythmic tasks with the bass and drums, also suggesting harmonic form.[47] Pianist Michael said that he focuses his hearing mostly on the rhythm section. He tries to listen to the whole, but it does not often work: "Being a piano player, I kind of need to listen to the whole spectrum. I don't think about it, though. I suppose I listen more to the rhythm section because I listen to the harmonic and melodic elements more intuitively."

Reflective of a similar arrangement, metal bass player Nathan said that he works off the drummer, with his hearing of the drummer's expression informing how he understands and treats the music. He is also conscious of how other players in the band relate to the lines that he lays down. Between the drummer and the guitarists, he described himself as the "glue": "Being a bassist, you're not ever flying solo; you're always gluing everything together, particularly in terms of forming the rhythm section with the drummer. Playing with a different drummer could totally change your playing style. I have played with some really good drummers, and somehow their creativity feeds mine, and I can play stuff that I didn't ever think I would come up with myself."

Nathan commented that he listens to the guitarists, too, "but they're a lot harder to lock in with." They cannot be his main focus. Players of melodic instruments describe using rhythm players as an aural focal point, at least in a rhythmic sense. Rock guitarist Andy said, "The thing I really notice is whether a song is dragging or speeding up. I think

I have a better relationship with the rhythm section than anything else in terms of the way I experience and think about rock music."The jazz vibraphonist Gary Burton said that the best advice he ever received was from the jazz drummer Shelly Manne, who said, "Listen to the drummer. Let the drummer be in charge of the time feel. Don't try to lead the band when you solo."[48]

This is not as simple as some leading and others following. Anthony, a Latin drummer, said that as a drummer, he typically works off melody players: "I tend to work more off the melody section than the rhythm. I think it is easier to work because it can be really difficult to listen to all of the rhythm section parts and play your part at the same time, but listening to the melody gives you a basis to work off and a reference without being too much." Anthony is suggesting that he focuses his hearing on the melody players to reduce the load on his ear. As with players of melody instruments, he takes as his reference the sounds that best help him to fit in.

Hearing Through Seeing Motions

The visual organization of musicians reflects how players "hear off" subsets of others. In the classical tradition, chamber ensembles of trios and quartets are arranged so that players can always see one another's movements, at least peripherally. Movements precede sound, for example, when the first violinist visibly breathes in and raises their instrument to signal an entry. In an orchestra, the players cannot all see one another, so seating is arranged in a semicircular fashion and often on a gradient to facilitate sight to the conductor and the leader (the chair of the first violin section, known as the concertmaster in North America), who is positioned at the midpoint of the straight edge of the stage. Seeing is equally important on the bandstand, where many players maintain a line of sight with and are grouped near the players they most need to see and hear with.

To direct players, conductors move in anticipation of the sound, using gestures to give an embodied foundation for players' hearing of the sound that they must form next. Schuller defined the art of conducting as using "minimum of conductorial (if you will, choreographic) gestures" to generate "a maximum of accurate acoustical results."[49] Moving ahead of the sound is no small feat. Schuller calls this hearing with a "third ear," meaning that conductors "hear" outside their bodies in order to attend to the effects of their gestures on the sounds played.[50]

Leaders adopt different choreographic gestures, to use Schuller's language, for different situations of visual perception. Conductors face a large group of players and must communicate a range of musical directions involving tempo, dynamics, timbre, and entry and exit points. Ensuring that their instructions are seen requires the conductor to move their hands in front of their body, one typically extended by a baton. The tempo is continuously gestured with beating hands, and other cues are added as needed. Conductors have individual stylistic approaches, but common visual devices include the exaggerated raising of the baton and their body to signal entry points. To indicate points of exit, conductors bring their hands in toward the center of their body or close their hands in a pinching motion. A rounder sound is gestured with circular movements at waist height, with patterns of crescendo (louder) and decrescendo (softer) indicated through variations in the height of the conductor's hands. For big sound, as in the opening chords of Beethoven's Fifth Symphony, conductors extend their hands widely and closer to head height.

Players form their sound off what they see of the movements of the conductor. Frank, a choral singer, gave an example:

> I have a real admiration for choral directors because they have such strong aural and communication skills. Our choral director . . . was recently in the States and was working with someone who talks about using different sorts of hand signals to produce different sorts of sounds

from the choir. The first couple of weeks after the course, he didn't tell us that he was going to use a certain signal to create this sound; he just did the signals, and they created that sound. That is what this American conductor has found over the years: that people just respond to this. So doing a circular movement with your hands produces a much richer, more round sound. People naturally follow that.

Frank said that he hears himself as he sings, just as he hears the other singers around him, but that creating a cohesive sound is also a matter of "who is directing the singing and their direction in terms of timbre." He adjusts his singing based on the conductor's gestures.

In terms of performing on a bandstand, Scott talked about paying attention to the gestures of the band and section leaders to support the aural work of "sitting in" with others. As in the orchestra leader's intake of breath, the section leader in Scott's horn section moves their instrument to signal the start and stop of a note. Because the following players are adjacent and the leader is also playing, the leader's visual cues manifest as exaggerated motions of playing. Such motions allow following players to "hear" the musical trajectory of the section leader:

> [The] main thing [is] listening, phrasing, and also cutting off notes, as well, where notes finish. Doing them together. . . . I did a gig recently with a really, really heavy sax player. . . . After each note he would give you . . . a flick for when to stop the note. . . . He was tenor sax, and we were playing lines together. . . . That was his conversation with me . . . moving his sax like that—there was no discussion needed. . . . Not just looking at where the note starts—that is crucial, too; you have to hit it together—but the end of the note; that is where it is supposed to be, and that is where you cut it off, right there, and that is what he showed me with that little movement.

Scott explained that even when playing off charts, this resource does not settle how the music should be played. Further coordination is needed to ensure note duration is consistent across players. The section leader embellishes his movements to signal the stopping of a note, aware that the section players will perceive these gestures peripherally. Scott, standing beside the section leader, sees these gestures and takes them as a cue to where they will end the note. This takes some of the load off his ear because he is able to see how he needs to alter his body movements to blend in with his fellow players.

Scott plays in bands with a band leader who typically plays an instrument. The band leader is positioned at the front of the ensemble and so can see, and be seen by, all the other players. The band leader's cues thus manifest almost as conductorial movements with both their instrument and glances at the players. In improvising traditions in particular, players contend with knowing when to transition from one section or one key to the next. The band leader signals transitions within a piece of music rather than providing direction on the formation of individual notes. In moving from one section to the next, Scott looks to the band leader to coordinate the transition: "Sometimes the cues can be very, very subtle, but it depends on the person. . . . Generally the person cuing is playing bass, and they'll give their bass a little raise or even give you a look. . . . A lot of guys have come and filled in for me, and I've heard reports back that it has been hard work because they didn't know what was coming up, and they weren't aware of his cues and his mannerisms." Seeing at least partially substitutes for hearing because the leader's gestures and glances signal transition points.

How Transitions Are Aided by the Collective Feel of the Rhythmic Pulse

Players' knowledge of where they are in the music owes a great deal to the feel of the rhythmic pulse. The gestures of conductors and leaders should not come as a surprise. They are interactive cues that aid what needs to be an aural-embodied sense of the music.[51]

Members of a jazz band talked about how their shared feeling of the rhythmic pulse guides their hearing of where they are in the music and so when to move on. Max (trumpet), Curtis (guitar), and Guy (bass) had been playing together for five years when we spoke. Their music was never scored, existing only ever as what they termed an aural "blueprint," meaning they maintained a collective aural memory of their repertoire of songs. Within this blueprint, they took liberties in the notion of what constitutes a song. Ideas that may have been originally a section in one song could be combined with those from another and reimagined into a new work for a particular performance. Onstage, they must then grapple with how, this time through, they are going to work their repertoire into songs. Guy explained that the band improvises with a riff or an idea, the challenge of which is "what you do in each little section and when you should move on." I then asked the group how they knew when to move on.

The first method that came to mind was via their feel of the rhythmic pulse. Curtis said their music was built on "climaxing" and that they could "instinctively feel when it is the right time to move on to the next part." Guy explained:

> You can really tell. Sometimes it is mathematical; like, a lot of the music that we play is based around groupings of four or eight. . . . for instance, if you're playing a riff, that rules out changing to the next section after we have played it three times because it just wouldn't feel right. . . . So you have got little things like that which kind of hold it together, and then as to whether it is the fourth time, eighth time, or thirty-second time that you change, it is more of a feeling that we can all feel, whether it has reached the point where it is at its climax or it is getting boring.

Here, Guy is describing a collective embodied sense of how all group members hear and feel the music. They also coordinate visually.

"Eyes," Curtis said. Guy added, "There might be a visual cue to say that we are going to do it now." Hearing is most important, they explained, because it tells players what is going on. They need to "get it" aurally and in their feel of the rhythmic pulse, but glances signal the transition points.

Trombonist Scott also talked about how his sense of the rhythmic pulse informs his hearing of the music. This sense of the feel of the music tells him where the group is in a four- or eight-bar phrase and when they are nearing a transition point. The music is organized around predictable patterns, though the specifics are improvised. As with Guy and Curtis, he attends to glances to achieve synchrony as the group transitions:

> There are a lot of open sections in Latin music, open chorus, improvised lead vocals and stuff, and the horn section will come in after that, like a mamba or whatever it may be, going into the next section and knowing the form and the general four-bar loop that is going on the whole time. It is generally sort of four- or eight-bar phrases, sometimes longer, but that is the general way, and just hearing where that sits, where the next line starts. . . . And you will have a lead vocal section. It's generally the same, sometimes it is longer or shorter, but kind of knowing. And it is just listening to it and knowing—generally on your chart, it will have written where you come in, after what, the chorus, the lead vocal, and just knowing where that bit comes in and waiting for the cue from the band leader.

Scott talked not only about feeling but also moving with the music. It is a way to "get that feel inside," Scott said. He continued, "If you just stood there and played, for me that wouldn't be the same. I move a lot when I play, and especially when I am improvising, I do all kinds of random movements with my body. It is just feeling and expressing it in that way."

Hearing Via Proprioception

One of the learning strategies described earlier involves students using their proprioceptive sense of their sound to reconfigure how they produce their sound and how they hear it. Players work on the feel of sound as it is produced to alter their sound production and then readjust their hearing of the new sound. Seasoned performers also described an intimate connection between hearing and the feel of playing but in the opposite direction. In the context of performance, hearing is not only retrospective but also prospective: players "hear" what *will be* heard. They hear ahead via their body's movements.

Players say this is a special kind of hearing. Trombonists Mark and Scott used the words "hearing in the head" to describe it. Mark explained its importance through a reflection on what happened when it was absent for his students:

> You have to be able to hear the music in your head. You *have* to be able to hear it in your head. You can tell when a student isn't hearing the music in their head first because the music doesn't flow, and it doesn't make sense. It isn't music; it is just notes. They don't understand the phrasing because they're not actually singing it in their head before they play it. . . . Unless you have a concept of sound in your head, nothing is going to come out. What you hear in your head is what is going to come out [of] the bell [of the trombone].

Hearing in the head is about flow. It helps with the challenge of playing the music *right now* so that it retains its coherence and meaning. What is called "hearing in the head" is a sense of proprioception: organizing the body to make a desired sound. It is a different modality from that of aural perception.

Improvisers like the violinist Lachlan used the term "ear-to-hand connection." Lachlan explained, "To be a free improviser requires a particular type of listening. . . . It is the ability to hear a harmonic, rhythmic, or melodic concept and adjust what you're doing to respond to it and answer it." The temporal challenges of improvisation are such that the ability to hear harmonic, rhythmic, or melodic concepts and make adjustments cannot mean only hearing what has already come. The hearing must be at least partly anticipatory. Conductors do this, too, hearing with their so-called third ear.

One way that proprioception is used by musicians is "hearing" a mistake ahead of its sounding. Players know some mistakes before they hear them by sensing proprioception gone wrong. Cellist Emily talked about this in the context of realizing that she was not prepared for a shift in hand position that would affect the tuning of the notes that followed:

> Shifting is the time I know I've stuffed up before the sound has come out. I have overshot. As soon as my hand moves, I know whether the sound is going to come out wrong. I performed the Elgar [the first movement of the Cello Concerto in E Minor] at a recital, and in the run leading up to the high E, I knew that it wasn't going to come out right; I knew it was going to be out of tune. As I started playing the quick run, my hand was jumbled, and as soon as I started, I knew that last note wasn't going to come out right. And it didn't.

This experience is sensed but not heard by the player or audience. Observing the playing, the anticipation of the error could have been seen in Emily's body as she squinted her eyes and tensed her shoulders. Reflecting on that point in the recital, she talked about the embodied experience of clammy hands and the rush of heat in her body in that moment, which then introduced a new battle to guard against further errors. Teachers often tell students not to let the audience know that an error is coming. Audiences hear the piece through the gestures and facial expressions of the players as much as through the sound they produce, so it is important to display the right sounds—with one's body—even when there are missteps. Of course, controlling one's body in the heat of the moment is another matter.

The opposite also happens, of course, as when Emily knows that her hands are precisely where they need to be for the sound to be heard as in tune. This feeling often comes outside the pressure of the performance environment, though. "I often have that feeling practicing scales quickly with a metronome. I nail them every time," she said.

WHAT WE LEARN FROM MUSICIANS ABOUT HEARING

The case of the musicians brings into focus the various social interaction frameworks within which musical hearing is developed and done. Musical hearing takes place within at least four social interaction frameworks: being assessed by judges, working with teachers in lesson environments, playing along with recorded others, and playing for an audience.

First, musical hearing is developed within a school-like framework in which students study for exams. The type of hearing developed in this context is mostly disconnected from playing, with sounds being removed from their musical context. A teacher or examiner plays isolated sounds, and students are assessed in ways that facilitate discrimination in the distribution of awards. There is an artificiality to teaching in this way. Many teaching and rehearsal techniques isolate moments and sounds. Working through mnemonics, as in the case of hearing intervals in a known song, can begin to place the hearing of intervals within a student's grasp. However, separating out these moments introduces the risk that students will learn to hear only to elicit a favorable judgment from examiners. The musicians I interviewed frequently pointed out that this kind of hearing has little to do with musicianship or becoming a competent performer.

Second, students work on hearing as a strategy to improve their playing under the guidance of instrumental teachers. This is done in anticipation of performance but not for an audience. Much of the task involves finding ways to develop a proprioceptive sense of how they will sound if they move their bodies in this way or that. They work at becoming musicians by disattending what they hear of their playing, instead focusing on developing a sense of their sound via how it feels in their bodies. In singing, the student's hearing of their vocal production is guided by teachers' cues about posture, air flow, and the engagement of various muscles, which they then internalize. The benchmarks are principally physical—for example, knowing where a vibration is felt in the body—because to describe hearing in aural terms is too abstract. Learning in this context can also involve attending to a sound pattern that can be explained via proprioception, as in the case of a flute teacher who coaches their student to adjust their embouchure, air speed, and air direction based on properties of the sound like "beating."

Teachers invite students into a relation in which they will transcend their own bodies. Students acknowledge that their teachers already have a sense of how to move their bodies to produce the "right" sound. They work on their hearing and playing by making themselves an appendage to the teacher's body, a process that also involves learning to hear differently through their own. This level of intervention in inner experience on the part of the teacher differs from that of other domains. In vipassana meditation, for example, the teacher directs the student's attention toward embodied experience but makes no attempt to align the student's experience with their own.[52]

Third, players cultivate their hearing by interacting with recorded musical others, either in the practice of transcription or by playing along. Learning to hear musically takes time, more time than is typically available in lesson and rehearsal environments. Transcribing recorded music and playing along with recordings can solve this practical challenge. Students must develop their ear in relation to an other, but it can be difficult to get other musicians to hang around and play for the time it takes to do so. Recordings are available anytime, anywhere. They do not complain when a section is repeated endlessly. They do not laugh when a learner gets it wrong.

The interactional meaning of the recording emerges through the work of the musician who takes on the roles of both student and teacher, assessing and directing their hearing and playing, attentive to the gap between their attempts and the recorded benchmark. As in a rehearsal or lesson environment, corrective sequences occur around contrast pairs.[53] But a recording does not stop on its own or offer critiques. Assessment and direction occur in a self-directed way as the musician presents themselves with the preferred sounds by pressing play, pause, and rewind. In transcription, hearing is tested by checking and rechecking, and sometimes by having the transcript checked by a teacher. Hearing develops iteratively. Students must continually encourage themselves to notice where they are falling short.

Working with recordings is synesthetic. In transcription, musicians hear, move to find the desired note on their instrument, and then move to write down the heard sound. The proprioceptive efforts involved in forming and writing down the sound, and the visual artifact of hearing, make the student's hearing more precise. When playing along, musicians hear and move to play or sing the sounds they hear. They slowly develop their hearing and their playing through their embodied consciousness of the gap between what they hear and play and the goal post of the recorded musical other.

Last, musicians cultivate their hearing by performing for an audience. Within this framework, the presence of the audience means that the music must go on. They are not incrementally working on getting their hearing and sound "right." The goal is to play together with others well enough this time through.

The cases presented in this chapter revolved around playing in a group. Playing together means that musicians must work on blending their sounds in real time. This challenge is not unlike that posed in the

Japanese martial art of aikido in which practitioners are coached to stay one-thirty-second of an inch ahead of the aggression of sparring partners or to maintain "sticky contact."[54] In aikido, blending requires fighters to prioritize the movement of the other's body and using some "cheats" to ensure that their bodies remain in the right relation. Musicians do something similar: they focus on hearing how others are treating the music rather than on the mechanics of their own playing. But they need ways to "hear" with more than their ear, ways to anticipate and coordinate the musical action. Musicians' "cheats" include narrowing the scope of sound that they respond to and focusing on adjacent players or another section. They also attend to seen gestures, using them as interactive cues to the embodied experience.

A difference in the perspective of time exists between the musician's hearing and what the audience hears that reflects the inaudible stages of the metamorphosis of body motions into sound for players. The audience hears what was played; they hear the past, or the end of the transformation from body motion to sound. The musician has to hear *before* producing what is to be heard; they hear the future. The case of the musicians uniquely demonstrates that hearing can and, in some cases, must be done without having heard a sound at all.

3

HOW ADVENTURERS HEAR

Ice climbing is so far outside common experience that nonclimbers may find it hard to grasp what a climber must do to climb up a face and back down again. While climbers love to talk and write about their experiences, they often take the practice of climbing itself for granted. Stories from adventurers tend to focus on climbing gone wrong, so those outside the adventurer community may have heard only of fatalities or near misses with gripping rescues.[1] As Ralph Storer explained, "The longer the fall, the more excruciating the pain[;] the greater spillage of blood, the more salivating relished the tale."[2] Sociologists concerned with such activities often ask questions about risk perception and how risk relates to adventurer identities.[3] Interestingly, the experience of climbing does not have a great deal to do with taking risks. Most adventurers do not have a death wish.[4]

This chapter tells another story. I ask: How are activities like ice climbing and walking in remote places performed? What role do the senses play in the practice? How do adventurers survive? Early in my research, I met a mountaineer named Emil who had been going out into the hills since childhood. He worked professionally as a guide, undertook many first ascents, and continued to climb into his sixties. Emil told me that we must have higher standards than losing a leg but living to tell the story.

Ice climbing and surviving are matters of expertise, close attention, and listening to what is happening in an environment. One's senses must be switched on. First, a climber needs the tactile and proprioceptive understanding of moving across a frozen surface vertically. They kick their legs into the ice to engage their crampons in a move termed "front pointing." Ideally, the kick will have enough force to place the crampon points into the ice about one centimeter (a bit less than half an inch). This is enough to hold the climber's weight given the strength of the ice; any more is wasted energy. Their movements must be adjusted to the different textures and qualities of the ice, so they continuously monitor how the ice feels, looks, and sounds from one step to the next.

Green ice, found at high elevations where it is always cold, is the hardest to climb and must be avoided. A surface this hard has drastic implications for the angle of ascent because the climber's crampon may only bite in a couple of millimeters, and the effort of kicking into such hard ice drains the climber's energy, making long ascents impossible. Emil explained that visually, green ice appears "kind of glassy, but not glassy in the way that glass is. You can see, so you're keeping a close eye on these things."

Every night, the mountain freezes into place. As the sun comes up, icicles start to free themselves and tinkle as they fall. If they hit a climber, they hurt, but just like the sound of running water under a snowpack, the tinkles also indicate instability and ultimately a risk of avalanche. The sounds of crampons and ice axes biting into a surface are instructive: Are they embedded strongly enough? Would a less firm placement suffice? Above the snowline, silence often dominates. For climbers, the experience of silence can expand the options of what they can do safely because it allows for the perception of fine sensory cues essential to understanding the environment.

The specialization of this sensory work is evident when we reflect on what someone less experienced might miss. Emil thought of

Australian rock climbers who travel to New Zealand for ice climbing only to find themselves quickly in trouble "because they're not
aware of all the clues around them." The sound of falling ice is not
subtle, but "it's also not necessarily a sound you would place," so inexperienced ice climbers might not be made aware of the danger indicated by that sound. Where an experienced ice climber can tell the
consistency of ice by its color, a rock climber may not and may fail to
adjust their route toward a friendlier surface. Climbers inexperienced
in New Zealand mountain environments may also pass evidence of
recent avalanches in a snow gully, which should tell them to turn
back, without seeing it for what it means. Novices may misinterpret
the scale of the activity and thus the time a trip will take. Faces in
New Zealand can be ten or twenty times greater than those of the
Australian Blue Mountains, and compounding the issue, rock climbers can fail to appreciate that the journey down is not a quick abseil
or a matter of walking out. They may not know that they need to get
going in the early hours lit only by a head torch, and they may belay
when climbing in pairs, which while technically correct takes longer
and may therefore introduce other risks.

I spent time with thirty-one adventurers based in Australia and
New Zealand. I went into the field as an interviewer and partici-
pant observer. While these activities were sometimes separate, what
mostly emerged was a melding of the two, in which I was able to
interview people while spending time with them in significant
places as per the "go-along" method.[5] We spoke about how they
initially came to appreciate the outdoors, which participants often
related through stories of early trips with family, friends, or school
groups. These stories often progressed to accounts of longer journeys in more challenging conditions. We spoke about times when
things went awry, when the weather turned bad, and when a slip
could have been fatal, as well as times of sublime pleasure and connection to place.

As an extension of these conversations, the adventurers were keen to take me places so that I could understand their world. They explained their experience and pointed things out as we went along as if I were any other novice. They drew links between the practices that they had described earlier and the aural and other sensory experiences that we encountered along the way, such as those indicating subtle changes in weather conditions. I mostly went bushwalking (or "tramping," as it is known in New Zealand) but also canyoning, skiing, and hiking on a glacier (figure 3.1).

When I asked adventurers how they developed their outdoor skills, especially their hearing of the environment, most answered that it was a matter of experience. There are two issues with this explanation. The first is pragmatic for the adventurers themselves. In short, getting that experience can be dicey. Adventurers tell

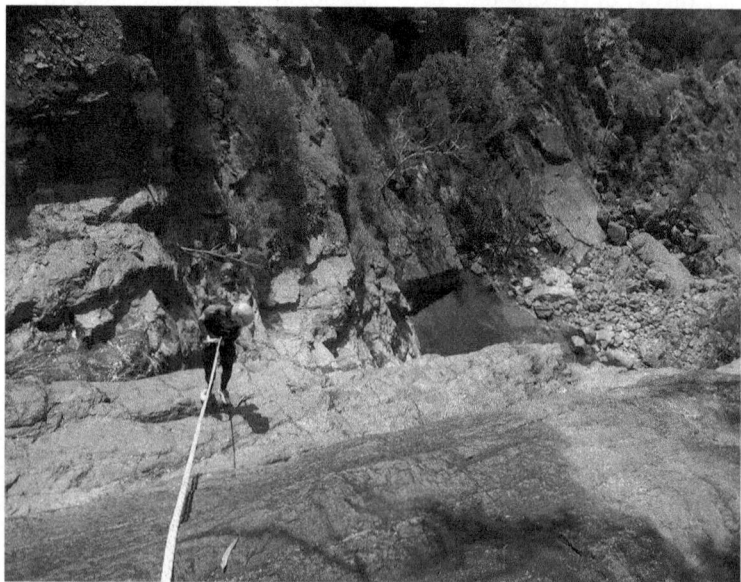

FIGURE 3.1 Abseiling through a canyon in Bungonia National Park, Australia.

stories about getting into dangerous situations; they might not have made it out, but they did, and they sure learned from it. We are reminded of the limitations of this way of knowing by the story of Christopher McCandless, who starved to death after entering the Alaskan wilderness alone with limited equipment, supplies, and expertise.[6] The second issue with the explanation of experience is a problem for the sociologist, namely, that it leaves the learning unexamined. This chapter reveals what makes up the experience that adventurers speak of.

My analysis first addresses adventurers' hearing fostered through stories, which can precede experience. The stories that adventurers tell are not limited to what the activity means for them or to questions of identity commonly addressed by scholars interested in narrative.[7] Adventurers use stories to deliberately transform their own embodied appreciations and dispositions, as well as those of others. Stories contain useful information about places and the interpretive work of moving through those places. In this, stories prime understanding, calling out experiences that may come to be significant, drawing the audience into the storyteller's perspective.

I then address how experience acts as a pathway to learning to hear, and to perceive more generally. Adventurers in training learn by going out with more knowledgeable others. When passing through a landscape, the more experienced party member narrates decision-making processes while pointing out cues. Novices are coached to attend to changes in sounds as evidence of the party's relative location and the developing conditions. Experienced others also pass on to novices "rules" for attending to place, for example, leaving mobile music devices at home to limit distractions. The lessons are not only about the significance of specific cues but also the value of sensory awareness given that no two trips are the same. Experts consider listening not only a matter of hearing but also a metaphor for humility and attention.

HOW ADVENTURERS TELL STORIES TO PRIME THE EMBODIED EXPERIENCES OF THEMSELVES AND OTHERS

Many of the adventurers I spoke with waxed lyrical about sharing their stories around campfires, in backcountry huts, or while traversing less difficult ground. They told me that this is how they communicate what they know and how they process their own experiences into memory. It is through storytelling, rather than through formal education or by continually taking risks, that they develop and share knowledge. In Andrew's words, "Stories become part of the lore of the tribe or the experiences that we share." Narrative guides where to focus in the adventure experience. It becomes "part of the chain of interpretation," as Emil put it.

The following describes two sets of stories. First, we hear from Emil, who talks about river-rolling boulders, and then we hear from Emil's daughter, Anna, who talks about hearing her father's stories and then shares her own. Second, we hear from Aaron, who describes the conditions for a snowpack collapse. The purpose of sharing these stories is to examine the relationship between stories and experience: the kinds of understanding that adventurers seek to share through stories, the work that must be done to integrate storied ways of knowing into embodied understanding, and points of tension or even failure. In seeking to disentangle narrative and practice at this level, we can get closer to appreciating the extent to which stories precede bodily experience in terms of understanding.

Hearing the River-Rolling Boulders

Because crossing a river is a point in a trip when things can go disastrously wrong, the objective danger posed by rivers features regularly in adventurers' stories. In his stories of the Southern Alps region of New

Zealand, Emil told me about the loudness of rivers after heavy rains and the muffled clunking sounds of the so-called river-rolling boulders that move beneath the surface of the water because of the overwhelming strength of the current. He shared this story as an example of subtle cues in the environment. This was part of an ongoing conversation that we had for many days about what expertise means in the context of adventuring. It was shared without a prompt for a story.

On a trip through the Landsborough Valley, Emil needed to cross the Landsborough River and Zora Creek multiple times. The first time he met the Landsborough, he crossed without difficulty. The river was only thigh high because the summer snow melt had passed. As he continued down the valley, however, the weather turned. Incessant rains caused side streams to swell and feed into the main river, which was then "roaring." His attention to the river heightened, he continued carefully, wondering where he would be able to find shelter. There was a hut on his map, but to get to it, he would need to cross Zora Creek. He saw that the creek was high and discolored. Its sound was overwhelming, and underneath its roar he heard river-rolling boulders. Describing the sound, he said, "It means, whatever you do, stay out of that river. If the river can be rolling substantial rocks, you know that you're not going to be standing up in that." While he could hear that it was dangerous, he did not know what he would do if he did not cross. He chose to try it, but his first three attempts ended in water-logged retreat. At that moment, he thought of Gerhard Mueller and Charlie Douglas and their party, who surveyed the Landsborough basin in 1887 and found a large boulder in the middle of Zora Creek that they were able to use to form a bridge after waiting for the water level to go down. Douglas said that being unable to swim had saved his life many times because it made him less willing to attempt river crossings in flood and more willing to patiently wait for the water level to go down.

Tired, cold, and anxious, Emil could not wait it out as Douglas had. He found a point where the river narrowed to only five meters. Ahead he could hear and see that it would only get worse; the roaring was even louder, and the river was foaming as it met the Landsborough. This was the best he could do, so he forded the river and made it. Just.

Emil has shared this story in many ways with many people. His daughter, Anna, grew up being taken on tramping trips and hearing her father's stories, including the one just related. She told me that her appreciation of rivers originated in these stories. She particularly recalled hearing about the sound of river-rolling boulders and said that the lesson from these stories is to stay out of the river if you hear the boulders.

If our conversation had stopped at this point, I could have concluded that stories capture sensory appreciations of an environment. However, this is not entirely the case. Because Anna had identified stories as a core aspect of developing her understanding of rivers among other environmental features, I asked her if she had any stories of her own to share. She responded by sharing her first experience of seeing a creek in flood and hearing the boulders, when she started working as a guide at Fox Glacier in New Zealand. Groups were making their way back along the valley floor after a torrential rain, and one of the side creeks was very high. One of the other guides called her to help their group cross:

> I looked at the river they were planning to cross, and I said, "No, I am not going to help you cross that. I want you to go back into the forest and tell your group a story until the river goes down." . . . The river was black with silt, and there were boulders rolling along the bottom. If anyone had fallen over, they would have been pushed into the main river, and they would have never been seen again. The risk was very high, and the rivers don't stay like that for very long. . . . They were only thinking of solving the problem by crossing the river, not solving the problem by waiting.

The last line of this story echoes Emil's retelling of Charlie Douglas's quip that being unable to swim had saved his life many times. Emil did not heed this lesson, though it taught both Emil and Anna about waiting as a strategy.

Anna continued by linking the lesson of waiting to another story of her own. She was once on a trip where there was heavy rain and the creek rose quickly. Testing the water with her foot, she found it being pulled by the force of the river. Recognizing the risk that she would be pulled into the main river if she slipped, she chose to wait in the bush for five hours, after which time the water had died down, and the crossing was safe and easy.

Having heard these stories, I asked a series of questions to try to disentangle the narrative aspects of Anna's sensory learning of rivers from embodied aspects: What do you remember of the process of learning to assess a river? When did you first encounter the river-rolling boulders? Could you identify them instantly when you heard them? While she reinforced that hearing and reading the stories of others were critical as a learning strategy, experiences of crossing rivers herself under many conditions—various flows, speeds, depths, and bottoms—allowed her to become comfortable crossing them. She explained, "I saw that [the side creek at Fox Glacier] in flood and heard the boulders rolling down and thought, 'Shit, that's what they [storytellers] mean.' You can hear them, and you can smell it, too. You can smell this silty smell in the air because of all of the soil the river is churning up."

Thinking back to the stories and reminders of the hazards in the area relayed to her by a senior guide, she recalled, "They just said that you would be able to hear them; they didn't say what the noise would be like. They also said that the river would be black, a sort of dark chocolate color. I have never heard anyone describe the sound. There are also so many other sounds when you are out there. There is the wind and the rain and the sound of the water rushing, and you can hear the boulders kind of clicking against each other as they come down. Generally, people just say that you can hear the boulders rolling down, though."

A gap exists between an appreciation formed through stories ahead of an experience and the embodied appreciation that can be formed only through it. In the stories that Anna heard, the teller did not describe the sound of the boulders. Descriptions of sounds were absent in the stories that the adventurers related to me, too, despite the tellers' awareness of my interest in hearing. Such stories instruct novices to listen for river-rolling boulders, but the focus is more on directing attention to the phenomenon than on seeking to capture the precise quality of the sound that adventurers must be able to hear. Stories also offer a guide to interrelating sensory information: when you see this or feel that, listen for this.

The "Whoomph" of a Snowpack Fracture

Another common sound portrayed in adventurers' stories was the "whoomph" of a snowpack fracturing. Climber Aaron told a series of stories about this "whoomphing" in response to a question I posed to a group of three climbers over a meal about how their sensory appreciation of the outdoors developed. While I did not ask the group to provide stories, our discussion became an extended story-sharing session, seemingly more for the climbers' benefit than my own. Aaron shared that he first heard about whoomphing and what it meant in terms of surface stability while taking an avalanche awareness course. He recalled his instructor presenting the phenomenon through a story in which the sound was described as an aural indicator of avalanche-prone terrain. As with the stories of hearing rivers, Aaron's instructor's story included a description of what can happen:

> If you're traveling over snow which has a weakness, a weak layer at depth as you travel over it, the snowpack that you're walking on near the surface might be quite a cohesive layer. And just all it takes is your weight walking on top of this layer, which will make the layer deeper

down just collapse, and it might only be going down a few millimeters, but it's settling, and it creates this big kind of "whoomph" noise. And you can't really feel it often. You just hear it in maybe a twenty-meter radius around you. And you think, "Oh, OK, this is not stable at all."

In this story, the instructor did not describe the sound itself or compare it to another sound, but Aaron went on to describe it using a story of his own. He was on an ice-climbing trip at Wye Creek, just outside the Remarkables Ski Area in Queenstown, New Zealand. The party went up to the ridgeline at the ski field boundary and dropped back into the Wye Creek basin. This was Aaron's first time in the area, and he found the first four kilometers or so of the trip "pretty mellow," the terrain not being very steep. As he walked across the surface, he heard a whoomph about every fifty meters, a sound he described as "unreal." He knew from stories he had heard, and from the avalanche awareness course he had taken, that on nearly flat terrain like this he was safe but that the sound was a warning of avalanche risk on steeper ground. The creek gradient increased to about thirty degrees toward the end, making it a "prime avalanche slope," Aaron said. The party turned back after hearing the whoomphing over the flatter terrain. As he finished the story, he said, "I'd heard about this whole whoomphing thing prior to that, but that's the first time I'd actually heard it. I definitely linked the two together [the stories of the sound and his experience of it] straightaway. It's like, 'Oh, this is what it sounds like.'" He was able to recall the narrative account and make the connection between the sound and the danger, but he lacked a sensory appreciation of the whoomph ahead of his experience of it.

As the audience of this story, I conceptually understood the sound and the risk it represented, but I could not imagine the sound itself. Perhaps breaching the tacit rules of hearing the story, I said, "I don't have any concept of what that must sound like," prompting Aaron to try again to articulate the heard cues: "It's a bit like if you've been walking along [a] footpath, and suddenly it settles. Big fright." Aaron was attempting to link the sound in his story to a sound I may have heard, but we did not have shared experience, and the common ground he was trying to establish was inadequate. Footpaths do not tend to settle or whoomph.

Aaron told me that while he had learned a lot from stories, putting experiences into words could be challenging: "Often I'll read something that other authors or other writers have said about their trip in the hills, and I'll be, 'Yes, that's the feeling.' But I've never been able to express it. So I often have to just quote people to describe what I think of situations." This challenge is enhanced when communicating experiences to nonclimbers like me. He had to go to extra effort to convey something of the experience but found that he was "always disappointed slightly in the end with the result." He said, "They [the audience of non-climbers] haven't quite got the idea, but that's the best I could do."

The Experience That Follows the Story

Most of the time, descriptions of environmental features like river-rolling boulders are shorthand for embodied experiences that will follow. Outside the context of an interview in which a researcher, such as me, may insist on a rendition of a sound, storytellers typically say something like, "You will hear . . . ," but the actual hearing of the sound, among other sensory cues, is left to experience. When Emil originally told me his story, I asked him what the river-rolling boulders sounded like. He answered, "It is a sort of muffled, clunking noise that you can hear above the noise of the water, 'clunk clunk clunk clunk' as something is knocking against other rocks." Adjectives like *noisy* and *loud* and onomatopoeic words like *clunk* awkwardly convey something of the sounds of a potentially hazardous river. However, the aural concept of the sound I had formed proved off the mark when I finally heard river-rolling boulders on a trip with Emil, who was there to ask, "Can you hear the boulders?"

Words can be inadequate because they cannot capture embodied experiences with enough detail and accuracy, a broad challenge that has been identified elsewhere.[8] Audiences must do interpretive work to translate a story, not only at the point of hearing it, as others have recognized, but at the point of encountering new phenomena that come to be interpreted partly through the lens of cautionary tales and partly through an adventurer's own embodied experience.[9] The embodied knowledge suggested in the narrative comes to make sense retrospectively as an adventurer who has heard a story about a particular phenomenon pulls together multiple strands of sensory information to test whether they are experiencing what they have only previously heard about. In their subsequent storytelling, the adventurer knows that words will fall short, so they do not usually attempt a rendition of a sound but rather focus on directing listeners' attention to the phenomenon indicated by the sound.

We see the significance of direct experience in cases where it is lacking. John had been interested in alpine environments since he was a child, but he grew up in rural Australia, where such places were not accessible to him geographically or economically; further, he lacked the necessary social networks that enable climbing. Instead, he got into bushwalking in local national parks with family and school groups. At university, he joined a mountaineering club only to find that they did not have experienced mountaineers, so he settled for cross-country skiing and rock climbing. These activities helped him develop some skills relevant to mountaineering, but he was conscious that without experiencing what a place feels, looks, and sounds like, his understanding was abstract at best.

John later decided to go to New Zealand, where he started with climbing courses because, without any experience of climbing environments and without knowing other climbers, this was his only option. The formal instruction he received in his climbing courses allowed him to gain rope and climbing skills but was unable to advance his understanding of real-world climbing environments. He read and heard stories from more experienced climbers that gave him some expectations of what he would encounter, but these stories could not translate into sensory understanding.

John told me about his attempted climb of Mount Darby toward the end of one of his first visits. From stories, he knew that the mountain froze in the morning and that he would therefore need to set out early to take advantage of the freeze. He described this as a kind of "vicarious experience." His party left their hut at two o'clock in the morning, but they had a long walk to the base of the climb and did not reach it until eight o'clock. By this time, the sun had been up for two or three hours, and the surface was becoming "mushy." This sensory appreciation of the state of the surface was retrospective. Where an experienced climber would not have started an ascent in these conditions, his party continued. By nine o'clock, there was a rockfall of about two cubic meters, which John both heard and saw as it was released three meters to his left, shattering on its way down.

This experience became a story that John now tells to explain the dangers of climbing on inhospitable New Zealand rock in the Mount Cook area in summer once the sun is up. From reading and hearing others' stories to becoming the storyteller himself once he had had an embodied experience, there was a shift in his narrative toward including a description of sensed cues:

> We always knew New Zealand rock was bad, but it was an abstract concept. We didn't have that minutiae of detail about snow melting and getting into the rock and loosening it up and actually being able to feel it and see how crap it is. By just standing on it, you were destabilizing it and making it move down, so you just had to be continuously moving. That really gives some detail and color to this very stereotypical notion that New Zealand rock is very bad. . . . All these experiences that happen, kind of in aggregate, give you a better understanding of

what's going on. . . . I guess it becomes a reality because you can read about mountaineering dangers and phenomena in books—this is how an avalanche happens, and this is how you climb in an alpine style—but it's a kind of intellectual exercise. If you're actually in an environment, then you're totally immersed in the reality of it.

Having been there, moving up the face, and seeing and hearing the rock fall, he understood the "mushy" surface in new ways. He described how "the ice starts to melt, and the water goes through the rock and in the cracks and loosens it up, and it falls off, so there was a fairly high likelihood of a rock fall." He did not articulate this point, but the water is something he could hear. By feeling the soft surface below his feet and later seeing and hearing the rockfall, he also came to hear the ice melting and understand what that meant.

Stories from others offer vicarious experience, but understanding their significance in an embodied sense requires adventurers to have their own experiences of hearing, seeing, feeling, and smelling environments as their bodies move through them. The adventurers I spoke with were committed to storytelling as a strategy for sharing and reflecting on their experiences, yet the relationship between the stories and the realities they attempted to describe was not straightforward. Embodied understanding is deeply embedded in experience. Stories say simply, "Here are the sounds that are there to be heard."

TRAVELING IN GROUPS: HOW GUIDES AND TRIP LEADERS ATTEMPT TO DRAW NOVICE ADVENTURERS INTO THEIR EMBODIED PERSPECTIVE

The adventurers generally agreed that the experience they valued so greatly should be initially gained under the guidance of skilled others. Adventurers often gave a narrative of their skill development in which they went out into the bush or the hills at a young age, often with family. They then joined bushwalking and mountaineering clubs, which radically expanded their experiences through the regular trips that clubs offer. These were the best ways to learn because the adventurers were walking or climbing under the "watchful gaze" of people who knew what they were doing, to use Manuel's words. This watchful gaze serves to limit fatal mistakes. As Jake put it, by going out with more experienced people, he "stood less chance of dying." Various strategies are involved in learning by going out with experienced others, as I will show in the following.

Naming-cum-Pointing to Cultivate the Attention of Novices

When I asked the adventurers to describe the learning strategy of going out with experienced others, conversations initially appeared to skirt specific mechanisms. Instead, they told me about going to different places, the challenges that they encountered, and what they perceived. They then took me on short trips during which we exchanged the odd word or story. Over time, what I came to understand is that this *is* the learning strategy. Novices learn what to listen and look for, and what value to place on various cues, by having things pointed out to them along the way. Michael Polanyi wrote about this kind of "naming-cum-pointing" teaching strategy to share ways of knowing that are beyond language. He wrote that the strategy relies on "the pupil's intelligent cooperation for catching the meaning of the demonstration."[10] Making the connection between directing one's attention to a phenomenon and understanding the significance of that phenomenon is the student's responsibility.

An adventurer who was able to articulate and demonstrate this learning method to me was Simon, a highly experienced and well-respected transalpine tramper and climber in New Zealand. But of course, he was once a novice. Thinking back to that time, he described a trip leader who greatly influenced him, a man who was "very mellow, quite chatty, and unassuming." Simon explained, "You would see him talking to someone, and what he would be saying would be something like, '[I'm] having a bit of trouble with this; could you give me a bit of a hand?'" This trip leader did not strictly need the less experienced adventurer to help him, he was giving them an opportunity to learn. Simon extended his bushcraft skills through his experiences with this person: "Some people you just end up having a lot of respect for just from being in the mountains with them and watching things. They are not necessarily trying to show you anything; you're just observing and seeing how they go about doing things. Just from observing their systems and talking about it, you come to learn a lot."

Central aspects of Simon's learning from this experienced other were observing his leader's methods and having sounds and sights pointed out. As they traveled through an environment, they looked at their maps together, and they saw things collaboratively that he had previously been unable to see on his own. He recalled learning to hear sounds like river-rolling boulders in this way: "I was probably with people who did know [what river-rolling boulders sound like], and they would have said, 'Hear the boulders?' And I would have said, 'Yeah,' and ever after I [would] know. . . . If you're in the hills for a week with someone, you have a whole week of coming across a river with someone and talking about this stuff all the time."

Such experiences are invitations for the novice to see, hear, and feel as the more experienced adventurer does. Simon tried to teach me to be attentive to the environment through a similar method. He was telling me a story about river-crossing deaths when he suddenly stopped and said, "Did you observe that change? The southerly [wind] has reached us." Because I was listening to the story, I missed the change in the weather: "I didn't notice, but I am freezing, and now [that] I look, it is quite clearly not sunny anymore." He joked that I had missed the change because I am Australian and so not attuned to New Zealand weather. He then quickly moved to point out the aural and other sensory cues of the change in weather so that I could be drawn into his perspective: "Back to noticing wind changes, sometimes I can suddenly hear things that I couldn't hear before, and that will be a southerly change because out here where I am out on the beach, I can suddenly hear the waves. And although the temperature and sky have not changed, I know at that point that the wind direction has changed, and I now have a southerly [wind] on me, and there will be cloud coming up on me shortly."

A person skilled in sensing these weather patterns can hear a southerly before they feel or see it. Simon gave me a list of other aural cues I might notice later on to prime my hearing. Sounds of thunder can be used to estimate time until a storm cloud hits. Sounds of fauna can draw attention to bands in the bush that are efficient for traveling through. By flagging these cues, he was creating an opportunity for me to engage my own senses later on.

Lucy described a similar process of skill development. She started going out into the hills as part of family camping holidays and later got into skiing and tramping through clubs. I asked her about the process of refining her hearing, and she said, "I think I've learned a lot by just doing it if that makes sense. Just being out in the mountains and particularly being out in a lot of stormy periods . . . hearing which direction the wind is coming from and hearing things like snow falling off trees or avalanches across the valley or rock fall." She went on to explain that it is "a great thing to go with people who are more experienced." At a minimum, it reduces the risk; learning from mistakes can be dangerous if not fatal. But more than that, as they encounter different situations together, members of a party articulate what they are feeling, seeing, and hearing, which serves to extend the sensory appreciations of novices. Lucy explained the nature of such conversations: "'Did you feel that?' or 'Did you hear that?' So it's sharing that sensory thing with someone else and verifying it."

This strategy for cultivating perception differs from storytelling in various ways. The obvious difference is that those involved are doing it collaboratively and sharing an experience, whereas in storytelling, storytellers are most often recalling experiences that the listeners were not present for. The subject matter also differs significantly. Stories typically take as their focus a challenging scenario. In contrast, the commentary and guidance offered by the experienced adventurer during a trip offers guides to hearing outside of emergencies.

How Adventurers Refine Their Hearing by Collaboratively Attending to Changes in Sound

Like doctors, adventurers must attend to changes in their environment. It is not so much the quality of the sound that is instructive, but rather its relative character. As Karen put it, "Often it is about a change in sound, so you have to hear the sound first, and then hear when it changes. . . . I guess you need a comparison, though, because it is about the change in sound as opposed to the sound itself." The comparative nature of sound provides information about many things: one's relative position in relation to an environmental feature such as a river or a ridgeline, the relative strength of a river or a rock formation, or developing weather conditions, as when a sound can suddenly be heard because of a change in wind direction.

Climber Kevin talked about being coached to attend to such changes by climbing mentors. Kevin grew up in Minnesota and mostly climbs in the United States are on "good" rock. When he started climbing in New Zealand, he was faced with crumbling rock and needed to learn how to climb these less stable surfaces safely. An experienced New Zealand–based climber told him, "You have to tap or kick the rocks before you use them." This tapping or kicking is not to dislodge the rock, though this could happen. Rather, it is more like the use of percussion in medical practice: tapping to hear what is beyond the visible plane. Kevin came to appreciate the difference in sound between stable and crumbling rock via aural contrast, as each type makes a unique sound. He said, "You may not know what is the correct sound, but as soon as you tap a rock and then have it fall off from your grasp, then you know that you want to avoid that kind of rock."

He explained this through the use of pitons (metal spikes or pegs driven into a climbing surface for support). The cracks in the rock produce different sounds as the piton is hammered into place, and by hearing these contrasting sounds, Kevin can hear the nature of the crack and thus the strength of his piton placement. He hears a ringing sound when the placement is strong. When he hears "a dull thud," he knows not to put too much trust in the piton.

The process of hearing via contrast also happens between peers. George talked about a canyoning trip he took with an experienced party in Kanangra Gorge in the Australian state of New South Wales. They were using their hearing of the water and wind to estimate the group's location. When they reached the bottom of the Kanangra Falls Canyon, they arrived at the gorge that they would follow upstream for about six or seven kilometers until they reached a creek that marked their exit point. George remarked that the group had been walking for quite a while before realizing the need to refocus on their navigation: "At some point, you think, 'Bloody hell, this is taking forever! Where is this creek?'"

This sudden interest in their location triggered efforts to hear collectively for it: "You are listening to the wind as it roars down the different gullies, and you are trying to hear how close you are to the next one. Then you try and listen for the stream to see where it comes in." When George and the other members of his party listened to the wind and water, they did so by attending to how the sounds changed as they moved over the ground. They heard the wind roaring through a gully and heard the volume of that sound increase as they grew closer. Hearing that change in volume refined their sense of space in relation to the sound and informed them of the distance to the next gully. They worked to distinguish the sound of the water from that of the wind and then estimated their distance from the creek based on the volume of the creek's sound.

George and his friends formed their judgments about the differences in sounds and their meanings collaboratively. He recalled, "We do generally have conversations, or rather we make comments as we go: 'You hear that?' 'How far do you reckon?' 'I reckon ten minutes.' 'Nah, I reckon it is closer.' 'Nah, there is another gully before it, so it is probably the wind coming down through that one that is confusing you.'" George was hearing partly through others' ears, comparing what he was hearing with what the others were hearing. He told me that by going through this process of collective hearing and sense-making, he and his friends formed an agreement that the creek was five hundred meters ahead, "and that was smack bang where it was."

This is a case in which a teaching strategy is also a technique used by experts to navigate their chosen activity. George was developing an aural skill that was directly connected to the context in which it would be useful, unlike the case of musicians who learn to identify intervals based on well-known songs, a skill that can help them pass an exam but not help with live performance. George was being coached to find meaning in the sounds of his environment via contrast because he needed that skill to become a successful canyoner. The experiential approach of attending to changes in sound as correlated to a specific set of conditions refines adventurers' hearing over long temporal scales as much as it gives them information in the moment.

Hearing Rules in Adventurer Communities

In general, the adventurers did not have good things to say about rules. They all bucked against the rules outlined by organizations such as the New Zealand Mountain Safety Council on matters such as river crossing, considering the organizations to overly simplify a skill that requires nuanced, qualitative judgment. The Council publishes educational pamphlets and runs courses that highlight hazards and teach techniques and "rules" for river safety. While rules—such as understand river dynamics, identify potential hazards, and know where, when, and how to cross—appear sensible, the perceptual expertise required to make such judgments far exceeds that which can be imparted through a pamphlet or training session.

While they likely would not use the term *rules*, the adventurers nonetheless seemed to have rules of their own related to hearing designed to put adventurers in a position where they can attend to their environment and their party. One such rule relates to the use of mobile music devices. Many adventurers explained that the type of listening they do in the bush or the mountains is distinct from modes of listening used in urban spaces. Smartphones and mobile music players are of the urban world and serve to disconnect people from their surroundings.[11] Adventurers seek a connection to a place, and the soundscape of an environment is part of the magic of being there. Transforming the soundscape of an adventuring environment with sound from a mobile device is therefore frowned upon.

George made a point of banning mobile music devices on trips for which he was the leader, and Andrew did the same. George went so far as to say that it was "unethical" to use a device in the bush, which he likened to watching videos on a phone during a recital. George and Andrew both said that experienced adventurers in their circles adhered to the no-mobile-music-devices rule but that novices often did not, risking ruining the experience for everyone. George explained,

> In [my previous club] it is unspoken. Everybody seems to understand it. [At my new club,] they're not very strong at bushwalking at the moment. . . . [They] seem to take with them all the trappings of urban life, so some of them will take an iPod. When I go on my trips, I really stipulate that . . . things like iPods are absolutely banned. I don't know

why we insist on it so much because it is not my ears that are listening to it; it is their ears. Maybe we're trying to educate them to understand what it [the activity] is about, or at least what we find appealing about it.

When we spoke, George had recently written an article for his club newsletter on the topic that opened with a rich description of the sensory aspects of a place. He drew attention to what adventurers would miss if they transported themselves elsewhere aurally. Wanting to connect with the immediate soundscape—created by the wildlife, the weather, the stillness—was commonly given by the adventurers as a reason to avoid bringing music players on trips.

Climbers, who typically find themselves in more challenging scenarios than bushwalkers, must attend to place, as opposed to a device, as a matter of not only pleasure but also safety. The climbers I interviewed uniformly agreed that climbing in an alpine environment requires one's senses to be alert. To climb with headphones on is a death wish, as John explained:

> I think there'd be a difference, say, between bushwalking and mountaineering. I think in bushwalking, it's generally fairly safe, and if you feel like . . . introducing a new element into your environment [such as music], then it's probably not going to distract your judgment in a way that will cause you to be unsafe. I think it would change the experience and it wouldn't be the type of experience that I would want. . . . Listening to music while you're actually climbing . . . would be very unsafe because you're not in touch with the snowpack and the potential for avalanches and the weather and how that could be changing. . . . There [are] so many factors that you should continually be focusing on that if you shove some other element in your environment, then it distracts you from those.

To say that the issue of using mobile music devices in adventuring environments was contentious would be an understatement.

All the adventurers had something to say about it. All were aware of the common philosophy against their use, and many agreed that it was not OK; however, some did not think rules should be "pushed" onto everyone.[12] For example, some said there were times that a music player could help relieve boredom at night or motivate them to keep going at the end of a long day.

Another rule of sorts related to clothing. Jacket hoods reduce adventurers' ability to hear. Karen showed this in her account of her trip to Antarctica, where, between her hood and the wind, she felt she was in a "bubble," unable to hear clearly. She was traveling with a group but said she felt that she could have been alone. Because of the conditions, hoods were needed, but that meant that she and her fellow adventurers needed to rely on hand signals to communicate.

The problem with hoods led to the creation of a rule about not wearing one while guiding, provided the conditions were amenable. Kate, a climber, received this instruction when she worked for a glacier-guiding company. The company owner told her, and a giant in the New Zealand climbing world had told him. She understood this prohibition as a cardinal rule passed down from one generation of New Zealand mountaineers to the next (figure 3.2):

> We were never allowed to wear hoods, like a jacket with the hood done up, because we couldn't hear. It was really important as the guide that you could hear what was going on. You had to wear, because it was pouring with rain [and] you didn't want water dripping down your back . . . a wide-brimmed hat and to have your hood down. I think that is probably the most significant thing that I can think of, somebody else saying, "This is what you need to do to make yourself and your clients safe." . . . And he [the company owner] used to tell us stories about people who were just oblivious. There were these huge rocks bouncing down the hill, and these people were sitting there having a picnic, and they looked up, and they said, "Oh look, rabbits!"

FIGURE 3.2 Glacier walk at Franz Josef Glacier, New Zealand. The guide wears a wide-brimmed hat as opposed to a hood to hear the environment and the party.

Again, the lesson here is about attention. Kate's story explains how important it is for guides to be fully aware of what is happening in the environment; their senses provide critical information that novices are likely to miss. Kate went on to explain that she also needs to have her hood down so that she can monitor how her group is doing without looking at them: "Of course, it's not just listening to your environment there but listening to what your clients are doing behind you. I certainly found as a guide that I listened very closely, like, how are they breathing? Are they able to keep up? I can hear them stumbling; are they OK? And it's partly because you're being discreet about it." In monitoring the group via hearing, as opposed to seeing, she can orient herself visually towards the surface she is traversing among other draws on her attention. It also communicates confidence to the novices, as opposed to the fear that may follow from someone obviously feeling the need to continuously check in.

One interesting aspect of adventuring rules is that they give some responsibility for doing hearing to the least experienced. Banning devices among novices in particular is a way of telling them that they must be contributors to the group from the start. It is not just the trip leader who needs to hear; all members of a group are responsible for attending to the environment. This differs from the classical music tradition, where in preliminary stages the teacher hears for the student to a significant degree.

LISTENING AS A METAPHOR FOR SYNESTHETIC ATTENTION

The purpose of this project has been to provide a micro-social analysis of hearing. At one level, the adventurers got it. They wanted to talk about it. They thought it mattered. However, they found it difficult to talk about their hearing as an isolated modality. They shared meandering, engaging stories. They took me on beautiful walks and lengthy drives. At some point during those outings, I would ask them to tell me about hearing. But their answers were vaguer than I had anticipated based on the narratives and the experiences that they had so far shared.

For instance, after talking to Veronica for about an hour, I explained that my specific interest was hearing. She acknowledged that, yes, it is important and rattled off the following:

> Yeah, you're always listening for rock fall; you know, where's that coming from? Is it coming from above me? Avalanches, you know, where are they coming from? Are they above me? Especially when you're climbing in the dark, which you do a lot of. And wind, listening to where the wind's coming from. Is the wind—because you can hear it

up above you often. Or how windy it is; the wind's picking up; I wonder how windy it's going to be on top. Because you might be sheltered because you're on the upper face, in the lee, but you can hear the wind picking up above, so you're listening and trying to gauge how strong is it up there.

Veronica's description tells us something about where hearing matters for adventurers, but it does not address hearing as a practice or how it is cultivated in this group. I could create a list like this from virtually any of our conversations. I felt an absence of meaning in these discussions, as did the adventurers.

What are we supposed to make of this? In this regard, something that Emil said in his mild-mannered way has stuck with me: "Listening is fine as long as you know it is a metaphor, too." It took me a long time to reconcile his meaning with my work. My gut-level response was, "It can't be a bloody metaphor! Can't you see what I'm trying to do here?" (Of course, I didn't verbalize that.)

The metaphor that he was referring to is the idea that listening means protecting one's perceptual connection to the world and being responsive to place. Or, as the adventurers might say, listening to place. The metaphorical use of the term listening raises a question about the attributes of hearing that lend it to this role, as well as what that implies about sensing and knowing more broadly. The composer and writer R. Murray Schafer's essay "Open Ears" provides some hints. It begins, "We have no ear lids. But this does not mean our ears are always open."[13] This is an idea that resonated with the adventurers; indeed, one observed our lack of ear lids, though he had not read Schafer's work. For adventurers, being good at listening means being open and responsive. However, listening is considered just one aspect of being open and responsive, no more or less important than others. When adventurers refer to listening, they mean a broader pattern of awareness, humility, and sensing as a pathway to understanding.

This is the lesson that they wanted to pass on. To me and to novices. They were trying to articulate a philosophy of adventure. Simon spoke at length about the importance of paying attention to the subtleties of a place, to the degree that sensory awareness is the foundation of bushcraft:

> Without sensory awareness, we have got nothing, haven't we? It is kind of everything. Ultimately, the standard thing I have long believed is that observation is the beginning. It is observation, observation, observation. It is taking it in and using it. It is critical. People who become competent in the hills are observant. . . . You're traveling through the land, and you develop a way of assessing the implications of things everywhere. You're looking at a river, and as you're keeping your eye on it, you're noticing what sort of volume of water there is in the river, whether it is up, whether it is not, what the rocks are like in the river, whether they are going to be greasy or not. It is not that you have any intention of crossing; they are just things to observe. It is just like traveling through the bush and noticing whether you're in an area with a lot of ferns or whether you're on the tops, how loose the rock is or isn't, what kind of rock it is, how it is all dipped and striked, what kind of fracture lines are running around, what kind of repeating patterns are happening as you're traveling around ridges. You might be traversing around the side of a range, so you need to think about patterns. If you're coming across slabs here, when you get around the corner, it is highly likely that you'll get something similar repeating because that is what rock does. All those little observations and awareness. It is part of developing no surprises. You might be traveling in mist, and you might not be sure whether the day is going to work out as one when you can travel reasonably safely or whether the weather is going to fall to bits, so if an airplane flies over [one did at this moment, and Simon directed my attention toward it], I would be listening to whether there was any variation in the sound of that because if there is a lot of pulsing, it is highly likely that there is a whole lot of wind. Whereas if it is all calm air, there

will just be a steady drone. Little things all the time that add up, none of them particularly important. You can tell people a few things, but it is like taking a horse to water: they either drink or they don't drink. If you're navigating on a ridge, you're listening for the wind. On the top, it is not a problem because you're going to be able to feel it straight away. In the bush, though, it is very easy to drop off the side of a ridge, and I would be listening for whether or not I am still in the wind. It is just a matter of having an ear out and listening to whether or not the wind is still coming across the ridge strongly, just keeping an eye, or rather an ear, on things.

Simon distinguished great adventurers from average ones by "how much they take out of their environment." He explained, "Some people will miss the strands. They are watching their compass, and basically following what they have been taught in a blooming course, as opposed to seeing and hearing what is going on around them, which is the guts of bushcraft. It is listening to the bush, hearing the bush." He moved between different ideas of hearing. One is aural, literally hearing what is going on around him. This hearing is mixed with other perceptual experiences. He hears and sees as he moves. Listening to the bush means something different again. It is about understanding and responding to place.

The idea that adventurers become competent by paying attention, via their senses as well as an awareness of geography and weather patterns, was commonly expressed. Unless novices are present, they primarily pull these strands together tacitly to make decisions. In one of this chapter's opening stories, Emil told me about rivers and what we can expect from them aurally to prepare our hearing ahead of an encounter with them. But he also explained that an appreciation of rivers is not only aural but also visual and tactile. Hearing, seeing, and feeling all contribute to an adventurer's assessment of a river: "You can tell a lot by the noise the river makes and, of course, while you're hearing the river you're looking at the water and you can see how turbulent it is. The thing is, often where the water is deeper it is making less noise; it has more room to move, say. But by interpreting the sound and the visual perception of what the water looks like together, you can come up with a pretty good idea."

Information about a river gained from hearing alone can be misleading. We see as we hear, and understanding comes from taking in place in this synesthetic way. This is not only about making an assessment in the moment. Adventurers refine their hearing by exploiting synesthesia.

Lucy gave a similar account. She worked in avalanche control, so both in her professional capacity and on her personal trips she was particularly attentive to the characteristics of snowpacks. She said, "You don't learn to understand and predict weather and how that's going to affect the snow without just being out amongst it a lot and being observant." There is a close connection between her hearing of sounds and her feeling of them. She described the "whoomph" sound of a snowpack fracturing as a "whole-body feeling." Awareness of this sound is critical in her assessment of avalanche risk; it makes her stop immediately. But she only came to know this sound by experiencing it, by being in places that offered the opportunity to hear and feel it. Another "sound feeling" that Lucy encounters is the "drummy" sound made when snow is hollow: "It's like a drum almost, which is when there's a hard slab over something softer. And it feels stiff, but it feels hollow, and it makes this hollow, drummy sound as well when you push down on it with your ski." When she encounters this sound, she knows that there is a slab formation (a cohesive layer of snow on top of a weaker layer and the main cause of avalanche), which she will examine more closely depending on the location and size of the slope.

You might have noticed that these accounts of hearing have become more interesting now they have been positioned to convey the meaning of hearing as understood by the adventurers: as one element, or strand, of the reasoning process in a given circumstance. Conditions can radically transform the embodied experience of and knowledge needed to negotiate a place. The specific time and place matter. This means that every new trip needs to be met on its own terms.[14] The following observation from Emil about how his hearing may have changed over time illustrates this idea:

This relates specifically to the area of sound, that you become much more acute at interpreting . . . the sound of wind. The strength of the wind, where it is coming from, what it means, of course, in terms of the weather because so much hinges on it, because the climate is so volatile there that you do take a real interest in this; there is no doubt about that. Interpreting the weather is something that you never stop learning [about] and probably improving on as long as you keep going out into the hills. One example comes to mind because it is so obvious. We were climbing the east ridge of Mount Cook, East Ridge, so it is sheltered from the west. It's a very long climb; the last part is up the edge of the Caroline Face. From the Grand Plateau, it is fifteen hundred meters, and it is a long way, [a] long way from anywhere. I have the memory of that particular occasion that as we got high up towards the summit ridge of Mount Cook, we could hear the wind roaring over the crest of what we were climbing. So powerful. And you know, well, if you knew anything, you'd know that when we get up there, we're going to have some serious problems. . . . We had to keep going up because it was much shorter to the top. When you get to the top of the East Ridge, you get onto the middle peak of Mount Cook. That means that . . . it is a long way from home. If you go to the high peak, it is a kilometer away along the icy ridge exposed to this howling gale, and then you've got to get back down off the high peak, so that option is out under these conditions. To the low peak, it is a bit less than half a kilometer away. If the weather isn't so good, normally we would proceed down to the low peak. That is the safest way under normal conditions; it is free of avalanche danger and so on. On this occasion, because of the gale blowing, what we did was once we got to the middle peak, we took the quickest way down off the summit ridge. Once we were off the ridge, the wind speed dropped markedly. We went down to the hanging glacier between the middle peak and the low peak. We were really looking for the quickest way down. What we did was something that you wouldn't do under normal circumstances. We found a big avalanche track. A big ice bulge had broken off and had roared down the side of the mountain, and we thought, "Well, if it can go down there, we can go down there, too." We ended up running down this avalanche track with the person at the back keeping an eye out in case anything else came down.

I asked Emil whether others with less understanding of that place might have made a different decision in those circumstances. He replied,

My guess is that they would have gone to the low peak. I think they would have been OK, but it would have taken them a lot longer than they [would have] expected. I can't remember what time we got onto the middle peak; it would have been midafternoon. . . . Anyway, it is a long way down, and it would take an inexperienced party a long time because they would be moving slowly. Because of the strong wind, they would be very nervous, and it would be well after dark before they got down, assuming that they would be able to continue after it got dark, which isn't self-evident.

Emil described many elements of hearing here, all of which are part of the adventuring experience. The adventurers told me that it is not so much that their hearing gets "better" with experience, but more that by hearing sounds in different places in different conditions they come to hear and understand more sounds over time. The development of their hearing is about making connections.

Veronica offered an account similar to Emil's. After she explained to me the many ways that hearing matters, I asked if she could give me an example of a time that she had used her hearing. She said,

Oh, it happens all the time. But the last time I can think of is just back in about January, and I climbed with a friend. We climbed the east ridge of [Mount] Cook, and we knew that the weather was going to be turning bad, but it was maybe, it was a big maybe, so [we thought we'd] go anyway. So we climbed, and the east ridge of Cook is sheltered from the nor-west [wind], but we could see there was . . . a halo around the sun, which is when ice crystals are in the atmosphere. And also we could see bits of ice blowing off the summit ridge and puffs of snow. And then the further we got up, we could hear the wind howling, the wind up above us, and the further we got towards the top of the ridge, it got worse and worse. But we just thought . . . we've got a fairly straightforward retreat straight back down the ridge. We'll just keep going until we hit the summit ridge and just check what it's like. And we stuck our heads over the summit ridge, and it was just horrible; it was a howling gale, so we just retreated all the way back down again. But I think it was because we were both experienced, and we knew we could move quickly. We knew that if we got to the top and it was too rough to go on, well, we could both quickly get down again.

Hearing is part of the climbing experience, but it is just one part of a wider reasoning process. Climbers hear in precise circumstances, in relation to their understanding of the geography, their understanding of the weather, and their awareness of their skills as climbers.

CONTROLLING THE STRESS RESPONSE

I started this chapter by saying that I was not going to talk about risk-taking, but I do need to address where risk and sensing meet. Some adventurers spoke about needing to control the stress response as a way to keep their sensory channels open. Stress narrows the focus of what adventurers can pay attention to, so controlling the stress response is critical. Much has been said about how adventuring requires great strength of mind as much as strength of body.[15] You need control over your mind to get through difficult situations.

Many of the adventurers described reaching a point where they no longer wanted to experience as much risk as they once had. For instance, Louise described going on trips with her local club that were becoming progressively more difficult, such as climbs and bushwalks with three-hundred-meter drops without being roped up. During these trips, Louise felt that she and her fellow adventurers were egging one another on. But at a certain point, she realized that she did not want that kind of danger anymore:

> [The] types of trips that I would probably do now are not as adrenaline pumping but longer, more [sedate], more journey type of things that involve a lower level of risk. But [these types of trips] are much more prolonged. I don't think it was an active decision; I think it was just [that] progressively the kinds of things that I had started to do and started to enjoy [changed]. I think I just moved away from those charged situations. Maybe [because of going out with] different groups of people; there were [fewer] influences. . . . I think there was a gradual realization that I wasn't actually getting excited by things, just very, very scared, and very unwilling, and just not comfortable.

I found it interesting that most of the people I interviewed also held this view, given the focus on risk in much of the sociological literature on adventuring.[16] I wondered whether it was because of my topic; by asking about hearing and listening, I had attracted those who took the metaphorical view of it. That is, adventurers who privileged connectedness over achievement.

Maybe it was partly that. But others gave me the impression that most adventurers do not want to be scared.[17] They think that the level of risk that climbers like Alex Honnold take by free climbing (i.e., without ropes or other protective equipment) sheer twelve-hundred-meter rock faces is abnormal, reckless even.[18] In their world, this is not how things are done. Most of the adventurers had come up through or were currently affiliated with mountaineering, alpine, or bushwalking clubs. In Simon's words, "In clubs, there is not that emphasis on pushing danger or perceived danger. They are not set up for it. People wouldn't join for those reasons."

What is interesting about these perceptions of risk and danger is that people who take the greatest risks, objectively speaking, do not feel as though they *are* taking risks. As accounted for in the concept of "edgework," there is a pursuit of both the intense emotions involved in voluntary risk-taking and a sense of control in it.[19] Going into the hills involves running near the edge without the potential embarrassment of needing to be rescued. Even Honnold speaks in these terms. He says that he is not taking risks. He prepares for climbs to the point that the risk is neutralized to an acceptable level.[20] That said, most climbers who attempt the climbs that Honnold does do not survive. There are many lost friends.

Some climbers from my research were doing the "harder stuff," as they might say, things that others would have thought of as too scary. Emil, Vincent, and Veronica were doing more dangerous trips than many and so were acutely conscious of the importance of controlling their stress response, or of not having the same type of stress response as others. As Emil put it, "If you haven't got self-control, if you can't keep calm in a crisis, if you can't think things through in a coherent way even when you're stressed, then you better stay at home."

The need to control the stress response in dangerous situations is evident in what happens to a climber's sensory awareness when stress takes over. Emil recounted an experience in which his sensory awareness shut down following a serious accident, requiring him to reengage his senses to get out of danger. He had been guiding a couple from Pioneer Hut on Fox Glacier across Governor Col, a passageway between Mount Haidinger and Mount Dixon. (The Col is a rather technical passage between the western and eastern sides of the Main Divide.) Emil fell over a cliff one hundred meters high on the eastern side of the Divide, where the snowy slopes are known to be prone to avalanching. He gave the following account of his experience as he came to:

> Where you really come close to killing yourself, your attention shrinks to that entirely, and this idea that people have of time slowing down. Your attention just narrows down to that one focal point. . . . It is just you falling through space, as it were. . . . When I came to, the thing I was aware of was pain, and that was all I was aware of. It took some time to become aware of more than that. I had this sense [at] first that what I was looking at was a negative of the world, that it was all dark, really. So certainly my vision didn't work straight away; it took a while to crank it up again. Then I became aware enough to start looking around me, and I saw a crampon lying there. Then sound [came back] after I had [gotten] up, seen the crampon, and tried to put it on or had put it on. It was only then that I heard the people shouting at me. Obviously, they would have been shouting all the while.

The clients he was guiding found their way back on their own. Emil crawled back to Haast Hut, a derelict hut nearby, and was rescued the next day. He thought of the closing-down of his sensory experience as part of the stress response. He said that "getting yourself out of that state is crucial." Without doing so, he could not have gotten himself to safety. He said, "What is important, I think, is remaining stress free because stress interferes with hearing, too, I'm sure of that. It is being open in a fairly relaxed sort of way so that you're not gripped up because that obviously interferes with the attention that you're able to give." For Emil, maintaining awareness is a matter of acquired "mental discipline."

It is not only accidents that can generate the affective experience of stress. Even for experienced climbers and cross-country skiers, simply being in extreme environments, especially when alone, can generate a sense of terror, having all sorts of peculiar effects on their sensory experience of the world. Frozen landscapes can be unsettlingly silent for many, even for expert climbers. Here, I am thinking of Vincent, who described experiences of climbing on objectively difficult terrain, including first ascents not quick to be repeated. He explained that solo climbing creates a state of hyper-awareness. He picks up more from the environment, which extends what he can do. He had an ambivalent attitude toward his solo climbing, though:

> The solos I did when I was younger I didn't like because I didn't like being by myself. Actually, the first time I did it, I climbed Mount Earnslaw just on a whim, and I got to this bivvy [i.e., a bivouac], and I had to turn the stove on because it was too quiet, and I was lonely [he laughs]. I do get incredibly lonely, and it is overpowering. I don't like it that much. It's a pretty intense thing to do. I suppose another reason why I am not that comfortable with it is that the solos I have done are really scary: technical things without ropes where if I fell off I would die, there is no question. There was one solo that I did, the full west ridge of Mount Tasman, and that was so cool because I was by myself for about three and a half days, and I got to Pioneer Hut, and I hadn't spoken to anybody, and I had been inside my head for that length of time, and I got to the hut, and someone said hello, and I couldn't talk to them. I had actually been so inside myself and so focused that I needed to go back outside and think about where I was at.

What Vincent was failing to control in these situations, what generated stress, is almost the opposite of what Emil described. He was hearing too much, seeing too much, feeling too much. Or, hearing too little. Emil was present when Vincent and I were speaking, and the difference between the two climbers' experiences became a reference point in our conversation. Vincent continued,

It is hyper-awareness. You can't put it into words, and I guess that is why it is so intense. People like [Emil] have been doing it [for] so long that they are used to being hyper-aware, but when I am doing it, it is [he shudders]. It's hard work, I find, because all your senses are going off. It is also different when you have not been there before; its slightly edgy. You are pushing the limits of what you can do. I mean, on that west ridge trip, I only had one ice axe. I didn't have a rope or a harness, and I was climbing stuff [for which] I should have had all that stuff. And I didn't know the ground, so I had to route-find, and [I] was hyper-aware. I think if you are going to do things like that, you have to be or you will die.

Silence focuses the mind. Emil embraces the silence. And he argued, as Vincent suggested here, that you need that silence and the hyper-awareness that follows to do the most extreme climbs. For Emil, the need for absolute attention and sensitivity to his environment was what attracted him to solo climbing:

[Going solo] does enable you to retain a consciousness or keep your attention focused, as it were, all around you, and that certainly includes sound. And again, the most obvious things are the most dramatic, like avalanches, like rock fall. It doesn't need to be an avalanche, but what happens is at night everything freezes into place, including icicles hanging from rocks and ice bulges. The sun comes up, and these things start to free themselves from where they're hanging, and they can hurt if they hit you. Just the fact that you have a responsibility for somebody else, and there is a lot of toing and froing of conversation, as well, whether it is encouraging the other person or saying, "For god's sake, hurry up, I'm getting scared here." You are so concerned about the other person that you're not listening to what is happening around you.

Not everyone can manage the silence of solo climbing, meaning both the literal silence and the inherent loneliness of the activity. For many, it feels like something is wrong. Along these lines, Louise said, "I don't think I really put much stock in sound unless it is absent, and it is *very* noticeable when it is absent. In those cases, it feels like there is something wrong, so you probably try and listen more intently to smaller things, like the sound under your feet."

Climbers under extreme stress also sometimes report getting a song stuck in their head or imagining someone else being present. When experiencing this type of sensory deprivation or discomfort, they often try to focus on something else to stop themselves from losing a sense of reality. They shift their sensate experience to manage the stress. Those who survive the near impossible often report what Ernest Shackleton termed the "Third Man": a sense of a physical presence, an unseen companion who shows, and encourages one toward, a pathway to survival.[21] Others report auditory hallucinations. The mountaineer Joe Simpson heard Boney M.'s "Brown Girl in the Ring" as he hopped and crawled his way back to base camp after a near-fatal fall on his descent of Siula Grande in the Peruvian Andes.[22]

Adventurers can also seek out sound to fill the void, as Vincent did when he turned on his stove at the bivouac. Controversially, others turn to a mobile music device. One of the most interesting accounts in this respect came from Karen, a cross-country skier who had completed many ice cap expeditions. She spoke about an expedition to the South Pole. She was with a party, but there was very little social interaction and very little sensory input given the environment. She explained that music gives you "something in your head" when the sensory deprivation might otherwise cause great discomfort:

> We would take iPods with us down there. . . . Some people would be walking along with their iPods on because it does give you something in your head, whereas if you don't have it, you haven't got it. . . . An iPod won't last a full day in those temperatures, so I used it right at the start of the day when I was feeling a bit creaky and tired and sore. Then I

used it right at the end [of the day] to help me finish off. Then it was about using music as a distraction in a way. . . . The role of music in these sorts of conditions is interesting. A lot of people do listen to the iPods because they don't want to be totally alone, I think. . . . The choice of listening or not listening, though, is interesting because it changes your connection to the space around you. When [I] don't want to be connected, that is when I put it on. When I do want to be connected, I turn it off.

Karen explained that when people do not have a device, they can imagine sound anyway: "I don't know whether you have seen that film *Touching the Void*, but at one point, when the guy [Brendan Mackey acting the part of Joe Simpson] is coming down the mountain, he says, 'I do not want to die to Boney M.' He had it going around and around in his head. It is a bit like that sometimes. You get sounds in your head that you don't want to hear. Your brain just gets stuck on them."

WHAT WE LEARN FROM ADVENTURERS ABOUT HEARING

Of the groups of people addressed in this book, adventurers have the most in common with doctors when it comes to hearing: both use hearing to collect evidence from the world to make decisions. In this sense, hearing means paying aural attention to cues outside the self. Adventurers attend to sounds produced by the environment or those that manifest as they move through it. Unlike musicians and Morse code operators, they typically do not use hearing as part of a feedback loop to produce a particular sound.

As for the doctors, hearing for adventurers is also a means to "see" beyond what is registered by the eye. The cues that adventurers are concerned with are often most crucial in cases where the adventurers cannot otherwise see or feel something that would explain the surrounding conditions. Just as doctors hear evidence of what is happening inside a patient's body, adventurers listen for sounds that are evidence of what is happening below a surface or beyond their current location, such as wind and unstable ice.

The adventurers found it difficult to consider listening as a single modality. For them, the language of listening expresses an approach that includes not only the hearing of sound but also much more. When they talk about listening, what they mean is paying attention to what is outside oneself and the interface between self and the world. Approaching a journey with bravado comes with an inner orientation, a sense of control, and a focus on one's own strength and endurance, not on how they meet the world. The adventurers that I spoke with said coming back alive requires something different. They attend to how they are organizing their body but always in relation to what is happening beyond them. They do not move without paying close attention to the conditions.

It has been suggested that an adventurer can attend to only so much. If you are paying attention to the talk of other party members, or even the sounds of their bodies to see how they are doing, then you are disattending other things, like subtle indicators of avalanche risk. Unlike the case of the doctors, this problem of capacity can typically be resolved by creating space for noticing.

It is hard to believe that the unconscious is left unused by adventurers. But their message is not to trust your unconscious. They say, "Notice. Attend." This means leaving your mobile device at home. It means controlling your stress response so that you maintain your ability to attend fully to your surroundings. It might even mean going solo so that you can remove the need to worry about and attend to others and bring more conscious attention to what is happening around you. The adventurers' message is to bring maximum consciousness to those things that others are likely to miss—those things that can save your life.

4

HOW MORSE CODE
OPERATORS HEAR

ontemporary Morse code operators sometimes affectionately refer to Morse as the "first internet."[1] Morse code made its way to Australia via a Canadian immigrant named Samuel McGowan shortly after the technology had been developed.[2] With the support of the budding administration, the first lines were installed in Victoria in 1853 and 1854.[3] Following the installation of a short proof-of-concept line, Morse connected the main settlement of Melbourne with the newly settled portside locale of Williamstown, closely followed by lines to the ports of Geelong, Queenscliff, and Port Melbourne; the gold mining fields in Ballarat and Bendigo; and, in 1859, to the Flemington Racecourse for transmission of the results of the Australian Champion Sweepstakes (which later became the Melbourne Cup). Other colonies followed this model of a publicly owned telegraph network, establishing lines among the colonies and with Britain—a priority but no small feat given the distance and conditions.

The social impact of this Morse network was massive. Messages from London that once took months to arrive now took only about seven hours. Telegraph offices became hubs of communication, connected to an expansive network of post offices transmitting official and private communications, weather reports, and news. Permanent telegraphists (telegraphers), known as "telegs," were positioned at cattle yards to quickly transmit sale prices, in the rail network to transmit passenger and cargo information, and at large factories to manage stock and orders. Telegrams were also sent and received by private citizens. Morse emerged before the telephone and radio, so if you wanted to let your mother know you were coming home, you would send her a telegram. In 1945, the Postmaster-General's Department (PMG) hit a peak of thirty-five million telegram messages transmitted annually.

With the important role played by the Morse lines for community communications, Morse operators held a unique and trusted position as mediators of this information. In the words of one of the operators I met, Alan, a telegraphist was a "listening post." Aware of everything that went on, telegraphists had to pledge to maintain secrecy, and breaches would lead to termination. "We'd take telegrams, a lot of personal information and things like that, [and] you're just not allowed to, and you didn't divulge it," Alan said. Operators needed to hear Morse to be able to send and receive messages, but they could not pay attention to the content of those messages. At the same time, operators were part of the community, so it could be hard to ignore what they heard. For example, those working during World War II somberly recalled receiving lists of the dead.

But technologies change. In Australia, Morse was phased out in the 1960s, with the last telegram being transmitted in 1968 between the Western Australian towns of Roebourne and Wittenoom.[4] In the age of the smartphone and Web 4.0, we have hardly any need for Morse code or those with the necessary embodied understanding to send and receive it. If we are to trust television and film, its relevance is limited to emergency spy or military communications, and only when the "bad guys" take out digital networks (think *Chuck*, *Under Siege*, *The Hunt for Red October*, and even *Interstellar*). The most common message in these representations:

$$\bullet\bullet\bullet \quad \text{— — —} \quad \bullet\bullet\bullet$$

S   O   S

While no longer practically important, Morse code operation is instructive for the social construction of hearing. The invention of the telegraph and Morse code also required people to invent ways of mobilizing the body to perform telegraphy competently. The case of the Morse code operators thus gives us historical insight into the cultivation of hearing. One novel aspect of this form of hearing is the folk understanding that competent Morse operation depends on changing the self, not simply acquiring a skill. Operators talk about changing what is happening in their brains, compared to the heightening of connections that the adventurers described.

I interviewed nineteen Morse code operators who trained and worked on the Australian lines before the networks were decommissioned. Most had worked for the PMG, including a mix of telegraphists, who had been full-time telegraph operators in capital cities' Chief Telegraph Offices or larger regional centers, and postal clerks, who had worked in post offices on general duties that included telegraph operating. The last cohort of PMG telegraphists was trained in 1957, but many were still in contact with one another at the time of my fieldwork. You might think of them as a historical reenactment community, like the hobbyist Civil War reenactors in the United States. They met up in uniform at communications museums, including the National Communication Museum in Melbourne and the Powerhouse Museum in Sydney, to staff the lines for demonstrations. They also staffed old telegraph stations, such as the Cape Otway Lightstation, the station at Alice Springs in the Northern Territory, and the Beechworth Telegraph Station (figure 4.1). Some operators have setups in their homes that use period Morse sounders and keys coupled with modified modems (necessary given the decommissioning of landline telegraphy), which they continue to use to communicate with one another.

I also met two PMG operators who had worked in Antarctica as part of the Australian National Antarctic Research Expeditions between 1952 and 1978. In Antarctica, they operated using

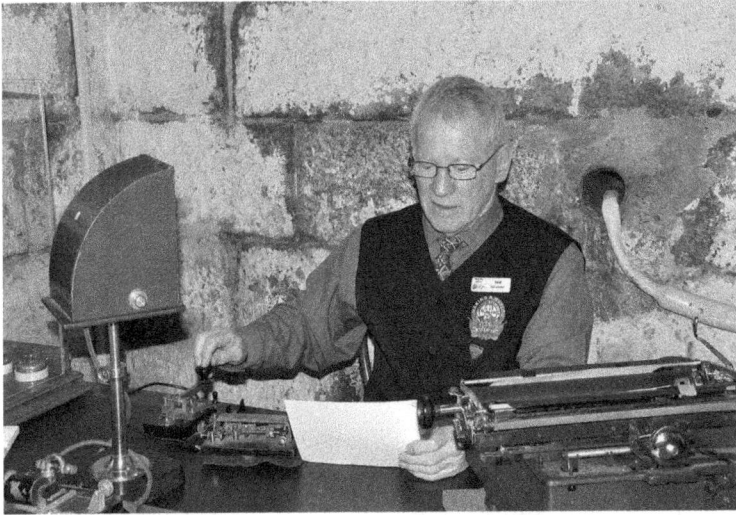

FIGURE 4.1 A Morse operator working with a straight key at the Bendigo Post Office Morse display.

radiotelegraphy, not electrical telegraphy, the significance of which I will explain shortly. I also spoke with a railway telegraph services operator (of note, the communication conventions of railway telegraphy differed, but the technology was similar), and a person with a military background who had also worked by radio.[5]

The following provides an introduction to the technology involved in Morse transmission and the sounds that the various systems generate. I then examine a variety of methods involved in cultivating an aural-embodied understanding of Morse. Many of these methods develop operators' hearing via proprioception and movement, but not because half the task of forming a Morse signal involves using an arm and hand. I then address the forms that embodied competency in Morse take, some of which do not relate clearly to the core task of sending and receiving messages.

AUSTRALIAN TELEGRAPHY SYSTEMS
AND INSTRUMENTS

Communication in Morse is theoretically standardized. All the operators I spoke with used International Morse Code (table 4.1), which is a revision of the original American Morse Code (also known as Railroad Morse).[6] However, various instruments are involved in the production and reception of Morse that affect its sound, and not all operators can understand one another despite the adoption of an agreed-upon language.

The sending and receiving of Morse can take many forms, which for our purposes is especially important because the systems and instruments used affect the Morse sound. *Sending* refers to operators' formation of Morse signals using a Morse key. *Receiving* refers to hearing the code transmitted by the sender and then translating that code into typed or handwritten characters in a telegram. The PMG (i.e., the postal system), the railways, and commercial operations from cattle yards to manufacturers operated over what is called the "electrical telegraph." In this system, Morse is transmitted over wires suspended on telegraph poles. In Australia, these lines can span thousands of kilometers, with mechanical repeater stations placed at intervals of about two hundred kilometers.[7]

The PMG operators were all trained to send and receive Morse by straight (or "hand") key with a sounder housed in an amplifying resonator box. At the sending end of the line, the operator taps on the Morse key with a downward motion using a combination of short ("dot") and long ("dash") signals to form characters that compose the text-based message. The hand key is a kind of electrical switch that sends electrical pulses according to the length of time that the operator holds the key down.[8]

On the receiving end, the sounder, amplified by the resonator box, makes a "click" sound to signal the start and stop of each signal. So, in effect, operators attend to the silence between the clicks, rather than

TABLE 4.1 INTERNATIONAL MORSE CODE

A •—	K —•—	U ••—	1 •————
B —•••	L •—••	V •••—	2 ••———
C —•—•	M ——	W •——	3 •••——
D —••	N —•	X —••—	4 ••••—
E •	O ———	Y —•——	5 •••••
F ••—•	P •——•	Z ——••	6 —••••
G ——•	Q ——•—		7 ——•••
H ••••	R •—•		8 ———••
I ••	S •••		9 ————•
J •———	T —		0 —————

the sounds themselves (figure 4.2). James tried to teach me: "We'll make a dash. When I make a dash with the sounder, you hear a click go down, and there's nothing. While ever I hold the key down, there's no noise. You can't hear anything, can you? You'll hear [click sound] . . . it should make a click back. It's not very loud [click sound.] Open up a bit. That's better [click sound]. Click down, and then when you release it [click sound], the spring brings it back, and you get a second click. It's the length of the time between the clicks [that] is what you register." Descriptions of Morse dashes and dots suggest that these signals are audible, which misrepresents the essential competence of Morse operators.

FIGURE 4.2 Vertical strokes above the Morse characters signify where the clicks generated by a sounder fall.

There was also a semiautomatic key called a "jigger." The jigger was broadly adopted in the PMG and in the railway telegraph services, provided that it was suitable for the line that an operator was working.[9] It automatically forms dots in the length of time the key is held in the required position. Fred explained, "For me, it [working on a hand key] was hard work. . . . And the jigger, if you held one side of a little handle, it would make dots automatically. And [on] the other side, you had to make your dashes. But if you had the letter 'H,' four dots, you'd only hold it, and it would make di-di-di-di-di-di-di-dit, and you'd take your hand off." These changes in orientation and the automation of forming the dots reduced the strain on the operator's hand and wrist and thus reduced the incidence of overuse injury. Dashes were formed as normal.[10] The jigger also increased the speed at which operators could send messages.

Some said, though, that jiggers, more so than hand keys, could render operators "bad senders." Fred gave an example: "Some fellas didn't realize that they weren't—well, we say 'good senders' or 'great senders,' and they'd send a bit of rubbish. . . . The letter 'H' is four dots, [but] sometimes they might put an extra one in and not realize it. Well, that becomes a figure 5, see":

↓ [extra dot]

••••   •••••

H   5

What is happening here is that the operator is moving the jigger to compose dots but then closing it without precision so that it is held for a count of five not four, changing the character formed entirely.[11]

Radiotelegraphy (wireless telegraphy) was developed later.[12] It had a variety of applications, but the operators I spoke with who had used this system had worked in military communications during World War II or on the radio link between Australia and Antarctica. As the name implies, rather than transmitting Morse via an electric current carried by wires, this form of telegraphy transmitted pulses via radio waves. The code itself is the same as that produced by electrical telegraphy; operators are still sending and receiving text-based communications via dots and dashes.[13]

The sound produced by electrical telegraphy and that produced by radiotelegraphy differs significantly. In radiotelegraphy, the transmitted code is generated by what is known as a beat frequency oscillator, referred to simply as an oscillator, which generates a beep when the key is held down (figure 4.3). When Morse is transmitted via a sounder, operators attend to *silence*; that is, to the gaps *between* the clicks. With an oscillator, they attend to *sound*, to the high-pitched beeps themselves. James demonstrated for me: "With an oscillator, [beep sound] while ever I hold the key down, [beep sound], you get tone. And it'll just sound like that forever. . . . That's the difference between the two styles. One, you're listening to the space between the clicks, and [with] this one [i.e., radiotelegraphy], you're listening to the length of the actual tone itself."

Radiotelegraphy is the form of Morse you are likely more familiar with because it appears more often in film and television. But among my operators, electrical telegraphy was more commonly used. Some of the PMG operators, like Gordon, called radio telegraphists "the buzzer people."

The difference in the sounds produced by the two systems is such that understanding one does not necessarily translate to understanding the other. Many commented that operators who trained on the sounder could typically "read" Morse from an oscillator, but the reverse

FIGURE 4.3 The oscillator tone sounds when the line is at the peak. It is held for three counts for a dash and one count for a dot.

was not true. The clearest example of this difficulty came from Cecilia and Gary, operators who were married. Gary had been a PMG operator and so had trained on a sounder. Cecilia, a Morse code instructor during World War II, trained on an oscillator. Cecilia initially said to me, "Morse is Morse is Morse, that's it." But it later emerged that Cecilia and Gary could barely communicate with each other in Morse. When Gary exchanged messages with friends from home, Cecilia would have no idea what was being said. She had worked in cipher and so was not familiar with the abbreviated plain English commonly used by PMG operators, and she could not make sense of the clicks of the sounder. Fortunately, they could communicate with each other well enough that once, when Gary had climbed onto the roof and promptly sent his ladder adrift, he was able to get assistance by tapping out an SOS to Cecilia through the roof.

In general, with a little practice, sounder operators could transition to an oscillator, but the reverse tended to be more difficult, and it was the PMG operators posted to Antarctica who needed to meet this challenge. Fred recalled the learning curve: "They said, 'Look, we're going to send you a couple of pieces on the oscillator and see how you go.' And [I] put the earphones on . . . and I'm typing, and gosh, it was a bit different. Anyway, I made a few mistakes, and they said, 'Well, how did you find it?' I said, 'Well, it was OK, but it wasn't too fast.' But for some reason, I just couldn't quite transpose the letter as I should. [It was a] matter of being used to it, anyway."

HOW INSTRUCTORS TEACH THE CODE

First Step: The Alphabet

Being an operator was skilled work. Those who came up through the PMG typically began in their mid-teens as telegram messengers, then trained informally through post office networks, trying to learn the

code in their off time. Eventually, they had to complete a formal quali-
fication at the Postal Training School, which they typically entered at
the age of sixteen or seventeen. But to gain admission, they needed to
be able to send and receive code at a rate of twelve words per minute.
So those who wanted to gain entrance had to learn on their own. Post
offices could not afford to pay for training, especially for those who
might not ultimately make the grade. Instead, there was more of an
incentive system. Those who could achieve the target rate of sending
and receiving were given a small sum of money in recognition but,
more importantly, the longer-term payoff of a secure government job
if they became fully qualified. Times were tough, so the prize of a government job was worth it. With that, one would be "set for life."

The first task for operators in training is to learn the alphanumeric characters used in Morse code, just as young children learn to
recognize the letters of the alphabet. Trainees first read the sounds
of the characters; their learning begins visually. They receive a copy
of the code printed on paper and work their way through it. James
explained, "To learn the actual code, though, you had to do that
yourself, [that is,] that 'A' was a dot and a dash, and 'B' was a dash and
three dots, and 'C' was a dash-dot-dash-dot. That sort of thing. You
had to do that yourself. Nobody can really teach you that; you just had
to read it off and memorize it."

Stanley gave a similar account, noting, too, the length of time it
takes to achieve mastery: "First of all, you had to learn the code, [and]
then you had to recognize the signals, which were very, very slow,
like a dot-dash. Then your little brain would tick over, and you'd say,
'Dot-dash. Oh, yes, that's an "A."' I suppose I learned that for probably
a couple of years."

They thought of this phase as an exercise in rote learning because
there was no internal logic for the combinations of dots and dashes
that made up the letters.[14] As Gordon said, "[You] just learn it. . . .
[it's] just slow, repetitive work. [There are] no tricks to it." Working
operators shared memorization aids with the telegraph messengers

interested in becoming operators. Benjamin emphasized that one needed to recite the code aloud: "I used to say them [the signals] out loud because it doesn't register when you just say it in your head." Trainees start by reading the code and vocalizing what they see:

A	•—	"A, dot dash"
B	—•••	"B, dash dot dot"
C	—•—•	"C, dash dot dash dot"
D	—••	"D, dash dot dot"
E	•	"E, dot"

Morse operators learn the signals that compose each character, but that does not help with understanding the rhythm or sound. That is, the word *dash* does not feel three times longer than the word *dot*—the terms were not adopted for that reason. Neither do the terms reflect the sounds that the signals make, which manifest as either a pair of clicks or a high-pitched beep. In many instances, an embodied experience precedes conceptual or abstract thought, but here, the conceptual is organizing what will become an aural and proprioceptive understanding of how to receive and send code.[15] In this respect, Morse is similar to medical education, which begins with a conceptual understanding of the functioning of healthy and diseased bodies, followed by clinical skills training.

The boys who worked as telegram messengers for the PMG were also encouraged by the operators to get into the habit of translating the written language they saw in their telegram deliveries into either Morse as imagined or Morse as spoken. While out on their deliveries, they would see street signs or billboards and translate the words as read into Morse. James explained his practice: "One of the best ways was to look at advertisements on the wall while you were on the train and convert them in your head to Morse. [You'd see an ad for the pharmaceutical company] Vincent's APC, and you'd convert it in your mind. . . . di-di-di-dah for the 'V.' . . . You didn't say it out aloud, of course, because people would have looked at you." And Alan said,

I'd ride through the railway yards . . . doing the telephone exchange at night. And coming home in the morning . . . I'd read all the signs and try and put them into Morse. . . . And each of the trucks as you go through the railway yard have numbers on them. . . . I'd go along the rows of trucks, and I'd be interpreting the thing, you know, dah-dah-dit [G], dah-di-dah-dah [Y], di-dah-dah-dah [J]. . . . Underneath they had the tare . . . so many tons . . . so I used to go along transcribing in my mind, just as you're traveling along. . . . It might sound a bit facile and simple, but indeed, I wasn't going di-dah-dah [W], di-di-dit [S], and all that kind of stuff straight off. It was trying to remember what I had learned, like, What was that? Dah-dah-dit [G]? About that level . . . just in my mind. I didn't want to appear to be completely stupid as I'm walking along, talking to myself.

After learning the signal combinations alphabetically, the next challenge is to identify signal combinations for letters out of order, that is, by working on words. Practicing with words acts as a kind of self-administered test. For example, trying to spell the name *George* means asking oneself, Can I recall what signals make up a "G" when it is not preceded by an "F"?

How Mnemonic Devices Are Used to Emphasize Syllabic Stress in Spoken Language

Once a trainee knows the Morse alphabet, they begin the long road of developing a feel for the Morse rhythm. The dots and dashes signify that there *is* a rhythm, but strategies and devices must be employed to find it. Operators recalled using or being aware of several approaches to find this rhythm. But regardless of approach, all trainees are trying to do the same thing: learn to hear Morse code in relation to the movements involved in forming it.

One strategy I came across involves the use of a mnemonic device in which each letter of the Morse alphabet is paired with a word or phrase with similar syllabic stress to the Morse character (table 4.2).

TABLE 4.2 MORSE MNEMONIC DEVICES USED IN WORLD WAR II MILITARY SIGNALS TRAINING

Letter	Morse	Mnemonic	Letter	Morse	Mnemonic
A	•—	a – las	N	—•	noo-dle
B	—•••	ba-by-ish-ness	O	———	out-side-door
C	—•—•	cal-cu-la-tion	P	•——•	pol-ice-sta-tion
D	—••	dub-i-ous	Q	——•—	queen-car-o-line
E	•	egg	R	•—•	re-cord-er
F	••—•	fed-er-a-tion	S	•••	si-cil-y
G	——•	green-gag-es	T	—	tool
H	••••	hes-it-an-cy	U	••—	un-ex-celled
I	••	inn-er	V	•••—	ven-om-ous-snake
J	•———	jap-an-tea-tray	W	•——	with-out-doubt
K	—•—	koh-i-noor	X	—••—	ex-cell-ent-work
L	•—••	lin-o-le-um	Y	—•——	york-shire-cream-cheese
M	——	mon-soon	Z	——••	zo-ol-o-gy

This set of mnemonics was used in signals training for military operators during World War II. The addition of a word or phrase not only acts as a memory aid for the signals that make up a character but also takes a budding operator inside their own body to produce short and long sequences that they already know. For example, the letter "W" is remembered as "with-out-doubt." The step between the phrase and the signal is the feeling of "short-long-long" as the trainee vocalizes the phrase. This is then translated to "dot-dash-dash." The trainee is now working on more than a sequence of signals; they are working on a sequence of tangible spaces in time.

FIGURE 4.4 A marked-up extract from Beethoven's Rondo in C Major, Opus 51.

I´ encountered a similar mnemonic strategy when I was learning the piano. My teacher would sometimes write a word or phrase over a sequence of notes that was causing me trouble rhythmically. One such annotation was on my copy of a Beethoven rondo (figure 4.4). A rondo is characterized by a theme that is repeated several times separated by episodes. When the theme reappears, there is often a variation. In the variation in question, the theme is articulated in triplets in the right hand while the left continues in quavers (a three-two polyrhythm, also known as a hemiola). My teacher had written "bibbity bobbity" on the score over the first two groupings of triplets along with a note that I should repeat this over the following groupings. "Bib-bi-ty bob-bi-ty" expresses short groups of threes—as in "si-cil-y" for the letter "S" in the Morse schema—the idea being that I sing and feel each grouping of three as I played with my right hand, disattending my left. It was a way to organize the rhythm I needed to hear and move to, bootstrapped to the embodied pacing captured in the word or phrase. This annotation from my teacher some twenty years ago is a rare survivor. My teacher erased most such markups ahead of exams, as it was viewed as cheating.

This example of a mnemonic device used in my piano training also foregrounds how this initial visual-to-haptic translation ("bibbity bobbity") involves a second haptic translation: playing the notes. A similar translation occurs in Morse code, from seeing to feeling the code as spoken before moving on to form the rhythm by working the key.

How Instructors Sing the Code to Trainees to Convey Morse Cadence

PMG operators often talked about needing to work with an experienced operator to develop the correct cadence in their sending and receiving. The Morse convention is that dashes are three times the length of dots, a space equal to one dash separates letters, and a space equal to seven dots separates words. The mnemonics I have just described are not that precise; they give just a broad sense of short and long and in what combination. Learning this basic structure is an important first step, but it does not teach operators to hear and move as needed to send the right way. Native speakers of a language often run words together, not pausing to distinguish one word from the next. In spoken language, words have a shape of sorts; they are more than the sum of their parts (i.e., the letters of which they are made). Morse is similar, though it is the letters that have unique shapes, subtleties in the rhythmic push and pull of the expression that characterize each letter.

Getting a sense of the shape of letters involves the guidance of an experienced operator who can vocalize their rhythms. Among themselves, operators do not talk about dots and dashes. When they speak in code—that is, when they vocalize words in the language of Morse—they speak in sequences of di, dit, and dah (as Alan did when he recalled translating alphanumeric characters into Morse in a railway yard). "Di" expresses a dot that falls at the beginning or in the middle of a character. "Dit" expresses a dot that falls at the end of a character. "Dah" expresses a dash. Alan explained, "The first thing I was told was, 'Here's the Morse code.' You learn it off by heart, and you might start off saying, 'Well, dot, dash, dash, dot, dot.' Very soon they told me, 'No, the dot is a dit, and the dash is a dah.' So, then you go off, and in parrot fashion I learned dah-di-dah-dah [Y], di-di-dit [S], dah-di-dah-dit [C], and so on—much slower than that, of course."

The letter "C" is one that training operators struggle with. James explained, "Some people, when they make a 'C,' which is a dash and a dot, dash and a dot, you don't send it like that. It sounds like two 'Ns.'" The problem here is operating at speed; when the gap between letters is reduced, an operator may form an incorrect assumption about where one letter begins and another ends. To address this issue, operators develop a sense of the right sequence as sung. James continued, "It's sort of dah-di-dah-dit. You can actually sing Morse if you like . . . it's got a rhythm to it. . . . Instead of just writing up the board and saying it's a dash and a dot and a dash and a dot for a 'C,' . . . they think, 'How does that sound? Does it go dah-dit dah-dit, or is it?' But it's not. It's dah-di-dah-dit. It's got sort of a swing to it."

↓ [pause]

— • — •   — • — •

C   N   N

Sung as "dah di dah dit"   Sung as "dah dit, dah dit"
(*not* dash dot dash dot)   (*not* dash dot, dash dot)

There is an emphasis on the "dahs." The "di" in the "C" is clipped, so it sounds and feels tightly joined to the "dah" that follows it and so cannot be mistaken for a dot that ends a word, the dash that begins the next character, or a continuation of the sequence for this character. The signals flow into one another. The "dit" at the end, however, has more space around it.

Another mistake could come in the distinction between "V" and the combination of "S" and "T." For example, did the sender mean "vain" or "stain"? The receiver would most likely know from the context if the message was given in plain English, as opposed to cipher, but the point I am emphasizing here is the significance of the subtleties in expression:

	↓ [pause]
••• —	••• —
V	S T
Sung as "di di di dah"	Sung as "di di dit, dah"
(*not* dot dot dot dash)	(*not* dot dot dot, dash)

With the importance of cadence in mind, James said that it helped to hear the cadence as sung before learning to send. Operators must know the sound in that way before they can move to form it. Cecilia, who trained pilots in Morse during World War II, recalled something similar. She began with singing them the code:

> They would send all these forty young men, they were about twenty-one, and they trained them here, and [they did] a bit of pilot training. Then they sent them to England, and they joined in the Battle of Britain. And from what I can work out, most of them were killed. But I taught them Morse. . . . And here I am two days a week with all these twenty-one-year-olds sitting in front of me. I was only about twenty-five and making them sing Morse to get it into their heads. Because it was about a year or two before they invented a board that you can plug into, like a telephone board, and they could plug into Morse, going all different speeds, and teach themselves. But before that, [I] taught them to sing it.

Allowing for subtle idiosyncrasies in the relative lengths of dots and dashes, as well as nuances in rhythmic pulse among operators, each letter becomes its own recognizable entity. As with the doctors' hearing of heart murmurs, it is the sound within the sequence that is critical. Operators must hear and vocally form the "di" that connects to the "dah," not a "dot" that may be separate from the "dash," which would introduce ambiguity over the intended letter. They must hear the whole sequence. Charles explained: "You just got used to the sound of them, yeah. I mean, an 'A' was an 'A,' and that's all there was to it. It was just the sound, and every sound had . . . you're going on the actual makeup of the character. . . . If you knew what the code was for a particular letter, well, then you were part of the way there, and it was just a matter of associating that to the sound that was coming out of these two brass rods hitting together."

Operators internalize the phrasing by singing it to themselves and moving their bodies to form the signal in anticipation of meeting live traffic. A: di-dah; B: dah-di-di-dit; C: dah-di-dah-dit. My operators said they needed to get these rhythmic sequences into their minds. Vocalizing is critical, that is, making the sound with one's mouth out loud. The training operator feels their body from within as they sing the sound. The vocal movements mirror a kind of lifting off at the end of the character's sequence, similar to a conductor signaling the end of a musical phrase. The throat constricts on the "dit" more than on the "di," for which there is a change in mouth shape, a movement of the tongue from one character to the next, not quite flapping in the mouth but a gentler movement than used for a "dit." For the "t" of the "dit," the tongue presses firmly into the roof of the mouth, cutting off the sound.

With this rhythmic or, as they would say, musical quality in mind, Benjamin and Harold told me about the operators from one of the Chief Telegraph Offices who played instruments. Benjamin said, "I was interested that you are speaking with musicians. With two violinists, you could tell them apart by their timing, just like with Morse. Tone wouldn't be so important." The last part is not true, but his understanding shows that in Morse, rhythm is the most important aspect given that it is not possible to control tone. Harold added, "There were a lot of musicians in the telegraph room. There were piano players and trumpet players; there were heaps of them!" I asked whether the ability to hear musically could help with hearing Morse. Harold answered, "I think it was [helpful]. It helps with the rhythm sort of stuff. It all gets back to the timing." Benjamin went on, "It is the same thing, isn't it? The timing is an element of music." The connection between Morse and music that the operators understand demonstrates that they do not think of rhythm as a function of movement; for them, it has a sonorous quality.

Tapping, Slapping, and Blinking: How Trainees Are Coached to Move Their Bodies to Get the Morse Rhythm

Operators recalled using various techniques of moving their bodies and of tapping on their bodies or objects to learn to form the Morse rhythm. When tapping, the trainees are not using a key, so the movements are not about making sounds but rather learning to structure lengths of *non*sound. Tapping is a way of getting the code into their bodies. Charles explained:

> You've just got to go and learn it and learn it and learn it until it's drilled into you. It's just automatic. I mean, [my wife] used to go crook at me [lose her temper], and I still do it if I'm resting my arm there and the TV [is on] or something, I'll be tapping it out. Just tapping Morse out, a word I've heard, and I'll tap it out in Morse. When [we were] on the trains, . . . sometimes we'd use our eyes to send Morse. Just, you know, you can flick your eyes. . . . Just simple stuff, you know, like if you're sitting in a train, and there'd be a pretty girl there or something, you'd just say, "Good sort," or something.

These methods of training via moving the body differ from the self-percussion and auto-auscultation used by medical students, in which nuances in feeling sound beneath the fingers are indicative of specific conditions. Morse operators do not interrogate the qualities of sounds, or what lies beneath the skin. In their case, movement is about finding the correct cadence by moving their body in the rhythmic pulse of Morse signals.

When tapping against the skin with a couple of fingers, the taps do not have differing audible lengths. The varying lengths are indicated only by the gap that precedes the next tap. William developed a more sophisticated version of this technique in which the intended signals varied in terms of how they felt as they were produced. William was a PMG operator, but his background was different from the others in that he grew up at a post office. His father was a postmaster in a country town, and, as was often the case at the time, the postmaster's residence was connected to the post office. William was thus surrounded by the sound of Morse from a young age. He and his sister made a hobby of communicating with each other in Morse through the wall between their bedrooms. They came up with their own way of signaling the dots and dashes: a knock for a dot and a slap for a dash.

The taps and slaps organize for shorter and longer durations. He explained, "A dash is three times as long as a dot. And the way I reckon you can get the best rhythm out—you've got to work at a rhythm. That's a dot [he knocks on his leg]; that's a dash [he slaps his leg]. You go [he touches to his thigh in time with his speech], 'Dot [knock], dot [knock], [pause], dot [knock], dot [knock], [pause], di [knock], dah [slap], dit [knock], [pause], dot [knock], dot [knock].'"

Repeating the movement and vocalization between the "di" and the "dah," he said "up" as he moved from a knock to a slap: "That gives you the best rhythm of that than anything." He continued, "You've got to come back [he makes a fist, then extends his hand flat] to the [he lowers his hand to his thigh] for 'slap' [he touches his leg with his hand flat] after, then 'knock' [he touches his thigh with a closed fist]. And that is just the right spacing." On the word "up," he would raise his hand about ten centimeters, change its orientation from a fist to a flat palm, and then lower his hand to his thigh or another surface like a table or wall. This journey, William reasoned, takes about three times as long as the movement of knocking used for a dash. "You get the right spacing and everything, but I've never heard of anyone else that does it," he said with a laugh.

Moving on to a Key

A lot of the learning of Morse happens at a key. In training schools, trainees were arranged in rows facing the front of the room, each position furnished with a Morse key, sounder, and typewriter. Trainees were presented with various drills and practice messages to send. They dutifully formed the characters while their instructor moved around the room, looking and listening over their shoulders. In terms of pedagogical sequence, moving on to a key happens after a budding operator has gotten the hang of the alphabet; however, they are likely still practicing various strategies of moving and vocalizing. For example, they may still work on tapping out signals on their leg or the arm of a chair in their off time, or an experienced operator may hear that they are not quite getting the rhythm yet and take them aside to sing them the code.

This aspect of learning would be easy to see as just more practice. Gary said, "The Morse, it was just repetition of daily practice. That's pretty well the whole secret." Operators told me about the vast amount of time they spent on Morse in the training school. In the PMG system, trainees spent three to four hours a day sending and receiving in both plain English and cipher, one block of time spent sending, another spent receiving. Albert gave this account of the process:

> Three hours a day would be sending and receiving Morse code. . . . For an hour and a half a day, you would send Morse. You would send it to yourself, or you would send it to somebody else on the other side of the room so they could set up—on the switchboard there, they could put any two people together, the bloke in that corner with him, and him with him, and you would send it to each other, and then the instructors could listen in. [They] had their set on it, and they could listen to the set there.

Or they would—they used Wheatstone tape . . . which is a tape with holes in it which sends perfect Morse code, and you can run that at two words a minute or thirty-five words a minute. So, they would just set that at the speed that they thought you should have been listening to at the time.

These methods were not specific to the PMG. Elliott, a railway operator, similarly said that spending time at the key sending and receiving is critical: "I used to go to the classroom. They had several instruments in there that you could use the keys to learn, and the instructor would help you with any problems that you were having. And he used to sit there for hours, just sending to me—for about [an] hour and a half a day, and I would just read the sounds. And I had to write it down."

Operating a key connects the sound and rhythm of Morse to the body positions and movements involved in forming signals. Sending is half the job, so we could see lessons in how to use the key, how to position one's hand in relation to the key, and how to move one's wrist only in these terms. But the operators gave me the impression that their hearing of Morse was intimately intertwined with their arm and hand movements. That is, sending is not an exercise just for the hand and arm, and receiving is not an exercise just for the ear. Both sending and receiving are a synthesis of hearing *and* movement. Morse operators hear *in* movement.

When sending, trainees work from a letter as visualized silently. The character is rendered audible via the movement of the hand and arm at the key. They think of the sound patterns first, ahead of the movements that will make the characters audible. Fred explained:

You've got to learn the alphabet yourself; no one can teach you the Morse alphabet. So once you get that in your mind, then you get onto a key, and you start practicing: "A," di-dah—and you do that lots of times—"B," and so forth. And then you have an instructor who takes over and sends to you. And then he might send the word *and*, and you hit "A-N-D" [on the typewriter]. . . . Everybody had a sounder on their desk and a key and an instructor at the front. And for two hours, I did this for about nine months, gradually bringing [my] speed up. Then at the end, there was the examination. And that was difficult because it was a pass-or-fail sort of situation.

Fred focused on the process of sending, but operators move between the activities of sending and receiving. Both activities involve translations among the visual, aural, and kinesthetic, albeit in different sequences. When receiving, the task begins with hearing the sound. Trainees type down what they have heard, making it visible to themselves and to the instructors who will evaluate their skills.

Instructors look for the points at which they can show trainees what they need to be doing as operators. Some operators, like James, said working on Morse movements was of much more value for trainees than was receiving verbal feedback about how they were hearing their sound or that of other senders. He explained how wrist position and action are demonstrated: "Most people found receiving a lot more difficult than sending, but as I said with the sending, it's a wrist action. You don't hold your wrist down like that. You don't hold it to one side. . . . You've got to have a flexible wrist, and you've got to form the characters correctly. As I said, if a chap's sending a 'C' the wrong way, you show him, [saying,] 'This is how it should be sent.' And [you] take his hand off again, [and] you do it for him. [Then he says,] 'Oh, yeah, I've got that. Righto, thanks.'"

James acknowledged that the hard part of Morse operation is receiving, the hearing-forward aspect of the practice. But rather than attending to receiving directly, instructors primarily offer correction in sending. They talk to trainees about body position and wrist action. Here, the pedagogical approach is mimetic. They show the trainees what a problem character sounds like by giving a demonstration with a key. In effect, they are saying, "To hear and move to form the character correctly, you need to copy my movements." They are trying to aid trainees' understanding of Morse, which is largely aural, via the movements involved in forming it.

Once they have mastered the correct body positions and sequences of movement, trainees must increase their speed. Albert summarized the whole training process as follows: "Start off slowly, and you get faster." The gradual process of increasing one's speed in Morse is similar to that of musicians who practice playing a piece using a metronome, starting out slowly and increasing the speed only once they are able to play smoothly and without errors. Each increase in speed is nearly imperceptible (e.g., from sixty beats a minute to sixty-three beats a minute). Moving this slowly, it may take the musician days or weeks to get their playing up to speed.

In Morse training schools, the process is even slower. Trainees go from sending and receiving at a rate of twelve words per minute to twenty or twenty-two and a half per minute over ten months of practicing three to four hours a day, five days a week. The Wheatstone tape described by Albert aids in this process by transmitting a perfect production of Morse at a manageable pace for trainees to try to interpret and ultimately embody. Trainees are also carried along by the shifting pace of their instructors and the adjacent sending and receiving bodies of others who are meeting the pace of the week. The operators felt that Morse was being drilled into their bodies this way. Charles reflected, "The training was excellent when you look back on it. It was disciplined and was drummed into you. I mean, it's just like the army, that type of thing; you just automatically react. It would not have left any of us; it's there for the rest of your days."

Speed increases were marked with monthly tests. With each test, one or two trainees would not make the grade. To their shame, they would end up in circulation or some other non-operating role. As in the military, masculine bravado pervaded the training schools, and shifts in pace were coupled with blokey pressure to meet the new standard. William recalled, "The quality of work was high. Most got into the job, and stayed in the job, due to a love of Morse, and you would have been badly embarrassed if workmates thought one couldn't cut it."

For their final test, trainees had to receive eighteen telegrams in twenty minutes and send at the same speed. But testing did not end with graduation. The telegraphist barrier exam assessed whether an operator had reached the rate of twenty-five words per minute; those who passed received a higher salary. Operators who had passed the barrier exam were also eligible to sit for the supervisor's exam (a small number pursued this path), which required an even higher rate of speed of Morse operation, as well as an understanding of traffic procedures, technical knowledge, and machine telegraphy.

The formation of signals at increasing speeds also needed to be accurate, though my operators tended to skip over this aspect beyond making reference to the number of allowed errors in tests. William was an outlier in this respect; he said an operator's focus should never be building speed despite the emphasis placed on speed in Morse training programs. William stressed that learning Morse should be focused on accurately producing the rhythm. If you focus on getting the correct pulse and accurately forming signals at the key, then speed will follow. Thus, speed is not the desired outcome but rather a by-product. William observed that those who pursued speed first did not develop their understanding of the code. When an operator focuses only on movement, on the speed of their motor action, they disattend hearing and thus make mistakes that they do not register.

How Transcription Exercises Stamp Out the Urge of Trainees to Anticipate the Message

Work at the key centers mostly around sending and receiving mock telegram messages. Such transmission exercises were especially concerned with holding the attention of receivers, effectively saying to them, "Hear *all* the letters, not just the first few until you think you know what the word will be." The importance of this message is obvious for trainee operators receiving in cipher. An operator had to listen to and transcribe each character. In plain English, however, the temptation was to jump ahead, moving from hearing each audible signal to making an educated guess. Stanley explained, "You've certainly got to read the words as they're coming through [and] try not to anticipate. That's one of the worst things: anticipation."

To discourage the tendency to anticipate the message, drills that work on sending often included words that were similar to but different from commonly expected words. Alan explained:

> When you first start learning, the sound is coming through, and you've got your pen poised—this is before you get on to typewriters—and you're trying to keep up with it. It will send "BENDIGO" and you've got "B-E-N-D," and you're going like that, and you're trying to anticipate. The instructors in the course would make sure that you didn't anticipate by doing things differently. . . . "FLINDERS NAVAL DEPOT" was a regular one. They'd [the instructors would] send a mock telegram. See, they'd sit up [at] the front, and they'd have these twenty-odd people all going through to their sounders, and you'd be writing it down. That's when you're learning to receive, and "FLINDERS NAVAL DEPOT," fifteen words at 10:15, just like an ordinary telegram, would be "MR J SMITH so-and-so," and you've taken "NAVAL" up there. Send "N-A-V," and you'd think, "Here's 'NAVAL,'" but no. [It would be] "SEND NAVEL ORANGES." . . . They did all those kinds of things to make sure that you didn't anticipate. . . . And "GOING TO FISHER"—start off with "FISH," and you think, "Oh, here's 'FISHING,'" [but it is] "FISHERMAN'S BEND." They do all things differently just so that you wouldn't anticipate. So, you got into the habit of sitting a word or two behind.

Receiving cipher especially demanded that trainees listen to what they were receiving, that they be "in the now," rather than moving beyond what has been said to what an operator predicts will be said.[16] James explained:

> A lot of the time they would give us groups of five letters, what you're calling in the military cipher. Just jumbled up, five letters. Space. Five letters. Space. That way, it stops you guessing. Because if you start off giving somebody "H-A," and he gets a "P," he thinks, "I bet the next two are 'P-Y,' and that'll make 'HAPPY.'" And then as soon as they start "B-I" on the next word, he's almost got "BIRTHDAY" written down, you see? So it defeats the purpose. But if you listen to five jumbled up letters, you can't guess anything. . . . And that made you pay attention.

One of the lessons here is to sit behind the message. While this is not always what happens in practice, while training, operators are told that they must hear the characters as they are being formed, resisting the urge to anticipate what will come next. Their typing hands need to sit even further behind, perhaps by whole words. Fred continued, "Look, I think you need a reasonable memory or a good memory. That's because when you're proficient and you're receiving a message, you're not typing down letter for letter. You're staying a few words behind. So there's where the memory comes in. . . . It might start off, 'IT WAS HOT IN WAGGA TODAY,' so you type that while you're listening for the next [word], which still continues. [It] doesn't stop."

In a similar vein, William said, "A good operator, when he's receiving, you don't receive letter by letter. And you really don't receive word by word. And a good operator can be a message behind and still put it all down. So, that's got to be a good memory." They type what has been while they listen for what is next. They must sit far enough behind the heard message that their typing hands do not get carried away and their ear does not move from listening to responding in the form of typing, thus missing the message. They work on keeping themselves in a "listening" state, rather than hearing in their heads what they expect to come next.

This practice is reminiscent of what jazz musicians do in transcription, though with important differences. In jazz transcription, musicians work on refraining from responding (in the form of notating what they have heard) in ever-increasing spans of music. Jazz transcription is specific to practice; holding off moving to transcribe is something they do only to shift their listening orientation to working on deconstructive hearing. They go back, over the line of the music again, hearing more in each pass, whether that involves a more accurate appreciation of the pitch, the musical expression, or otherwise. When transcribing, musicians anchor themselves to one note to better hear the next.

This type of repetition does not feature in the Morse case. Operators in training are essentially doing a dry run of what they will need to do professionally. They are not going back to try again. Harold recalled the unforgiving margin of error: "You couldn't afford to make a mistake." There is no going back because *there will be* no going back. Operators must get it right the first time. A typed message is not a resource for them to rehear but rather a test of whether they have heard correctly in what is almost a sudden-death scenario; if errors occur too often, they will be kicked out of the program. For Morse operators, hearing right means maintaining attention, hearing each character—not just getting the gist—before moving on to typing.

THE PRACTICES INVOLVED IN WORKING LIVE TRAFFIC

Operators Pass on Tricks of the Trade to Trainees for Hearing Morse Through the Noise of "the Room"

As in other fields of activity, real-world practice differs markedly from classroom practice. After graduation, operators posted to a

Chief Telegraph Office recalled being struck by the palpable noise of "the room" (figure 4.5). In Sydney, the Chief Telegraph Office could accommodate as many as five hundred telegraphists over two floors, each with their own key, sounder, and typewriter. In the 1950s, about three hundred and fifty operators staffed the office each day. In addition to the noise of the room, there was also noise from teleprinters and the pneumatic tube system. Fred recalled, "When you went into a big telegraph office like Sydney or Melbourne, and let's say mid-morning and midafternoon, you can hear this tremendous clatter of sounders and machines [and] teleprinters going, and electric belts with telegrams whizzing around, and there's a huge noise. And when you first come out of the school, you think, 'Gee, how will I ever put up with this noise?' And then, of course, . . . there might be six or eight people on a long bench, all with their own sounder and key and relay, [and] everything's clicking."

In the training school, trainees received a single message at the same time, and the noise coming from the sounders was thus a synchronized sequence of code. But when dealing with live traffic, operators were faced with the noise of competing clicks of various volumes

FIGURE 4.5 The Chief Telegraph Office in Brisbane, Australia, December 24, 1929.

and timbres—as if making sense of electric telegraph signals was not hard enough! The change was off-putting. Operators described achieving a good level of fluency in the language of Morse by the end of their training, but hitting live traffic was another matter entirely. "You thought you were a good operator until you got into the telegraph branch, and you found out you weren't so good," Gordon said.

Post offices had their own background noise and distractions, with customers needing service at the counter, the chatter of voices, and the sounds of various machinery. Benjamin, a postal clerk, explained the woes of the post office operator: "The telegraphists had terrible noise all around them, but they could at least focus on their sounder—which is why they had the 'Morse deafness'—whereas at the post office, we had the post stamping machine, the telegraph messengers were all around you, and people kept calling you from the counter, which broke your concentration. So it was a different kind of noise to the noise that [telegraphists] talk about. It was terribly distracting, but no one cared because they didn't do Morse."

Operators in both settings needed to find a way to dial in their hearing. Just as doctors use a stethoscope partly to close off other parts of the medical interaction, Morse operators must grapple with how to block out the noise around them. In the Chief Telegraph Offices, new operators were paired with experienced operators to help with the transition from school to workplace. This was done under the guise of familiarizing newcomers with traffic procedures, but in reality, it was more about the experienced operators sharing tricks of the trade with the newcomers and building their confidence as they worked through the initial panic. Albert shared that when he first encountered live traffic, he did not have a clue what was being said:

> Oh, it was a big learning curve. In the first day, I went to the Chief Telegraph Office, and they sat me down on the Morse line to Orbost, and he [the experienced operator] called up [opened the line] nine o'clock, and he would have had the weather readings. And I said,

"Go ahead," and he started to send, and I didn't have a clue what he was saying. Like, there was nothing there that I could recognize. It was just a jumble of sound. So, the supervisor just walked over, and he opened the key, and he said, "Hang on for a second," and he said, "Take six deep breaths." He said, "Now, what was that coming out of there?" And I said, "Morse code." And he said, "Can you do Morse code at the required speed for the final examining?" I said, "Yes, I passed it." So, he [said], "OK." So, he said to the fella, "Go ahead," and I was right [able to operate].

The telegraphists in particular talked about needing to find ways to focus on their sounder, blocking out other sounds, almost as if in a romantic comedy in which the focus narrows to the intimate moment. Fred said that he eventually stopped hearing the Morse coming through the neighboring station: "You don't hear the one next door unless you want to. And it doesn't faze you." Most accounted for this ability in terms of concentration. Benjamin reflected, "You just got to a stage where they could have set off a bomb and I would have still heard the Morse. You focus on it, but it is not so much hearing; it is your concentration. People could talk to you, and you wouldn't even know they are there." Harold agreed: "Yes, exactly. You block everything out." For Morse operators, *not* hearing is essential to hearing.

This concentration could be aided by a spatial shift, by adjusting one's body position to be closer to the sounder. "You have to have your ear right in the sounder, really," Gordon explained. Operators also described finding idiosyncrasies in the sounds that they needed to attend to to help block out extraneous sounds. They would try to tune into the nuances in the tone of their sounder as opposed to those of the operator's next to them. Harold said, "The sounders all had a different tone. Some of them would ring, some would have a duller tone, some would have a ding about them, [and] others would go, 'Plonk, plonk, plonk.'"

When there was no obvious difference in the tones of the sounders, operators could manufacture one by placing an object on their sounder to change its timbre. James recalled,

> I remember a couple of chaps in Sydney used to put a penny on the top of the sounder . . . and it would give it a more distinctive noise to the one either side of him, where you might hear it a little bit. . . . Then another trick was, there used to be a certain type of tobacco [that] was sold in a tin, and the Americans used to do this a lot, but I have seen it done in Sydney, too. They would cut a hole in the top, and they would fit that on so it used to rattle the tin and it made their . . . resonator . . . sound different to the other ones around them.

How Operators Use Speed to Test the Hearing of Receivers

Among PMG operators, speed was a major preoccupation. As the writer Tom Standage described, "Telegraph operators were members of a closed, exclusive community . . . [with] their own customs and vocabulary, and a strict pecking order, based on the speed at which they could send and receive messages."[17] Throughout training, and in their relationships with their local colleagues, operators are generous with the support that they provide to one another. When it came to message transmission, in which an operator's relationship is first and foremost with the operator at the other end of the line, consideration of the recipient's needs fell by the wayside.

PMG operators gained a reputation for the volume of traffic they could handle, a reputation that others wanted to emulate. While some of the speeds claimed were contentious, the reputation of "gun" operators entered Morse legend as something to aspire to. Where telegraphists were officially required to operate at twenty-two and a half words per minute, and operators who reached twenty-five words per minute received a raise, "gun" operators were cited as operating at thirty-five words a minute or even higher.

In receiving, too, the ability to make sense of fragments was interactionally salient beyond the immediate task at hand. Fred explained:

> And the word we used was *gun operator*, like *gun shearer*. Some men you knew, that fellow over there, he's much better than I'll ever be, sort of thing. But you're trying to aspire to get up there. . . . There was a fellow over at Goulburn, Jack somebody, and he was a wild man on the key, and they'd be fighting all the time with him from Sydney. . . . It was a matter of pride, and getting on there for an hour and not breaking or taking fifty messages and not breaking the man. That was just one of those little things that—I suppose that was part of the enjoyments of the job. It was a repetitious job, but there was competition all the time, I suppose, friendly competition among your mates. And as my old boss . . . says, telegraphists are basically skites, show-offs.

James, who had worked as an operator at the Sydney Chief Telegraph Office, recalled the fastest senders in the state: J. A. P. ("Jap") O'Neil, and Callaghan, the "Mountain Lion." The story goes that on a "classic" Saturday morning, Jap and the Mountain Lion were working the line from Sydney to Katoomba. On this particular Saturday, more weddings were being held than usual, so the typically busy line was pushed to its limit. James recalled, "I think they did five hundred telegrams one morning in Morse. And Jap got a standing ovation off the boys in Sydney." While these stories influenced and inspired James, he did not know the operators personally: "I think he [Jap] was just about retiring when I started then. I can only remember him vaguely." Of the Mountain Lion, James said, "I saw him once. I didn't actually meet him."

Operators would challenge themselves and others by setting up demonstrations of prowess. James recalled once challenging a telegraphist he was friendly with: "I saw this telegram. It was addressed to the Wingecarribee Shire. And I thought, 'He won't know this' [the message would be challenging to receive]. And I went like the clappers.

And sure enough, he missed it. So I gave him a burst, you see? I said, 'What's up with you?' I just said, 'Type it down.'" Working with the same operator late one evening, James was asked by his supervisor to jump on the line and receive a press telegram with greyhound race results. He got on the line and said, "Get into it!" (meaning "Let's see how fast we can go!"), which he explained was "a silly thing to say" because of the difficulty involved in accurately reporting all the dog names and race results. But he "never missed a thing," he told me proudly. However, he played on the likelihood that he would have missed things and mischievously chose not to acknowledge receiving the message. After exasperating his friend, he announced, "'Course I got it! Go home!" "You had a little bit of fun," he said. He was being difficult to show off, and to challenge the receiver. The operators often laughed telling such stories.

A railway operator named Elliott also described this kind of "testing" culture: "The railways used a lot of code words, four-letter code words with meaning, things to cut down the length of the telegrams. I did receive ninety telegrams in sixty minutes from one young bloke at Adelaide. He was trying to see how fast he could send and [whether] you could keep up."

The operators were sending at their top speed, looking for where the receiver's hearing would fail. Clyde shared a story of two "gun" operators in Melbourne:

One of the guys was the best operator. His photo is downstairs [in the National Communication Museum]. There were two brothers, and they came from up Gisborne way, the Colliver brothers. They were crash hot! One of them became superintendent of the telegraph branch. They were the complete opposite, though. One was relaxed and would have a smoke, and you wouldn't have heard the other swear. But they were top operators; they were kings. They would send so many messages, and they would get crook [lose their temper] in Sydney because they couldn't receive them. And then you would have to cop it [be punished] the next hour if you were taking over that line!

Most Morse operators saw the practice of sending faster than could be reasonably received as a problem of ego. Harold, a postal clerk, said that the gun operators "all had pretty big egos, and some had giant egos and wouldn't slow down." Fred said, "They were egocentric, most of these blokes, the good operators. And they used to get reputations; it was like a sheep shearer: 'I can do two hundred sheep a day.' They might be able to send a hundred—well, that's an exaggeration, but let's say eighty telegrams in an hour on the Morse. And that was good going. The average, the others with the same messages might do forty, which is still not bad. Yeah, so I think ego came into it."

Tempers could run hot, with one's manhood at stake. Oliver, a telegraphist, said that "sometimes something like road rage could occur: telegraph rage." The greatest insult—"Put a man on the line"—was received when an operator was falling behind and "breaking" the sender. Charles explained:

> You'd get fined or reprimanded for all sorts of little things, and if you got on the line and got into a fight with somebody, sometimes the ultimate insult was, especially when you were young and just fairly new, was the country operators would say, "Put a man on the line." They'd say. . . . some of those guys out there were top operators, too, and they couldn't suffer us slower ones. Or if we broke them, opened the key up, oh, they'd abuse you. "Put a man on the line." And if you persevered and weren't going, they'd . . . ring the boss up and get you taken off.

Gordon was no stranger to such a scenario: "I can't remember how many lines I was kicked off, and I wasn't the only one. You'd get on a line, and the fellow at the other end would immediately know that you were new at it, and you'd continually break him because you couldn't keep up. And he would say—the favorite question was 'Get a man.' . . . But they were merciless because they had their traffic to dispose of, and they're not going to muck around getting broken all the time."

And Fred:

> If you weren't confident and you got on a busy line, the word was "booted off"; you couldn't handle the traffic. And that happened to me a few times. A fella was just too fast, too busy, too much traffic on hand to worry about a trainee, as we were known for the first couple of months. And they'd say, "You better go over there and do that. We'll get Charlie Blogs; he'll handle that." So you lost face, then, too, you see. Yeah, so it didn't pay to go in being [a] big shot and then [you] couldn't do the job.

This harsh treatment was specific to those at the other end of the line. Adjacent colleagues were only too happy to help, swapping the busy line for one with less pressure if someone was having trouble, or shooting back some harsh words in defense of a new operator. Walter explained: "It's the face-to-face bit. I mean, it's very easy to abuse somebody, say, over the phone or over a telegraph line, but when you're face-to-face, things are a lot different. . . . And you, of course, get to know the person when you're face-to-face. On the other end of a line, he's just somebody that's incompetent."

In recounting such scenarios, the operators I spoke with explained that the context sometimes justified the pressure to be quicker—for example, busy Saturdays or high-traffic lines—but just as often, I was told that the operators tended to have just one speed: fast. They were going like the clappers even if they did not need to. It was often speed for speed's sake, coupled with interstate rivalry.

Making Sense of Fragments as Another Test of an Operator's Hearing

Simultaneously existing with the obsession with speed was a great anxiety about making mistakes. Almost all the operators I spoke with said they could not afford to make mistakes. However, avoiding mistakes did not mean following processes that would ensure precision. They were going so fast that sending errors were inevitable. They were sending in fragments, too—that was the game. In the world of telegraphy, it is the receiver who is responsible for taking down the correct message (i.e., correct in intended meaning, not necessarily in the exactness of what was sent). When speed and error anxiety meet, what follows is a kind of reversal of operators' training in receiving, which often involved sitting ahead and guessing. They are trying to cobble together a message out of the bits and pieces that come through.

The operators used the term *journalizing* to describe the practice of anticipating a message based on the flow of the English language and commonly used words that start with particular combinations of letters. Fred explained:

> If you're guessing, and most of the time you're right, it's called "journalizing." Sometimes you can type the stuff down and think, "The next word is going to be this and that," and you type it down beforehand. You'll anticipate it because that's the flow of the English language. In the training school, they used to trick you. You'd have little exams, and the instructor would start sending the word— M-E-L—[and] everybody would type "MELBOURNE." No, M-E-L-T-O-N, "MELTON," which is a town, and so you'd muck that up. So you really had to be careful in exams, but that's what journalizing does to you.

Anticipating is a problem only when you're wrong. If you're right, it is some first-class journalizing. All the PMG operators described moments of taking some artistic license when receiving plain English messages, especially on predictable topics. Charles described such an instance: "Like the time I had nineteen telegrams under my typewriter, I made up a few that day, too. As long as I had the general [idea] because most of them were, you know, best wishes on your wedding or something." In this scenario, Charles was working as a postal clerk, and messages were coming through while he was serving customers at the counter. He was not thinking, "How many messages can I roughly remember before I type them out?" He was simply run off his feet, so all he could do was get the gist and then fill in the gaps.

Journalizing was also a valued skill in the context of receiving in poor conditions, such as when rain, wind, or auroral activity interfered with the signals. Charles explained:

> If you were working, say, places like Brighton, Mount Beauty, or you might be going down Gippsland to Sale and places like that, particularly if the weather was bad, the lines would be in very poor condition, the signal would be weak, [and] sometimes it wouldn't get through because it was the electric telegraph, not radiotelegraph. . . . So it had to be connected by copper wires, so you had telegraph poles of wires. Of course, when wire gets wet, the electricity then goes down the poles into the ground and earth, and you lose your power.

In such conditions, good operators knew how to adjust the relays, a technology that amplified the electrical signal, to increase the signal strength. Great operators might also be able to read off the relays, watching rather than hearing for the clicking. But as often as not, this was another scenario in which the operators needed to imagine the intended message. Gordon explained: "With experience you can guess a lot. See, some lines you get on sometimes, [on] some of the country lines . . . you'd get a lot of interference, wet weather and that, leakage on the lines, and you've got to work through a lot of difficulties, and you can guess a lot. And most of the times you're right. But whereas a completely inexperienced operator might say, 'No, I couldn't handle that,' [but] you could struggle through it if you're experienced."

Receivers must also deal with imperfect senders. In the classroom, trainees work with "perfect" Morse, especially those messages transmitted via Wheatstone tape. But that is not what they are working with on live traffic. Charles again: "When you came out of school and you went on a Morse line, I'm not joking, you thought, 'What the hell's that noise?' because you're not dealing with good senders in a lot of cases. A lot of postal clerks didn't get a lot of traffic, so they weren't necessarily good operators."

Returning to our earlier discussion of the possibility of making errors when sending on a jigger, I asked Fred, "Now when an extra dot is involved, and there's a debate over whether it's an 'H' or a '5,' how do you know?" He explained:

> Well, if you're sending what we call plain language—we used to send information to and from the newspapers in country [rural] Victoria. *The Mildura Express* might have been a newspaper. And we would send up something from, let's say, *The Age* newspaper, intended for the Mildura paper. And it might be just a story about what was happening at the time. . . . And in plain English, you're just telling the story. So what the fellas would do, you more or less turn off, and you're not thinking. . . . So if there's a bit of a mistake in the middle of a word, you wouldn't even interrupt . . . he's misspelt it, [but] you just type it down, you know.

When receiving plain English, the operator is interpreting the whole meaning of the message, not listening only to individual characters. The ability to do this did not take on the same near-mythical status of the speedy gun operators, but it was considered a special, even extra-sensory skill. Elliott remembered:

> I can remember some of the good operators there [on the railways]. [One man], he used to talk to you while he was sending; he used to talk to you while he was receiving. I was having difficulty to understand . . . the signals coming through because they were dropping out on the line just because of the quality of the line. He said to me, "We're here

to interpret what he's trying to say to us," and he hardly ever queried the bloke at the other end, and he still got the message. And I suppose that was from experience because the type of message we were sending was in code, and you had a sixth sense of what they were trying to send to you and then interpret it OK. . . . We had one operator that used to fall on the "M" and "E" of "MELBOURNE", pretty close together and didn't form it correctly. Well, it always was sent as a "G," so it'd be "G-L-B-O-U-R-N-E," [but] you would still know that he was trying to say "MELBOURNE." And another operator used to run the "I" and "N" together, which formed an "F." If you were reading the word as he said it, you would end up making a mistake. You would have to try and sit a little bit behind what he was trying to send you and to read it as the word rather than the individual [letters of the] alphabet.[18]

It was not only transmission difficulties that gave rise to this need to "sense" the message. PMG operators often made use of abbreviations (termed "cutting it up"), some well known, others the invention of the individual operator. They said this is kind of like text speak. James explained how this "cut-up" language was typically used:

Mother's Day was a classic example. Invariably, on the Saturday morning of Mother's Day, nine out of the ten telegrams would start off, "HAPPY MOTHER'S DAY." And then it might say something else, and then it would be, "LOVE JEAN, LITTLE HARRY, TOM, DICK." So if you had a good bloke at the other end, you'd just go, "HMD." And that really sped things up no end. . . . And the same with Christmas time. You'd just get "MERRY CHRISTMAS AND A HAPPY NEW YEAR," so you'd just go "MXAHNY." And put a little bit of a deliberate space between it, and he'd have it all down in full. . . . "COMMONWEALTH," you could safely abbreviate that to "CWLTH." And that was used a lot.

Most of the operators I spoke with mentioned the Mother's Day and Christmas abbreviations. But other abbreviations were less widely agreed upon and so could trip up new operators, especially because, in shortening a word to a single character or dropping parts of the signal such as the dashes, the receiver can very quickly fall behind. For instance, Clyde shared how operators working at the cattle yards would drop the "extra dashes" off numbers, so the number 1 would be shortened from •———— to •—, and so on. Because they were sending in numbers, the receivers would know the meaning was "1," not "A," which is also signaled as •—. Common words like *and* and *would* could also be abbreviated, but variation in expression across operators, cliques, and localities (i.e., social groups who develop their own ways of doing things) introduced a risk of misinterpretation. As Harold observed, "The Western Australians would always say 'WUD' for 'WOULD,' where we would say 'WLD'":

•——	••—	—••		•——	•—••	—••
W	U	D		W	L	D

The use of such abbreviations was not allowed in the training schools and was thus picked up on the job. James said, "[It was] not quite by the book. Nothing was by the book. Book, it all went out the window I think." Fred put it memorably: "You learn other things once you get into the system. It's like going to prison, I suppose; you learn the ropes." The prison reference is telling: the use of abbreviations had little to do with the core task; rather, it was about learning who was "cool," who the top dog was, and putting down or excluding the people who were not part of the "in" crowd. Cutting it up was done partly in the service of speed. If you send only parts of words, then you can move through messages considerably faster. But it is more than that. Some people could be fast senders without pushing the boundaries of cut-up language.

And cut-up language, if too obscure, could slow things down if a message needed to be repeated.

As with fast sending, operators tested one another's ability to receive cut-up language in order to establish a pecking order. One Saturday, William was working a line between Sydney and Nyngan, where flooding had caused a backlog of traffic. Despite the volume of telegrams, William and the operator at Nyngan (himself a "good operator") were proceeding at a "normal pace." It came to William's attention that people were starting to gather at the supervisor's office, and he guessed that they were there to assess his skills. William said to his Nyngan counterpart, "Come on, get into it." When the others then listened in, both William and the operator in Nyngan were going "flat out." William then directed the Nyngan operator to "cut it up." The supervisor came over to William and said, "We heard you were good, and we wanted to find out how good you are." William confessed that the speed of that exchange could not be maintained all day. That William and his counterpart in Nyngan were proceeding at a normal pace before their colleagues listened in also shows that their speed and use of abbreviations were not needed to address the traffic backlog—however, they were important for William to demonstrate his expertise to his colleagues.

Charles, familiar with James's sending style, commented on his signal formation and the difficulty of reading his messages: "See, [James], again, is a good example. He doesn't space between words. He just goes one continuous stream and, not only that, because you've heard us say we cut words up, well, he cuts up like we all do; he cuts the words up, and he streams them. So, that takes a particular skill to read that. You've got to be a fairly good operator to be able to read that." Operators who send like this shift responsibility for making sense of a message onto receivers; if a message is garbled, it is not the fault of a "bad" sender but of a "bad" receiver, one who cannot make sense of a message.

Operators outside the PMG system typically had great difficulty following cut up language. Elliott, a railway operator shared the following:

> I remember [my] first times on the railways: we had a Morse code opera-tor at Ballarat, and he used to talk in abbreviations and things. He would use the code for the station it [a message] was going to. If he was talking about Burrumbeet, he'd send "B-T," and you'd have to be on the same wavelength to know what he was talking about. And "about" might have been "A-B-T." . . . And if he's transmitting at a fairly fast speed, well, it's a bit difficult. You get lost. . . . and it's not like today's text, [where] you can sit there and think about it. When they were transmitting in Morse, it was instant, and [it was] gone. And [it] didn't allow you to go back and ponder five seconds or ten seconds later to look at it three times.

All this guesswork was necessarily limited to plain English. Messages like bank telegrams and military communications were sent in cipher; such messages were encoded into blocks of five characters and had to be decoded at the receiving end. Fred explained that trans-mitting cipher involved repetition, in place of an educated guess, in cases of error or uncertainty: "You couldn't do that [i.e., guess] with bank code; you must have it right. In that case, the letters would be repeated. But if the man was sending bank code, or he made a mistake, he would stop and then go, 'What was the signal?' He'd send a string of dots, about eight, and the man at the other end would know a mistake had been made. The sender would go back to the last correct word, do the correct word, and keep going again."

Idiosyncrasy and Its Security Implications

Operators typically have their own idiosyncrasies, which means that individual operators can be identified based on their cadence.

Among the PMG operators, some were good, steady senders. There were those who "clipped" their dashes, shortening them closer to two, rather than three, times the length of a dot. Some had a slight push or pull in their formation of particular characters. For example, James said that he could tell when he was talking to a particular operator because that operator always put a slight pause in his "Y," and as a result would send "N-M" instead:

<table>
<tr><td></td><td>↓ [idiosyncratic pause]</td></tr>
<tr><td>— • — —</td><td>— •   — —</td></tr>
<tr><td>Y</td><td>N   M</td></tr>
</table>

Another operator ran the "A" and "N" of *and* together, thus sending "P-D":

<table>
<tr><td></td><td>↓ [pause missing]</td></tr>
<tr><td>• —   — •   — • •</td><td>• — — •   — • •</td></tr>
<tr><td>A   N   D</td><td>P   D</td></tr>
</table>

Speaking of James, Charles commented, "Morse is just like human beings: each one's a little bit different. For instance, [James], when he sends, he's got a distinctive style of sending. In his telegraph days in Sydney, he was called 'Hammer' . . . because he only has one speed, and that's flat out. . . . In some ways, Morse is a little bit like an extension of the characteristics of an individual. [James] even in real life is flat out."

With hundreds of telegraphists working at the Chief Telegraph Offices, not every operator could be identified based on their idiosyncrasies. Rather, operators were aware of particular friends' idiosyncrasies; for example, an operator might notice an error in cadence and think, "Oh, that's this bloke I know." Charles explained that they adapted to whoever was sending pretty quickly; regardless of particular sending quirks, receivers could still identify the characters being formed. Rather than creating a problem or being a help, idiosyncrasies were simply noticed and a way to identify certain senders.[19]

In the PMG, some idiosyncrasies in the use of code and in the cadence of signal formation were allowed, but in other operating contexts, such as with the use of cipher in the military, idiosyncrasies were considered a major problem, and operators had to be careful to form each character with exactitude. In a military context, Morse operators were stationed with a military unit, and troop movements could sometimes be tracked based on the sending style of the Morse operator posted to the unit. It was thus critically important that the Morse signal sent by such operators was uniform and adhered exactly to protocol. Personal idiosyncrasies were like an aural signature and therefore had the potential to divulge military secrets.

For this reason, military operators used only hand keys, never jiggers. The jiggers were too hard to control and too likely to generate an idiosyncratic rendering of code. James explained:

> They didn't use them [i.e., jiggers] in the services very much. They frowned on them for a start . . . mainly for security reasons. They're pretty easy to pick [identify the operator] from a hand—well, so they reckon. . . . If you keep everybody on a Morse key, they all sound the same. What the Germans in particular used to do, they could tell if people had idiosyncrasies in their transmission style. . . . Well, this didn't apply at the post office. There were a lot [of operators] there that had idiosyncrasies, and possibly we all do, either . . . in the style or the way they're sent or the way they [i.e., operators] handle the procedure. Now in the military, they were very strict on procedure, so that you would all sound the same. Because if you do something that was just unique, now the Germans would listen in and they'd say they know that bloke over there is from an armored battalion, this radio operator. And he's got this distinct thing he does at the end of each [session, i.e. sign off] when they finish the circuit. And then they might pinpoint another one over here, and he's from over here. They know that. And they know where they are. And suddenly one day, they put the direction-finding gear [on], and they find this armored bloke is over here, and the

bloke that used to be over here, he's with him. And another one over there, he's with him. And they said, "Now, why are all these armored battalions getting together? It must be a big offensive coming up." And they start flying a few planes 'round, taking photos and things like that. All through somebody not doing the right thing.

Cecilia recalled the limits that were placed on military operators' expression of code. Whereas PMG operators would chat with one another in between sending telegrams, chatter among military operators was prohibited: "I only worked in code [cipher]. . . . But see, [Gary, her husband] didn't operate in wartime; only I did. And you couldn't talk. You were supposed to keep quiet because the [Japanese] listened into us, and we listened into them. And you're supposed to, you know, not talk so they wouldn't know where you were." She confessed that trying to erase operators' idiosyncrasies was almost a losing battle, but they all tried their best: "You could tell [who] everybody [was]. There's Bill on tonight, or everyone sounds personal, that's got a certain swing. . . . I've got [Cecilia's] Morse."

WHAT WE LEARN FROM MORSE OPERATORS ABOUT HEARING

The case of Morse operators' hearing, as with the other forms of hearing addressed in this book, demonstrates that what we think of as hearing is more varied in its meaning and practice than is typically acknowledged. For musicians, so much of hearing is bound to proprioception as a strategy to shift perspective and in the service of bodily organizing ahead of producing sound. Adventurers use a metaphorical notion of listening as a multimodal pattern of responsiveness to place. Doctors rely on both conscious and unconscious hearing, and displayed hearing as opposed to inner forms of attention that are realized elsewhere.

Morse operators add to these notions the idea of hearing as civic-mindedness. The role of acting as listening posts is not seen in other contexts of hearing; Morse operators are responsible for secret-keeping and calls to action when a message received demands it. In the context of Morse, value is placed on specialized aural skills. In contrast to the doctors, who felt that their aural clinical skills have been devalued over time, the Morse operators felt that their ability to interpret code aurally was always valued, and they continue to take pride in their skills and their service to their communities.

More so than in the other cases addressed in this book, the Morse operators show us a social hierarchy in the doing of hearing. By operating at great speed and transmitting code in fragments, they jostled for position and recognition. They tested one another's abilities to hear code to establish a pecking order rather than to advance their skills. Indeed, the "tests" involved in this friendly competition are antithetical to the principles of Morse operation. Operators were meant to prioritize accuracy and efficiency, but by sending incomplete information and sending so fast that receivers would miss the message, they achieved neither. The activities of the gun operator were less about message transmission than displaying aural prowess.

This is not to say that degrees of expertise in hearing are not recognized in the other cases addressed in this book. Cardiologists claimed to have the strongest aural skills of all medical specialties because of their heightened connection to auscultatory hearing. Doctors in other specialties contested this claim, demonstrating their own forms of aural expertise. The musicians used the term "good ears" to acknowledge players with strong aural skills. But what the musicians and doctors typically do *not* do is test one another's hearing.

The fragmentary nature of message transmission—whether owing to "tests" of skill, "bad senders" garbling the message, or the effect of environmental conditions on the signal—gives rise to another variety of hearing: listening for meaning, not the exact identification of characters sent. This is another manifestation of the idea of hearing for "all practical purposes," as we saw in the case of the musicians.[20] Interpretive work is involved in Morse operation. Operators do not type down exactly what they have heard; rather, they try to get the gist. The final typed message should include the intended idea of a transmission if not the exact wording.

The case of the Morse operators also offers us insight into the temporal aspects of hearing. Many of the operators I spoke with were conscious of the techno-historical context of their practice. They observed that memory was a key part of their hearing. They heard a sound in a moment, and they needed to understand a sound in a moment. But the primacy of memory has receded with the development of recording technologies that allow for a momentary sound to be replayed.

The operators were also aware that the significance of their skills had changed over time. I met the operators when they were involved in the Morsecodian community toward the end of the first decade of the twenty-first century. They had all stopped operating many years earlier but got back into Morse recreationally in the mid-1990s when one of them had the idea and drew in others who were keen. Those who joined had an enduring love of hearing Morse code—the sound of it—as well as a great pride in this special thing that they could do.

But they were also aware that their skill was nearing the end of its history. Some were a bit trepidatious with the language of its being a "dying art"—too close to the bone considering their aging bodies—but they were nonetheless facing the end of their aural culture. Their broadly expressed sentiment was that it was simply a matter of the march of technological progress, but they could not help feeling a little sad about it. They wanted not only to record their stories but also for the embodied skill of Morse operators to have its place in history.

Many made a point of saying that the skill had stayed with them throughout the years. Even after a break of decades, they quickly got back into it. Though many had developed some degree of hearing impairment, none had any trouble with Morse, often turning off their hearing aids when operating. But they acknowledged that their sense of the rhythm of Morse was something that could leave them, not in terms of receiving, of hearing the rhythm, but in terms of sending, of forming the characters with the "right" pulse. They hungered for the code, and they sought opportunities to use it, but their bodies had gotten out of sync.

When I was interviewing the operators, they spoke of others who were unwell or no longer with us. Though the Morsecodians were active at the time of our interviews, there was discussion of ending things. The annual meetings in Morse held in Sydney appear to be no more. The operators were acutely conscious of their age, and I understand that some have since died and that others are unwell. We are getting closer to our farewell to Morse code.

5

TURNING TO THE SENSED UNCONSCIOUS

T he idea that I have been working with in this book is what we can term the *sensed unconscious*.[1] The concept describes aspects of our embodied experience that remain concealed from our reflective attention as we orient our behavior outward. As people shape their behavior with an eye to how others will respond, they disattend the processes of embodying it. In face-to-face interactions, we might be self-conscious about how we will appear to others, but we are mostly unaware of how we are using our bodies to shape others' perceptions of ourselves. In a similar way, when painting, glassblowing, or wood turning, artists and craftspeople typically direct their focus to the unfolding object they are creating, rather than to the movements of the body and hands involved in creating it. Doctors, musicians, adventurers, and Morse code operators also do this as they organize their bodies to hear in ways that will make their behavior effective. Among other often unconscious aspects of sensed experience, our hearing seems to us to be passive, even though many cases suggest that hearing is an activity, a way of sensing that is not just had but *done*. Hearing seems passive only because it is carried out outside our reflective awareness.

The sensed unconscious has been recognized in many ways by theorists and researchers. To determine where this study fits in a long and evolving tradition of trying to understand how people unconsciously use their sensed bodies as foundations of their behavior, I describe three turns on the sensed unconscious. First, philosophers and social theorists have recognized that people unconsciously draw on their bodies as they shape their conduct. They had to fight against an overly rationalized, cognitive image of human beings as they developed their arguments. Second, researchers in various fields have described how people can "turn on," or bring consciousness to, their unconsciously deployed bodies to alter their behavior. Mentors, teachers, and senior practitioners help novices by showing them how to become aware of how they use their bodies unconsciously to construct their actions. The substantive chapters of this book have been part of this second turn.

I end with the beginning of a third turn. If, across substantive fields of social life, such as medicine, music, sports, art, and meditation, people turn on their previously unconscious embodiment of behavior to improve what they can do, are there common strategies that they employ? Can we identify "ethnomethods" to exploit the sensed unconscious?[2] In this chapter, I identify some promising candidates for a pragmatic sociology of the sensed unconscious. That is, I specify common methods that people, as folk sociologists, have discovered to be fruitful ways of turning on the bodily resources that they previously used unreflectively to produce their behavior.

THE FIRST TURN: PHILOSOPHERS AND SOCIAL THEORISTS RECOGNIZE THE SENSED UNCONSCIOUS

Many strands of philosophy and social theory speak to something like the sensed unconscious. Each philosopher and theorist has developed a unique vocabulary, but, when read together, their work encourages us to grasp a universally applicable idea. Much of the work that has grappled with aspects of experience that are "in" the body yet disattended has done so through the lens of habit. We acquire our dispositions, but, once learned, they recede from our conscious attention. Some scholars have adopted the term *habitus* to emphasize that these habits are a matter of acquired competence, not a conditioned response.[3]

Early contributions in the late nineteenth century from the American pragmatists leaned into the idea that our habits are modifiable, subject to conscious reflection, and bound to the environment in which they play out. William James showed how we adjust to and integrate with our surroundings. He used the example of walking, pointing out that we do not adopt the same habits of musculature when walking across a room in public that we use in the privacy of our own homes. In public, we are self-conscious of our gait, feeling the eyes of others upon us.[4] John Dewey wrote that we "know" via our habits, which "do all the perceiving, recognizing, imagining, recalling, judging, conceiving and reasoning."[5] In Dewey's philosophy, we are continually called on to alter our habits, though not all at once, reworking our knowing and action to meet the demands of the interaction in front of us. These cycles of revision are fundamental to the process of human learning.

In the 1930s the French anthropologist Marcel Mauss demonstrated that different "techniques of the body" are learned in different cultures and then taken for granted as the "natural" way of performing familiar activities in given cultures. These techniques are often rhythmic patterns used in the dynamic production of conduct.[6] American and French people walk differently from each other. Even our patterns of breath are unique to our cultures.

Norbert Elias, a German sociologist who spent much of his working life in Britain, developed a theory of civilization around the same time. His major work, *The Civilizing Process*, traced how postmedieval European standards regarding violence, sexual behavior, bodily functions, table manners, and forms of speech were gradually transformed by increasing thresholds of shame and repugnance, working outward from a nucleus in court etiquette. Customs that persist today, such as the use of a spoon as opposed to a fork for eating soup, seem so natural as to be beyond our conscious awareness, yet they were "established infinitely slowly. . . . standardized only step by step."[7]

Taking as his focus perception and ontology, the midtwentieth-century French philosopher Maurice Merleau-Ponty also turned his attention to the sensed unconscious. He was concerned with the relationship among our minds, bodies, and the world. In one discussion, he recalled being taken with a slow-motion film of Henri Matisse painting.[8] Seeing himself on film, Matisse became aware that he was moving his hand in a way that somehow held what he was painting, even before his instrument hit the surface. Reviewed in slow motion, the film suggests that Matisse was testing out possible courses of action through his gestures. In real time, he was not reflecting on alternative ways of painting; the alternatives were being debated in his brush motions. Matisse's attention was focused on where his gestures met the canvas, not on the critical creative choices that produced what would become static deposits of paint.

Others have similarly appreciated how people use their bodies to design what they project and objectify as speech. David McNeill, a psychologist who began developing a line of research at the University of Chicago in the 1970s, illustrated that gestures are the "growth point" of thought, guiding the reflective mind. Beyond our consciousness the hand supplies an idiosyncratic expression of inner discourse as speakers organize thoughts that manifest in spoken words.[9]

In the realm of tacit knowledge, Michael Polanyi, a Hungarian-born British chemist, economist, and philosopher who worked mainly in the United States and Canada, illustrated how people attend "to" the world "from" bodily processes to which they could, but do not, attend. For example, when a person focuses on repeating a word, they pay attention to the movement of their tongue and lips and the quality of the sound produced when they speak, but the word itself loses its meaning to them.[10] Similarly, if a pianist were to shift their attention to the biomechanics of their fingers when playing, they would risk losing their sense of the flow of the music. The human body is "the ultimate instrument of all our external knowledge," yet if we pay attention to how we use our bodies to construct our behavior, we lose our capacity to act effectively.[11] Even when we clarify our purpose and meaning through talk, in our work, and making ourselves useful to others, we create a mystery about how we are doing it.

Spanning over a century, across continents and traditions of thought, these thinkers and researchers have shared in a common effort to uncover what sits behind the focal attention of actors but is used as an essential foundation for competent behavior. To use Merleau-Ponty's language, once acquired, these ways of knowing are "in the hands."[12]

The French sociologist Pierre Bourdieu's articulation of habitus is perhaps the best-known contribution to the tradition. He argued that social class and level of educational capital determine the music we listen to, the art we appreciate, the food we have a taste for, and that our preferences reproduce existing power and class relations.[13] Bourdieu's theorization has been influential in sociological circles, becoming a dominant way of thinking about practice within the discipline. But Bourdieu's perspective was that habitus is "beyond the grasp of consciousness" and thus cannot be deliberately transformed.[14]

Following Bourdieu's argument, if people cannot consciously turn to their habitus, neither can analysts. This interpretation is supported by the paucity of writing detailing the workings of habitus. Researchers who have taken up Bourdieu's theory of practice repeatedly assert and provide examples to show that people draw on a distinctive habitus. But they stop at the point of recognizing the deep well of understanding that resides in our unconscious and guides our action, leaving unexamined how people draw on the bodily foundations of their behavior. Their contribution remains on the level of theory or philosophy.

For instance, a refrain throughout Loïc Wacquant's autoethnography of his experience as an apprentice boxer is that the making of boxers involves a "(re)socialization of physiology," yet Wacquant describes only snippets of what that entails.[15] Echoing Bourdieu's claim, he wrote that "the rules of the pugilistic art boil down to bodily moves that can be fully apprehended only in action and place it at the very edge of that which can be intellectually grasped and communicated," requiring participation to understand.[16] We see moments of work on the body, as in his account of working the pads, in which he identifies the snapping sound as an indicator that a boxer is landing punches.[17] Coaches call out what the drills should be, providing cues like "Keep your right leg back an' turn your foot inside."[18] Wacquant suggests that watching how others move provides instruction about how he should move himself.[19] But he does not present a sustained analysis of the cultivation of the sensed unconscious.

Matthew Desmond also took up Bourdieu's work in his ethnography of the practices of wildland firefighters. He approaches questions of the nature of human knowing, distinguishing between book learning and embodied know-how. The latter poses a challenge to rules for guiding and accounting for practice. Yet he falls back on a gloss, the claim that, as country boys, "we were already ready . . . before we set foot on the fireline."[20] On the sensory knowing of firefighters, he reverts to what his fellow firefighters already knew: "We knew how to observe the forest because our eyes had been searching the tips of pines and the trunks of oaks for years. Our ears knew what to listen for; our noses knew what the forest was supposed to smell like. Our footing and balance, posture and hiking style, sense of touch and movement were attuned to the forest, and this heightened awareness, this woodsy know-how inscribed in our histories and in our very bodies, allowed us to adapt quickly to the challenges of the fire."[21]

As readers, we are convinced that Desmond's fellow firefighters came to their work with a developed, relevant competency, but we do not see how they turned to that distinctive habitus when carrying out their work. What were the semiotics of sounds, what was the range of smells, and what were the variations of proprioception that the firefighters drew on in a particular instance to recognize a telltale sensual difference? It is Bourdieu's *The Logic of Practice* that informs the unsatisfying conclusion to the line of thought here: "The habitus is precisely this immanent law, *lex insita*, inscribed in bodies by identical histories, which is the precondition not only for the coordination of practices but also for practices of coordination."[22] The Forest Service thus cannot lay claim to the knowledge of firefighters, at least in full. It is a product of history to a significant degree, for example, playing in the dirt as children and responding to barked commands from football coaches.

Similar statements are often made outside academia in the folk commentaries that people invoke to explain how they developed a distinctive competency. When Australians talk about their swimming skills, they often give their nationality as an explanation, as if Australians collectively know how to swim by virtue of living together on an island. But competency is not a matter of growing up in a particular culture or place. By observing swimming teachers, we can see how they work with students in particular ways to help them produce particular patterns of movement. Even seemingly simple concepts, like moving one's legs up and down to kick, are typically beyond the comprehension of beginners. Teachers work with students using exercises that they know will put swimmers' bodies in the right position to effectively propel themselves through the water. They manipulate students' arms and legs. They coach students to glide without moving their legs. They have their students use aids like kickboards to focus on their kicking. They associate various words with patterns of movement. Students learn to swim by being supported to put their bodies to work in these ways. Once patterns of movement have been learned, swimmers do not need to direct conscious attention to them. They disattend, even forget them, but they have acquired a specific strategy of embodiment. Researchers can make more of a contribution to the study of the sensed unconscious if they look for those strategies and relate them.

Collectively, these theorists encourage researchers to acknowledge, as they have, that the sensed unconscious is a resource in social action. If researchers acknowledge only the backgrounded body, then they dwell in the first turn. To advance this analysis, researchers must study how actors attend to the ways they embody their conduct. If we step back from the theoretical project, we should all immediately be aware of the existence of our sensed unconscious and that we adopt strategies to develop its capabilities. Nearly every time we develop a new skill, whether intellectual, athletic, or artistic, we engage in the process of gaining knowledge that will ultimately take its place in our unconscious. When we teach, or watch others being taught, we also see this process at work, as instructors adopt various techniques to pass on their knowledge. The second turn requires researchers to take on this work on the body.

THE SECOND TURN: RESEARCHERS DESCRIBE HOW PEOPLE CAN ALTER THEIR BEHAVIOR BY TURNING TO THEIR PREVIOUSLY UNCONSCIOUSLY SENSED BODIES

The key to recognizing work on the sensed unconscious is acknowledging that it is variable. As Polanyi rightly pointed out, when we focus on the embodied experience of talking or engaging in a motor action, the experience comes to feel strange, and our ability to continue interacting or engaging in an activity effectively becomes compromised.[23] Erving Goffman wrote about a similar issue when distinguishing between main and side involvements, an example of which is knitting while listening.[24] Competent knitters can carry on a conversation while knitting, but if they drop a stitch, they can find themselves losing the flow of what they are saying or what is being said while they turn their focus to how their hands are using the needles to fix the error.

We all know that we can successfully and readily turn to our previously backgrounded bodies to improve our conduct. If, when reaching for the door handle, we do not grasp it, we turn our gaze to where our hand is going. If we slip as we walk, we turn to how our feet are hitting the ground.

Studies of expert practice capture many such instances of turning to the sensed unconscious. Take the adventurers. While they aspire to have their senses "switched on," meaning that they are consciously monitoring place and how they are meeting the world via their senses, this monitoring slips into the background at least some of the time. When an adventurer is climbing with a group, their conscious awareness is focused on their fellow climbers and those parts of the landscape that are currently most demanding, such as what they can see of where they will next place their feet. Their proprioception is backgrounded, as is their hearing of surface stability—as long as things progress smoothly. If they reach a section of a face that they cannot climb easily, they turn to how their body moves when climbing. If they were to sense a change, such as being hit by a falling icicle, they would redirect their attention to the sounds of the melting surface, which they had previously been disattending. Hearing comes to the fore so that they can evaluate the risk of the situation and alter their course of action as needed.

The psychologist Gary Klein captured a story from a fireground commander that points to something similar.[25] The fireground commander was describing an experience that he had had as a lieutenant. At a simple house fire, the crew followed their standard strategy of dousing the flames with water, but they found that it was not working. For the fireground commander, this was a story about how his extrasensory perception (ESP) saved the day. He said that something about the situation did not feel right, so he ordered the crew to evacuate the building—moments before the floor collapsed. It transpired that the seat of the fire was in the basement. Klein questioned the fireground commander about his decision, dissatisfied with the explanation of ESP. The commander had assumed that the house did not have a basement, but the fire felt hotter than he would have expected given what he could see. It was quiet, too. For a fire with that much heat, he would have expected it to be much louder. By momentarily bringing to his consciousness what his senses had provided, he reasoned through possible causes of the disconnect among what he could see, feel, and hear, leading to the decision to retreat.

Another case that shows how adepts turn to their sensed unconscious comes from the musicians. Musicians grapple with the problem of time. To paraphrase the flautist Alex, it is not that they must play a piece but that they must play it *right now*. During a performance, musicians cannot hear the music as the audience does because it comes too late, after the bodily movements that produce the sounds have been made. To "hear" what will become sound, they must attend to the proprioceptive processes through which they organize their playing.

Cases of expert practice show turns to the sensed unconscious but not its production. Novice musicians develop competencies in teaching sessions and in solo practice separate from the social situations in which they will be put to work. Teachers and students alike suspend concern for the version of themselves that is perceptible to others in social settings. Novices are often coached first to turn toward their body so that they can ultimately turn away from it. They shift their concentration to the body behind and producing the self, later relying on what we call in the vernacular "muscle memory."

An early contribution that takes us into these moments of rehearsal comes from David Sudnow, who applied Merleau-Ponty's thought to the experience of learning to play the piano. He demonstrated that the ability to play is not so much naturally or spontaneously "in the hands" as Merleau-Ponty put it.[26] Rather, it is *worked into* the hands through the practice strategies adopted by players. Drawing on his own experience, Sudnow found that he needed to develop a visual appreciation of the composition of scales and chords to develop his skills as an improviser; sound was less important for him in these early stages.[27] Once he could visualize chords, he started the awkward process of grasping for them, turning his attention to his hand movements. At first, his fingers needed to hunt for their assigned key, and he battled to find a hand position that would prevent him from hitting adjacent keys in error; in this process, he was challenged with the problem of balancing the weight of each finger.[28] He then expanded the scope of his visual work from a focus on the score and the keys to include his hand positions and the movements between the constellations he formed. The changing configuration of his hands became a phenomenon in itself, not an abstract feel for the music but a "hands-on" feeling. Once he could play, he did not need to see his hands moving as part of a process of consciously finding the notes. If he looked at his hands, he had the sense that "the fingers are making the music all by themselves."[29]

We can find observations that parallel Sudnow's in the ways that teaching and solo practice are done in many areas. Working with Polanyi's notions of subsidiary and focal awareness, the sociologist Erin O'Connor showed that glassblowing instructors encourage students to bring momentary focal awareness to their manipulation of the blowpipe, followed by a call to then refocus on the glass, not the movement involved in forming it. When gathering glass at the glory hole (a furnace used to reheat glass while it is being blown), O'Connor's instructor tells her to keep her pipe level or to twirl it at an even pace, such cues serving to shift her attention to how she is moving the pipe in her hands. Her instructor then gives a counter-instruction to attend to the glass, requiring that she disattend how she is working the pipe.[30]

The anthropologist Einat Bar-On Cohen also describes how teachers bring consciousness to students' backgrounded bodies. In the *kiba-dachi* exercise in karate, instructors coach students to hold a squatting position as if riding an imaginary horse for an hour and a half at a time to sharpen the connection between mind and body. The exercise generates intense physical pain, causing students to dissociate within a matter of minutes. Pedagogically, the aim is for students to neither move from the pose nor disattend the feelings it generates but rather to dwell in and accept the discomfort. To this end, the instructor walks among the students, physically manipulating the bodies of those who have fallen out of the pose and striking the shoulders of those who look like they might faint, forcing consciousness back into the practice.[31]

Recall Polanyi's example of how words lose their meaning when we focus on the feel of our tongue and lips moving.[32] In Morse code education, instructors direct students to pay attention to the mouth feel of syllabic stress. For example, they may ask students to suspend a focus on using the word *calculation* in a sentence so that they can appreciate how, when enunciating it, they are using a long-short-long-short pattern.

Various techniques and strategies are involved in turning to the backgrounded body in practice phases, some of which have been described in this book, such as exercises that work on a skill indirectly or those that exploit synesthesia by shifting one sense perception in relation to another. As researchers continue to examine how people turn to the processes of embodying behavior used in diverse fields of action and to access a range of senses, they expand the base of evidence on which to advance theories of social action.

THE THIRD TURN: TOWARD A SOCIOLOGY OF FOLK PRACTICES FOR TAPPING INTO THE SENSED UNCONSCIOUS

The studies presented in this book are meant to guide researchers toward a third turn: developing a sociology of the sensed unconscious that identifies commonalities in the practices people use to change their behavior by attending to their usually backgrounded embodied selves. In various fields of activity, instructors use techniques to guide students to cultivate ways of perceiving that they will ultimately come to use unconsciously. The teacher's focus is field specific. As sociologists, we can take the next step by searching for commonalities and differences across substantive areas of behavior and in the tacit embodiment of the various senses. This third turn may have value to practitioners by explaining what competent performers in various fields of behavior do to access and alter their usually tacitly mobilized foundations of performance.

In the following, I identify some ways of turning to the sensed unconscious that are commonly used in developing competency to enact types of social behavior that vary widely in substance and interactional context.

The Outside–Inside Process of Imitation

Used fruitfully to develop competency across a range of substantive activities, imitation is a universally known "ethnomethod," a way of producing a version of self that lives in folk interactions and understandings. Imitation is a process with multiple phases of intertwining; that is, it is a process of first focusing on what is outside and then enacting behavior in a way that will elicit an internal feeling.

Writing in poetic and, for many readers, almost inaccessible language, Merleau-Ponty has shown that people produce all moments of their experience through being intertwined, or in a chiasmic relationship, with the context in which they act. We are at once inside and outside ourselves, outside and in the world. The idea is hard to grasp because our language seems to defy the point. We think, talk, and write of what is "inside" and "outside" the self, and of the self and the world as separate, as if we could ever be separate from our context. Merleau-Ponty uses metaphor to try to convey the idea of intertwining.[33] To describe the point of existential overlapping, he uses the image of a single amoeba in the process of becoming two. The human example that he returns to time and again is that of one hand touching the other; here, the touching hand reveals the contours of the touched hand, and the touched hand reveals sensitivities in the touching hand. But, apart from explorations in child development, Merleau-Ponty's early demise left out the extension of his work to the social world.

Sociologists have picked up the challenge in various ways. Brian Lande offered the example of the cultivation of breathing in a military context. Breathing is usually done in the background of awareness. Cadets are taught that their breathing is no longer just a personal matter; rather, their breathing must now be paced to match that of their commanding officer. Imitating this pattern of breath is not something that simply happens. Cadets are called to attend to their breath when told that they are not performing well in running, shooting, or vocal projection because of their pattern of breathing. They are then coached to orient their attention toward the breath of their commanding officer: "In through your nose, out through your mouth. With me, in . . . out . . . in . . . out."[34] They take the other's movement as the basis of their turn, feeling for and controlling the movement of their diaphragm in the direction of long, slow breaths. When students fail to find the desired breathing pattern, imitation can be aided through seemingly ritualistic but subtly pedagogic strategies, such as when cadets are instructed to punch one another in the stomach so that they can hear and feel where to project their voices from. This is a way for cadets to locate their diaphragms. Once they have discovered this form of proprioception, they no longer have to observe or attend to their bodily doing, taking it for granted at least most of the time.

Michal Pagis offers another example of attending to breathing, in this case to cultivate the practice of vipassana meditation. Practitioners of vipassana are not expected to achieve a singular experience through the practice. Yet, paradoxically, meditators find that practicing together helps them attend to their own experiences as separate from those of others. For the novice, entering a new social context and sitting with strangers can make it challenging to let go of self-consciousness. Aware of this challenge, communities arrange meditation spaces with the teacher and experienced volunteers positioned at the front so that novices can see practitioners who are accustomed to disattending their neighbors. Novices see that the experts are not consciously attending to the movements or sounds of those around them.[35] This realization thus allows the novices' self-consciousness to recede, supporting the turn inward.

Musicians use imitation to improve their performance too, for example, when playing along with recordings. Through repeated passes, players focus on different elements of the recorded other such as the timbre of their instrument, the articulation of the notes, and the notes themselves. When they find themselves not imitating the recording perfectly in a given respect, they change the dynamic proprioception through which they create sound. What was once hidden in the interplay of unreflectively employed motions emerges as singular aspects of movement.

Puppeteering

Developing competency often involves working off another's body. One of the most extreme examples of this is puppeteering, in which instructors physically manipulate the student's body or move with the student so that what the adept sees and feels structures what the student sees and feels. Moving together means that a task is completed cooperatively, or within a student's "zone of proximal development," to use the psychologist Lev Vygotsky's language.[36] The instructor takes on large parts of the work at hand, at least in the early stages, while the novice becomes acquainted with the proprioception involved in competent performance. As Vygotsky theorized, this type of practice not only allows the novice to participate in activities currently beyond their skill level but also relays how the novice should interpret their inner and outer worlds.

The psychologist Patricia Greenfield described the use of puppeteering in the context of weaving apprenticeships among the Zinacantec Maya community in Mexico. In this community, adults, typically mothers, teach young children to weave in a hands-on fashion. Children first watch experienced weavers work and are then given their first projects via a practice such as "four hands on the loom."[37] In this practice, the child sits in the adult's lap and, like a puppet, is guided through movements on the loom. The child senses the interrelated movements of the adult's two hands, the generation of hand movement from the arms and the torso, and movements in the seat that are outside the range of visual focus.

I have been teaching my five-year-old to quilt with a sewing machine in a similar way, moving my arms and hands with my daughter's, progressively letting go as she finds the correct hand position and degree of contact with the fabric and the way to manipulate the fabric to maintain the desired line of sewing (figure 5.1). As we work together, I narrate how we're moving and what I sense of her body position and movement in relation to the fabric and the machine. A video of us working together captured me saying to her, "You're putting too much tension; relax your arms." I then lift her arms from the bed of the machine and flop them up and down to help her find the feeling of relaxed arms before she places them back on the fabric. I give the instruction "less tension" twice more, and after the second instance, she adjusts her seat to take some of the tension out of her arms. I then feel in the places our bodies touch and see in her body and in her stitching that she has relaxed, so I say, "That's it! You've got it." She then continues sewing the line smoothly. Our joined bodies, coupled with my narration, teach her about her relation to the unfolding object. The practice also

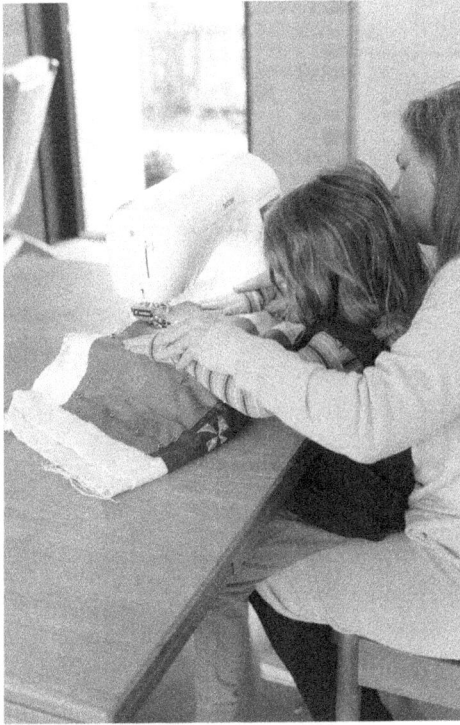

FIGURE 5.1 Four hands at the sewing machine.

encourages her to turn to the inner side of her conduct: her sense of her body position and how it feels as she moves her body freely rather than with tension.

Puppeteering is not just child's play or a matter of apprenticeship in craft work. A surgical apprenticeship often involves a strategy in which the surgeon "wields" the body of the surgical student who is still refining their skills. For example, the anthropologist Rachel Prentice observed a scenario in which an attending surgeon and a surgical resident were both applying pressure to the hand of a surgical student who was holding a drill to insert the final screw in a complex wrist surgery.[38]

This technique, perhaps more so than others, requires humility of the student. Ceding control over one's body is something that people often resist. However, an age difference between novice and expert, as with Greenfield's weavers, or a hierarchical arrangement, as with experienced doctors and medical students, can help establish an appropriate context for humility. That said, my five-year-old tolerates puppeteering only in short bursts before insisting she has got it!

Breaking Down an Ongoing Activity to Focus on a Part

We often study and train in a "take-it-apart" way. Then, more subtly, indirectly, there is a "putting-it-back-together" phase of learning. These types of learning are common methods of mastering the performance of a process by identifying and focusing on elements within it. One way to take a process apart is simply to repeat a single phase of it. Another, often complementary tactic is to transform a dynamic activity into static parts, or to change verbs into nouns.

Communities often document processes in ways that are abstracted from the doing of the activity itself. Many music communities use scores or charts to transform the actions of playing a piece of music into an abstract form. A musical note is an artificial device—a noun. It is a mark that stands still on a page but whose only raison d'être is to aid in an activity that is dynamic (i.e., singing or playing an instrument). Similarly, the Morse alphabet is abstracted from the sounds of the code and the motor action involved in forming it. Students memorize the alphabet as a foundation for what will become embodied action.

Other examples of creating nouns out of verbs involve breaking a complex action down into its component parts. For example, in gymnastics, various handstands are the foundation of tumbling sequences and handsprings used in vaulting. To learn the "L" handstand, or half-handstand, a beginner gymnast's hands are planted on the ground with their tailbone and one extended leg pointing upward, the other leg placed at a right angle to the floor. When an activity like a handstand is broken down into separate forms and represented diagrammatically, teachers have a way to demonstrate what a student must do with their body.

Armed with these nouns, teachers coach students in mini-processes through demonstrations with verbal commentary. In learning a new pattern of movement, breaking down a complex sequence into parts works on the visual-to-motor translation. The breaking-down is important because we can readily code only those elementary movements that we can see.[39]

The anthropologist Greg Downey has documented the breaking-down of the *rabo-de-arraia* ("stingray's tail") kick in capoeira, in which the practitioner's body begins in a crouching position with their trailing leg swinging around at hip height.[40] Naming the kick as a form tells students something of what the form involves, but there needs to be a second stage in the learning in which the noun effectively becomes a verb, a doing. This kick is too complicated for a novice to comprehend as one continuous movement. The student does not understand how their supporting leg must be positioned as they move into the kick, how they move out of the kick, and the footwork that precedes and follows. Teachers instruct students by working on the entry and exit of the kick as separate movements. When the student stops at the end of the entry, they must balance crouched on one leg, with their other leg extended into the kick. Kinetically, breaking it down presents a different challenge from that of kicking, more akin to mastering advanced balance poses in yoga. The student is not practicing the move. The instructor has the student pause during each element so that they can see and feel the body positions in freeze frame before combining them into the whole.

In many areas of practice, students build their skills through training exercises based on the principle of focusing on individual phases. For example, brass and woodwind players do what is called "tonguing," in which they move their tongue to the roof of their mouth to interrupt the airflow. Such interruptions allow the next note in the sequence to start with more precision, creating a crisp articulation. Teachers typically teach tonguing as an isolated exercise, instructing students to move their tongue as if saying "ti-ka-ti-ka" (on the flute), "ta-ka-ta-ka" (on the trumpet) or "too-koo-too-koo" (on the clarinet). "Ti-ka" is a noun to describe a process once it is put to work. A student can practice saying these sounds aloud before picking up their instrument. However, when playing, they do not vocalize the sounds; rather, they focus on the tactile rhythm of their tongue in their mouth. This technique is a way for students to learn the tongue action involved in producing the notes with the correct articulation. Once mastered, these tongue movements mostly recede from players' consciousness, allowing them to focus on other matters, such as how adjacent players are forming the notes, so that they can adjust their playing as needed to blend in.

While the archetypal examples of exercises focus on motility, they also apply to other aspects of sensation. For example, the cellist I observed and interviewed spoke about using scales as an exercise to develop her aural-embodied sense of pitch. She names each pitch (e.g., C, D, E flat) and then switches her focus between the feel of the notes and her hearing of them; based on what she hears, she can determine whether she is playing in tune and make adjustments to her body as needed. This type of exercise is an opportunity not only to build strength and control in the hands but also to understand the proprioception involved in producing the correct sound. What players are working on is getting the inner sense of the outer sound, or what it feels like to play the notes correctly. Indeed, students who perform these exercises as disconnected from their hearing develop poorly as players.

Learning to Attend to Part of a Sensed Sequence by Attending to the Whole

Conversely, we can develop control over our sensed unconscious by learning to attend to an entire sequence so that we can grasp a part of it. Poetry provides an example of this idea: we tend to remember poems better than works of prose because of the patterns of syllabic repetition and stress in poetry, which affect proprioception.[41] In an analysis of the poet Felicia Hemans's "Casabianca," the English professor Catherine Robson explained that we know that our sense of meter acts powerfully on our memory of poetry because it can easily overpower the meaning of the words. As an example, she describes the opening lines of the poem as understood by aficionados versus schoolchildren tasked with recitation:

Hemans opened her poem with an irregular line, which places its second strong stress on the word *stood*: "The BOY STOOD on the BURNing DECK." If mimetic meter is a feature of the work of "good" poets, then Hemans earns her stripes, for we are pulled up short by two adjacent stresses, and movement is arrested in the line as it is for the boy, who is literally going nowhere. And yet who, outside the hyper-educated elite, says it this way? Half knowledge of the words as a derided remnant of another age or as the beginning of something like a smutty limerick dictates that a singsong rhythm override the sense of the line, and so most English people, at least, would chant "The BOY stood ON the BURNing DECK." How would a child in a state of bodily anxiety have recited it? Not slowly, not with feeling, not thinking about how to fit sense to the syllables, meaning to the meter—instead, when you have to get through something, you gallop along with your eyes on the finishing post, with no desire to introduce significant pauses or reversed stresses or indeed anything that might hamper the progress of your thundering hooves. When finally at the end, would not the reciting child also be likely to murder the tender pathos of Hemans's final irregular, meditative stress on "that YOUNG FAITHful HEART" by chucking in for good measure an unstressed "and" between "young" and "faith" to regularize and thus speed up the line?[42]

Robson says that English educational praxis throughout the nineteenth and into the twentieth century drilled meters into schoolchildren's bodies via the requirement to memorize and perform poetry of increasing lengths under threat of humiliation and corporal punishment. Children who have not had such pedagogical experiences will not have developed this sense of syllabic stress and will thus be less carried along by the meter in their recall of a poem.[43] For children forced to memorize poetry in the manner described, it is not that the words are recalled simply by virtue of the meter; rather, the meter itself has been drilled into their bodies.

In medicine, clinical skills educators and supervisors coach students to learn a part through attention to a longer sequence when they vocalize heart sounds. They express a given heart murmur as "lub-dub-bi-di-dub," a sequence that includes elements of a regular heartbeat as well as the part that signals the presence of a murmur (i.e., the "bi" in the middle of the sequence). The student learns how to hear for the murmur by imitating the supervisor's vocalization, getting the feel for the whole sequence via the movement of their tongue and mouth. Like instrumentalists, medical students develop their inner understanding of the outer sound. The pattern of movement that they can feel in their mouth when they vocalize a heart murmur becomes a resource for how to hear for the murmur in a patient's body. Learning in this way allows them to identify pathological signs by feeling and hearing for an entire sequence.

Using an Abstract Analogy

When we encounter a new situation with new perceptual demands, we can find ourselves lost, unable to locate important information.

A novice may find that the sounds they pick up in the background of their awareness merge with other sounds, so they must learn to bring them out of the blur. Imagine a person conducting a bird survey in a forest teeming with wildlife. Novices can find it nearly impossible to separate and identify the calls that they can hear. Veterans have various "tricks of the trade" that they pass on to novices to help with this challenge, for example, associating a particular call with a "sounds-like" phrase or focusing on elements of the rhythm and pitch of a call rather than trying to memorize the call in its entirety. Tricks of the trade often come in the form of metaphor or analogy. Adepts support novices to learn that which is strange by averting to that which is already known.

Analogous ways of getting at the sensuous character of new phenomena are common in medical training, such as the use of pear-drop candies to simulate the smell of ketotic breath or likening the feel of cutting through a cancerous tumor to slicing an unripe pear.[44] Such strategies work on the body by highlighting a trait of the new that the novice can hunt for. Heart murmurs are named analogically, as we saw with the seagull murmur. The reference thus directs attention to the unique characteristic of the sound; for the seagull murmur, this is a sound with a higher pitch than the other sounds of the beating heart.

Tastes blur together, too. The amateur wine enthusiasts that Geneviève Teil studied described a process of moving from "tasting stupidly" to tasting in greater or more specific detail. Wine guides and course instructors encourage amateurs to pay attention, to question what they are perceiving, part of which involves providing them with terminology for the aroma of wines: "While repeatedly sniffing their wine glasses, they attempt first to unearth and smell the 'grapefruit' odor of chardonnay, followed by 'salty' or 'mineral' notes."[45] Such terminology is not shared with enthusiasts simply to provide them with the relevant lexicon for their hobby. The terms reference traits of wine that the enthusiast can hunt for. However, wine enthusiasts do not deal in absolutes; for example, one person may identify an aroma of pear and another rhubarb. What they find is also a function of their knowledge beyond the world of wine and ahead of tasting. When they share what they find with others, they widen one another's perceptions.[46]

Placing Self Outside Self

Paradoxically, turning to the backgrounded body requires strategies that allow a person to step outside themselves. This serves to aid us in attending to what previously was sensed but not within our reflective reach. There are many contexts in which we cannot see or hear ourselves as we will be seen and heard. With this in mind, communities adopt various tools to support the regarding of self. Among instrumental students, especially those in the classical tradition, corrections typically come from teachers during lessons. But teachers can also audio-record a performance in a lesson environment to capture how a performer sounds to others. Similarly, working musicians sometimes record themselves to hear their performance as the audience did to assess where they need to concentrate their attention in rehearsal.[47]

Some forms of training, such as dance, make use of a mirror to show students, as well as experienced practitioners, what they look like so that they can assess where they may need to alter their movements. In the sociologist Sibyl Kleiner's account, dancers use studio mirrors to work on their movements by observing their bodies in relation to those of others who are more closely meeting the mark.[48] Dancers sometimes describe a disturbing self-consciousness that comes from watching themselves. Self-consciousness, Kleiner says, is first visual. Dancers cannot tell from within where their body positions are falling short, so they take their reflected image as a ground for making a change inside.[49] This turn to the backgrounded body should occur only in rehearsal; onstage, it should be replaced by an embodied "flow."

There is an irony to the practice of perceiving the self externally as a strategy for making hidden, internal adjustments. Turning to our sensed unconscious requires us to make contact with aspects of our experience that we not only typically disattend but also cannot readily "see." Recordings and mirrors can show us how we appear to others, but these tools are a step removed from the backgrounded body that creates the performance. To adjust self-presentation, people work from the "outside," as reflected in a recording or mirror, to develop their sense of proprioception, typically through the coaching of teachers. The purpose of using these kinds of tools is fundamentally one of critique, which has its own irony, too: attacking to create. We must perceive that something is wrong to negate it and move toward a preferred version of self.

Enacting One Sensing Process to Access Another

Communities turn to the sensed unconscious by exploiting synesthesia. Our senses, typically conceived of as isolated, actually operate in an intertwined way. They are interrelated and frequently active. For example, when you go for a run, you do not stop hearing or seeing as you move.[50] Teachers exploit the synesthetic nature of experience when they support students to grasp one perception as grounded in another. The contrast pairs used by musicians when transcribing or playing along to a recorded piece of music work on this logic. The musician compares a musical phrase from two sources, whether in relation to a recording and the transcript, or the student's playing and that of a teacher. By comparing the two, the musician aims to discern any flaws in their work.[51] Similarly, adventurers do hearing by attending to changes that they perceive in sounds, as when they identify how securely a piton is embedded in the climbing surface by the sound it creates: a ringing sound indicates secure placement whereas a dull thud means that the piton has not found its mark.

Using one perception as a ground for another is not just a matter of aural contrast. There are interesting cases in which novices are coached to explore one sensation via another, such as when seeing or moving is used as a ground for hearing in new ways. An example of this is the orthopedic surgeon who got me to feel his arthritic knee to "hear" arthritis.

The case that advances thinking on this notion most is that of the vocal student, whose teacher focuses on correcting tongue position and the shape of the mouth and throat rather than addressing the student's hearing directly. The teacher recognizes that the student cannot readily hear themselves as they will be heard by others, so they encourage the student to disattend their sound and focus instead on the proprioception involved in forming it. This is the inverse of using a tool like a mirror to regard oneself. Here, the teacher coaches the student to disattend their sense of their outside and attend only to their hidden inner workings.

Armed with the knowledge of the reality of synesthetic experience, teachers and seasoned practitioners often comment on the sensations that will be present together in significant moments. The linguist Charles Goodwin wrote about this idea in relation to the work of geochemists who are trying to determine when to halt a chemical reaction with the fiber they are working with. Students working with fiber in a reaction tank handle the material, squeezing and manipulating it. Doing so, a student may comment that "when the fiber is done, it not only has a particular color, but also a distinctive texture."[52] They are arriving at the possibility of a new assessment criterion beyond sight, weaving together the haptic and the visual. The lesson is to look but also feel.

Adventurers are coached to be aware of the combinations of cues available for registration. We see this in the stories of the river-rolling boulders: the boulders make a sound, the river is a dark chocolate color, and it will have a peculiar smell, the color and odor resulting from churned silt. Adventurers say that if they were to try to isolate the strands of available information—that is, to attend only to what they can perceive via a single sense—their judgment of a situation would be incomplete. Ahead of a river crossing, they must interpret what the river looks like, hear the sound it is making, feel its movement against their bodies, and even smell it as part of a process of estimating its depth and level of turbulence. The notion of listening as synesthetic attention stems from the acknowledgment that an adventurer should never engage with just a single strand of information.

A FUTURE FOR THE THREE TURNS

Distinguishing among the three turns discussed here and establishing what each means for researchers is critical for the progress of the sociology of the sensed unconscious. To date, most well-known work has concentrated on the first turn, which recognizes the unconscious foundations of conduct as an element of the development of the philosophy of social action. Many social scientists have failed to move beyond this point, however, taking habitus in particular as an explanation for human knowing and behavior, not as a call for inquiry into its constitution. The second turn encourages us to investigate how actors attend to their unconscious bodily organizing. A growing body of evidence explains that adepts shift momentary attention to their backgrounded bodies and illustrates the techniques and devices that teachers use to transform students' embodied selves.

Moving from the first to the second turn is partly a problem of method. Work based on historical cases describes examples as "of" a particular time and place. While we can learn from historical analysis, as in the examination of training manuals and student textbooks, we cannot go back in time to identify the idiosyncrasies among various ways of perceiving or investigate the process of learning beyond what has been written down.[53] Quantitative methods, as adopted by Bourdieu in his work with social survey data, tell us something of broad social patterns but not what it looks and feels like to be in the bodies being investigated. Such methods also gloss over deviations: those who are well educated but have a penchant for the "wrong" music, those from lower social classes who are drawn to and understand "high art," the cultural omnivores described by Tony Bennett and colleagues.[54] Grand theories are tantalizing. But we lose something in our attempt to account for competent performance when using these scales of analysis. We must get closer to bodies in movement.

The ability to describe the procedures of competent performance has been greatly improved through the availability of video for social research. This is a method that remains important for the study of how people turn to their unconsciously sensed bodies. While this is not the approach I adopted, the evidence from many domains compiled in this chapter demonstrate that video is a powerful resource in the project of discovering the sensed unconscious because it allows the analyst to slow down and endlessly review events that pass quickly in the moment. With the capabilities of video, we can see up close what is organizing behavior as far as that is visible: moments in which an actor directs their gaze or adjusts their body position and those in which an interaction threatens to break down and must be managed and worked through.[55]

We see, too, only the moment, not the history woven into the decisions. A focus on events rather than biography has long been viewed by leading thinkers as the pathway to advancing social theory. In the late 1960s, Goffman's iconic call to attend to "moments and their men" rather than "men and their moments" reflected broader interactionist leanings and the commitment of conversation analysts dedicated to the close study of specific events in social life.[56] While such an approach has been fruitful, an absolute focus on the moment misses the resources that actors bring to it and the fact that a moment is a part of a longer course of social action. The sociologist Michael DeLand examined this problem in relation to playing pickup basketball at a public park. DeLand demonstrated that one's understanding of a rule dispute captured on video is advanced meaningfully by considering the biographical history of the player who responded to a foul call in anger. If we look only at the video, what we see are the interactional steps involved in the resolution of gameplay, not the far longer chain of events that informed the player's response or the ongoing implications of the situation for the angry player's sense of self.[57]

This is as true for embodied competence as it is for our social relations. The competence that is woven into our bodies is not the product of a moment. We see only a fraction of it in a video-recorded music lesson or cheese-tasting course, however instructive these moments may be.[58] What we primarily see is the conduct of the interaction, whether that is the form of correction techniques and their organization or how the body is constituted in the interaction.[59]

We develop our bodies over long temporal scales. Alone. Together. In one place. In another. For changing roles and purposes. Developing various competencies. Working on various aspects of mastery. Experiencing our bodies with varying degrees of attention. Adopting various tools to bring conscious awareness to our performance. All to deliberately, with concerted effort, change our embodied selves.

The people involved in a particular community are an important resource for the development of our understanding of embodied knowledge.[60] Speaking with them provides insight into the perspective of those "in" the action. With respect to embodied competence, speaking with group members is a way inside the body, too, providing insight into what is invisible. This is tricky, of course, because we are talking about matters that are often not only invisible but also unconscious. We must grapple with how to encourage self-reflexivity among research participants in the process of working on the body.

In my research, I found it helpful to talk through the navigation of "problems," such as difficult situations that can emerge in practice, or the challenges faced by teachers when helping students to correct and improve their behavior. These are the moments in which people turn to their sensed unconscious, effectively because it has failed or been found wanting in some way and so rises to the surface. Such conversations typically involved some role slippage between interviewer and student as I adopted the role of the learner to facilitate a demonstration of a problem in and around its narration.

However difficult these conversations are, without this pathway into the body, we cannot understand how musicians do the invisible "hearing ahead" that we cannot see in observation or even in a video that we can endlessly pause and replay. We cannot know what it feels like to attend to proprioception as a ground to change what is heard.

Many cases are ripe for inquiry through a combination of video and interview-based methods. Music-making and medical practice have attracted the most attention in previous work, though there is more to learn in those contexts. The cases that have interested me the most in finalizing my analysis relate to the skill acquisition of young children. Though not without research ethics challenges, teaching young children various athletic pursuits such as swimming and bike riding are especially interesting and worthy of video analysis. These are cases in which there are rich folk traditions of supporting the turn to the sensed unconscious ahead of turning away from it as we orient toward the world, yet little has been written on them sociologically.

Additional cases of specialized embodied knowledge also provide insight into the cultivation and operation of the sensed unconscious. One such case is the work of field biologists involved in fauna surveys. I met some field biologists in the course of this project and learned enough to know that it is something to investigate further. Cases in which there is a tangible difference between how we perceive ourselves and how others perceive us also promise to be productive, one such case being the people and processes involved in accent coaching.

On the back of this work, the third turn is intellectual. It is a search for commonalities across substantive areas of behavior and the senses in terms of how actors turn to or draw upon the body while keeping it in the background. This level of analysis must transcend specific cases but also examine what techniques or devices are a case of. For example, using a tool like a mirror is a means to place the self outside self; the point is not simply that tools aid in cultivating the body. It is the development of the third turn that will provide a pathway to a fuller understanding of the first turn: the philosophy of social action.

NOTES

INTRODUCTION

1. On tennis, see Greg Noble and Megan Watkins, "So, How Did Bourdieu Learn to Play Tennis? Habitus, Consciousness and Habitation," *Cultural Studies* 17, nos. 3–4 (2003): 520–39, https://doi.org/10.1080/0950238032000083926. On bike riding, see Michael Polanyi, *Personal Knowledge: Towards a Postcritical Philosophy* (Routledge and Kegan Paul, 1958); Harry Collins, *Tacit and Explicit Knowledge* (University of Chicago Press, 2010).

2. This physicality can be seen in the aggressive posturing of young Mexican American gang members who purposefully position themselves below others through poor posture or by squatting then tilt their heads back and glance down their noses. A version of this type of body positioning also exists in the context of driving, in which low-riders deliberately lower their car's shock absorbers and then position their bodies in a way that reduces their height while also allowing them to look down their noses. See Jack Katz, *Seductions of Crime: Moral and Sensual Attractions in Doing Evil* (Basic Books, 1988), 90–92.

3. Charles Goodwin, "Professional Vision," *American Anthropologist* 96, no. 3 (1994): 606–33, https://doi.org/10.1525/aa.1994.96.3.02a00100.

4. Guidance for parents of children with autism describes how to increase their children's eye contact, including strategies like the parent placing their own face in their child's line of sight or placing a toy between the child's face and the parent's face to direct the line of sight in the direction of the parent's face. See Brooke Ingersoll and Anna Dvortcsak, *Teaching Social Communication to Children with Autism: A Practitioner's Guide to Parent Training* (Guilford, 2010).

5. In his ethnography of Orthodox Jewish life in the Beverly–La Brea area, Iddo Tavory recalled his first experience of wearing a yarmulke in public and being aware of non-Jewish women "not looking" at him. See Iddo Tavory, *Summoned: Identification and Religious Life in a Jewish Neighborhood* (University of Chicago Press, 2016), 135.

6. For example, when greeting senior members of the British royal family, it is customary to bow or curtsy while maintaining eye contact. Eye contact should also be maintained throughout a conversation. See Elizabeth Wyse, ed., *Debrett's Handbook* (Debrett's, 2014).

7. Spencer E. Cahill et al., "Meanwhile Backstage: Public Bathrooms and the Interaction Order," *Urban Life* 14, no. 1 (1985): 33–58, https://doi.org/10.1177/009830398501400002.

8. Brian Lande, "'Laying Hands' and Learning to Touch and Grab in the Police Academy," in *The Oxford Handbook of the Sociology of Body and Embodiment*, ed. Natalie Boero and Katherine Mason (Oxford University Press, 2020), 447–68.

9. Joan Emerson, "Behavior in Private Places: Sustaining Definitions of Reality in Gynecological Examinations," in *Readings on Ethical and Social Issues in Biomedicine*, ed. Richard Wertz (Prentice-Hall, 1973), 221–35.

10. Rachel Prentice, *Bodies in Formation: An Ethnography of Anatomy and Surgery Education* (Duke University Press, 2013); Anna Harris, *A Sensory Education* (Routledge, 2021).

11. Aug Nishizaka, "Touch Without Vision: Referential Practice in a Non-technological Environment," *Journal of Pragmatics* 43, no. 2 (2011): 504–20, https://doi.org/10.1016/j.pragma.2009.07.015.

12. Lorenza Mondada, *Sensing in Social Interaction: The Taste for Cheese in Gourmet Shops* (Cambridge University Press, 2021).

13. Greg Downey, "Scaffolding Imitation in Capoeira: Physical Education and Enculturation in an Afro-Brazilian Art," *American Anthropologist* 110, no. 2 (2008): 204–13, https://doi.org/10.1111/j.1548-1433.2008.00026.x.

14. Brian Lande, "Breathing Like a Soldier: Culture Incarnate," *Sociological Review* 55, no. S1 (2007): 95–108, https://doi.org/10.1111/j.1467-954X.2007.00695.x.

15. Sibyl Kleiner, "Thinking with the Mind, Syncing with the Body: Ballet as Symbolic and Nonsymbolic Interaction," *Symbolic Interaction* 32, no. 3 (2009): 236–59, https://doi.org/10.1525/si.2009.32.3.236.

16. Murray Schafer, "Open Ears," in *The Auditory Culture Reader*, ed. Michael Bull and Les Black (Berg, 2003), 25–39.

17. Karin Bijsterveld, *Mechanical Sound: Technology, Culture, and Public Problems of Noise in the Twentieth Century* (MIT Press, 2008).

18. Erving Goffman, *Forms of Talk* (University of Pennsylvania Press, 1981).

19. Luis-Manuel Garcia, "Beats, Flesh, and Grain: Sonic Tactility and Affect in Electronic Dance Music," *Sound Studies* 1, no. 1 (2015): 59–76, https://doi.org/10.1080/20551940.2015.1079072; Evelyn Glennie, *Good Vibrations: My Autobiography* (Hutchinson, 1990).

20. This orientation toward sound and its meaning, rather than hearing itself, is reflected in the scholarly literature. See, for example, Karin Bijsterveld, "Breaking Into a World of Perfection: Innovation in Today's Classical Musical Instruments," *Social Studies of Science* 34, no. 5 (2004): 649–74; Paul Hegarty, *Noise/Music: A History* (Continuum, 2007); Catherine Strong, *Grunge: Music and Memory* (Ashgate, 2011); Richard Peterson, *Creating Country Music: Fabricating Authenticity* (University of Chicago Press, 1997).

21. On wildlife or traffic noise, see Don Ihde, *Listening and Voice: Phenomenologies of Sound*, 2nd ed. (State University of New York Press, 2007), 73–83; on sounds used to time our lives, Alain Corbin, *Village Bells: Sound and Meaning in the Nineteenth-Century French Countryside*, ed. Lawrence D. Kritzman, trans. Martin Thom (Columbia University Press, 1998).

22. Laura Mauldin, *Made to Hear: Cochlear Implants and Raising Deaf Children* (University of Minnesota Press, 2016); Stuart S. Blume, "Histories of Cochlear Implantation," *Social Science & Medicine* 49, no. 9 (1999): 1257–68, https://doi.org/10.1016/S0277-9536(99)00164-1.

23. Worker safety standards define hazardous noise as noise levels at an average of eighty five decibels over an eight hour period, or noise that hits peak levels over one hundred and forty decibels.

24. Tia DeNora, *Music in Everyday Life* (Cambridge University Press, 2000); Samira van Bohemen, Luna den Hertog, and Liesbet van Zoonen, "Music as a Resource for the Sexual Self: An Exploration of How Young People in the Netherlands Use Music for Good Sex," *Poetics* 66 (2018): 19–29, https://doi.org/10.1016/j.poetic.2017.12.001.

25. Hanns Eisler and Theodor Adorno, "The Politics of Hearing," in *Audio Culture: Readings in Modern Music*, ed. Christoph Cox and Daniel Warner (Continuum, 2007); Marc Perlman, "Golden Ears and Meter Readers: The Contest for Epistemic Authority in Audiophilia," *Social Studies of Science* 34, no. 5 (2004): 783–807, https://doi.org/10.1177/0306312704047613; Antoine Hennion, "Music Lovers: Taste as Performance," *Theory, Culture & Society* 18, no. 5 (2001):1–22, https://doi.org/10.1177/02632760122051940.

26. Daniel Levitin, *This Is Your Brain on Music: The Science of a Human Obsession* (Dutton, 2006).

27. Becker observed this in the context of the dance hall musicians he studied, who played repertoire based on the "squares" in their audience. See Howard S. Becker, *Outsiders: Studies in the Sociology of Deviance* (Free Press, 1963), 89–95.

28. On the practices of these professional connoisseurs, see Erik Nylander, "Mastering the Jazz Standard: Sayings and Doings of Artistic Valuation," *American Journal of Cultural Sociology* 2, no. 1 (2014): 66–96.

29. Christian Heath, "Body Work: The Collaborative Production of the Clinical Object," in *Communication in Medical Care: Interaction Between Primary Care Physicians and Patients*, ed. John Heritage and Douglas Maynard (University of Cambridge Press, 2006), 185–213.

30. Erving Goffman, "Where the Action Is," in *Interaction Ritual: Essays on Face-to-Face Behaviour* (Penguin, 1967).

31. In the study of human physiology, proprioception is typically distinguished from kinesthesia based on whether it is a static sense of our body positions that is being referred to (proprioception) or dynamic patterns of movement (kinesthesia). Recent work in embodied cognitive psychology emphasizes that proprioception and kinesthesia are coupled, reciprocally generating possibilities in human movement. See Ximena González-Grandón, Andrea Falcón-Cortés, and Gabriel Ramos-Fernández, "Proprioception in Action: A Matter of Ecological and Social Interaction," *Frontiers in Psychology* 11 (2021), https://doi.org/10.3389/fpsyg.2020.569403.

32. Uwe Proske and Simon C. Gandevia, "The Proprioceptive Senses: Their Roles in Signaling Body Shape, Body Position and Movement, and Muscle Force," *Physiological Reviews* 92, no. 4 (2012): 1651–97, https://doi.org/10.1152/physrev .00048.2011. Despite its absence from everyday vernacular, proprioception has attracted substantial interest within the fields of embodied cognitive psychology and phenomenological philosophy. Of particular concern is whether we should recognize proprioception as a matter of the mind, meaning neural processing, or as coupled with bodily experience and social relations. On the former, see Alvin I. Goldman, "A Moderate Approach to Embodied Cognitive Science," *Review of Philosophy and Psychology* 3, no. 1 (2012): 71–88, https:// doi.org/10.1007/s13164-012-0089-0. On the latter, see Shaun Gallagher, *How the Body Shapes the Mind* (Oxford University Press, 2012); J. Kevin O'Regan and Alva Noë, "The Origin of 'Feel'" in *From Animals to Animats: Proceedings of the Seventh International Conference on Simulation of Adaptive Behavior*, ed. Bridget Hallam et al. (MIT Press, 2002); Eleanor Rosch, Lydia Thompson, and Francisco J. Varela, *The Embodied Mind: Cognitive Science and Human Experience* (MIT Press, 1991).

33. Edward M. Hubbard and V. S. Ramachandran, "Neurocognitive Mechanisms of Synesthesia," *Neuron* 48, no. 3 (2005): 509–20, https://doi.org/10.1016/j.neuron.2005.10.012; Romke Rouw and H. Steven Scholte, "Increased Structural Connectivity in Grapheme-Color Synesthesia," *Nature Neuroscience* 10, no. 6 (2007): 792–97, https://doi.org/10.1038/nn1906; Devin Blair Terhune et al., "Enhanced Cortical Excitability in Grapheme-Color Synesthesia and Its Modulation," *Current Biology* 21, no. 23 (2011): 2006–9, https://doi.org/10.1016/j.cub.2011.10.032. Other forms of synesthesia have also been reported in the literature. On the tactile sensation of shapes in tasting food, see Richard Cytowic, *Synaesthesia: A Union of the Senses* (Springer-Verlag, 1989). On experiencing tingling sensations in response to hearing sounds, see Michael S. Beauchamp and Tony Ro, "Neural Substrates of Sound—Touch Synesthesia After a Thalamic Lesion," *Journal of Neuroscience* 28, no. 50 (2008): 13696, https://doi.org/10.1523/JNEUROSCI.3872-08.2008.

34. Mike J. Dixon, Daniel Smilek, and Philip M. Merikle, "Not All Synaesthetes Are Created Equal: Projector Versus Associator Synaesthetes," *Cognitive, Affective & Behavioral Neuroscience* 4, no. 3 (2004): 335–43, https://doi.org/10.3758/CABN.4.3.335.

35. With advances in neuroimaging, neuroscientists have begun mapping the neural basis of synesthesia, though contradictory results dominate the research program, perhaps because of individual variation among participants and neuroimaging methods. Two primary hypotheses account for synesthesia. The first relates to direct cross-activation between adjacent brain regions; see D. Brang et al., "Magnetoencephalography Reveals Early Activation of V4 in Grapheme-Color Synesthesia," *NeuroImage* 53, no. 1 (2010): 268–74, https://doi.org/10.1016/j.neuroimage.2010.06.008; V. S. Ramachandran and E. M. Hubbard, "Synaesthesia—A Window Into Perception, Thought and Language," *Journal of Consciousness Studies* 8, no. 12 (2001): 3–34, https://www.ingentaconnect.com/content/imp/jcs/2001/00000008/00000012/1244. The second hypothesis attributes synesthesia to hyperbinding or disinhibited feedback in the multisensory regions of the brain, such as the parietal cortex; see Peter G. Grossenbacher and Christopher T. Lovelace, "Mechanisms of Synesthesia: Cognitive and Physiological Constraints," *Trends in Cognitive Sciences* 5, no. 1 (2001): 36–41, https://doi.org/10.1016/S1364-6613(00)01571-0; J. Neufeld et al., "Disinhibited Feedback as a Cause of Synesthesia: Evidence from a Functional Connectivity Study on Auditory-Visual Synesthetes," *Neuropsychologia* 50, no. 7 (2012): 1471–77, https://doi.org/10.1016/j.neuropsychologia

.2012.02.032; Anna Zamm et al., "Pathways to Seeing Music: Enhanced Structural Connectivity in Colored-Music Synesthesia," *NeuroImage* 74 (2013): 359–66, https://doi.org/10.1016/j.neuroimage.2013.02.024. Others have interpreted synesthesia as a result of functional reorganization, as in the patient who experienced auditory–tactile synesthesia following a thalamic stroke; see Beauchamp and Ro, "Neural Substrates of Sound."

36. John Harrison, *Synaesthesia: The Strangest Thing* (Oxford University Press, 2001).

37. Maurice Merleau-Ponty, *Phenomenology of Perception*, trans. Colin Smith (Routledge, 2002), 266–67.

38. André J. Abath, "Merleau-Ponty and the Problem of Synaesthesia," in *Sensory Blending: On Synaesthesia and Related Phenomena*, ed. Ophelia Deroy (Oxford University Press, 2017), 157.

39. Alva Noë, *Action in Perception* (MIT Press, 2004).

40. Hervé Munz, "Les doigts fertiles," *Socio-anthropologie* 35 (2017): 75–91. In another example, marine scientists relate to cup corals with what Hayward terms "fingeryeyes" in a blurring of the optic and haptic. See Eva Hayward, "Fingeryeyes: Impressions of Cup Corals," *Cultural Anthropology* 25, no. 4 (2010): 577–99, https://doi.org/10.1111/j.1548-1360.2010.01070.x.

41. Barbara Pentimalli and Giampietro Gobo, "'Hearing with the Eyes': Visual Hearing in (a Trio) Music Rehearsals," *Senses and Society* 18, no. 3 (2023): 254–72, https://doi.org/10.1080/17458927.2023.2232621.

42. Anna Mann et al., "Mixing Methods, Tasting Fingers: Notes on an Ethnographic Experiment," *HAU: Journal of Ethnographic Theory* 1, no. 1 (2011): 221–43, https://doi.org/10.14318/hau1.1.009.

43. Paul Carter, "Ambiguous Traces, Mishearing and Auditory Space," in *Hearing Cultures: Essays on Sound, Listening and Modernity*, ed. Veit Erlmann (Berg, 2004), 43–44.

44. Jonathan Sterne, *The Audible Past: Cultural Origins of Sound Reproduction* (Duke University Press, 2003), 19. Smith uses the analogy of software and hardware to express the difference between hearing and listening; see Bruce R. Smith, "Listening to the Wild Blue Yonder: The Challenges of Acoustic Ecology," in *Hearing Cultures: Essays on Sound, Listening and Modernity*, ed. Viet Erlmann (Berg, 2004), 38.

45. Eisler and Adorno, "The Politics of Hearing," 74.

46. Robert Walser, *Running with the Devil: Power, Gender, and Madness in Heavy Metal Music* (Wesleyan University Press, 1993).

47. Harris Berger, *Metal, Rock, and Jazz: Perception and Phenomenology of Musical Experience* (Wesleyan University Press, 1999).

48. Norbert Elias, *The Civilizing Process: Sociogenetic and Psychogenetic Investigations*, 2nd ed., ed. Eric Dunning et al., trans. Edmund Jephcott (Wiley-Blackwell, 2000); Marcel Mauss, "Techniques of the Body," *Economy and Society* 2, no. 1 (1973): 70–88, https://doi.org/10.1080/03085147300000003; Pierre Bourdieu, *The Logic of Practice*, trans. Richard Nice (Stanford University Press, 1990); Michel Foucault, *Madness and Civilization: A History of Insanity in the Age of Reason*, trans. Richard Howard (Routledge, 1967); Michel Foucault, *Discipline and Punish: The Birth of the Prison*, trans. Alan Sheridan (Penguin, 1977); Michel Foucault, *The History of Sexuality*, vol. 1, trans. Robert Hurley (Pantheon, 1978); Erving Goffman, *The Presentation of Self in Everyday Life* (Anchor, 1959) Judith Butler, *Bodies That Matter: On the Discursive Limits of "Sex"* (Routledge, 1993); Judith Butler, *Gender Trouble: Feminism and the Subversion of Identity* (Routledge, 1999).

49. Iris Marion Young, *Throwing Like a Girl and Other Essays in Feminist Philosophy and Social Theory* (Indiana University Press, 1990); Elizabeth Grosz, *Volatile Bodies: Towards a Corporeal Feminism* (Allen & Unwin, 1994); Merleau-Ponty, *Phenomenology of Perception*.

50. Alain Corbin, *The Foul and the Fragrant: Odor and the French Social Imagination* (Harvard University Press, 1988); Elaine Scarry, *The Body in Pain: The Making and Unmaking of the World* (Oxford University Press, 1988).

51. Jack Katz, "On Becoming an Ethnographer," *Journal of Contemporary Ethnography* 48, no. 1 (2018): 16–50, https://doi.org/10.1177/0891241618777801.

52. David Sudnow, *Ways of the Hand: The Organization of Improvised Conduct* (Harvard University Press, 1978).

53. Melissa Van Drie, "Training the Auscultative Ear," *Senses and Society* 8, no. 2 (2013): 165–91, https://doi.org/10.2752/174589313X13589681981019.

54. Margarethe Kusenbach, "Street Phenomenology: The Go-Along as Ethnographic Research Tool," *Ethnography* 4, no. 3 (2003): 455–85, https://doi.org/10.1177/146613810343007.

55. Kusenbach, "Street Phenomenology," 469.

56. For an argument on the resources people bring to interactions beyond the moment and their methodological implications, see Michael F. DeLand, "Men and Their Moments: Character-Driven Ethnography and Interaction Analysis in a Park Basketball Rule Dispute," *Social Psychology Quarterly* 84, no. 2 (2021): 01902725211004894, https://doi.org/10.1177/01902725211004894.

57. Kleiner, "Thinking with the Mind."

1. HOW DOCTORS HEAR

1. Christian Heath, "Pain Talk: The Expression of Suffering in the Medical Consultation," *Social Psychology Quarterly* 52, no. 2 (1989): 113–25, https://doi .org/10.2307/2786911.

2. Dawn Goodwin, "Sensing the Way: Embodied Dimensions of Diagnostic Work," in *Ethnographies of Diagnostic Work: Dimensions of Transformative Practice*, ed. Monika Buscher et al. (Palgrave Macmillan, 2010), 37–92; Cornelius Schubert, "Making Sure: A Comparative Micro-analysis of Diagnostic Instruments in Medical Practice," *Social Science & Medicine* 73, no. 6 (2011): 851–57, https://doi.org/10.1016/j.socscimed.2011.05.032; John Gardner and Clare Williams, "Corporal Diagnostic Work and Diagnostic Spaces: Clinicians' Use of Space and Bodies During Diagnosis," *Sociology of Health & Illness* 37, no. 5 (2015): 765–81, https://doi.org/10.1111/1467-9566.12233.

3. Harry Collins and Robert Evans, *Rethinking Expertise* (University of Chicago Press, 2007); Gary Klein, *Sources of Power: How People Make Decisions* (MIT Press, 1998); Tim Ingold, *The Perception of the Environment: Essays on Livelihood, Dwelling, and Skill* (Routledge, 2000).

4. Nelly Oudshoorn, "Diagnosis at a Distance: The Invisible Work of Patients and Healthcare Professionals in Cardiac Telemonitoring Technology," *Sociology of Health & Illness* 30, no. 2 (2008): 272–88, https://doi.org/10.1111/j.1467-9566 .2007.01032.x; Sarah Maslen, "Sensory Work of Diagnosis: A Crisis of Legitimacy," *Senses & Society* 11, no. 2 (2016): 158–76, https://doi.org/10.1080 /17458927.2016.1190065.

5. Specialties included general practice, orthopedic surgery, general surgery, anesthetics, gynecology, obstetrics, cardiology, ophthalmology, and neurology.

6. Michael Eraut, "Transfer of Knowledge Between Education and Workplace Settings," in *Knowledge, Values and Educational Policy: A Critical Perspective*, ed. Harry Daniels et al. (Routledge, 2009), 65–84; Rosalind Driver et al., "Constructing Scientific Knowledge in the Classroom," *Educational Researcher* 23, no. 7 (1994): 5–12, https://doi.org/10.3102/0013189X023007005; John Seely Brown and Paul Duguid, "Organizational Learning and Communities of Practice: Toward a Unified View of Working, Learning, and Innovation," *Organization Science* 2, no. 1 (1991): 40–57; Alice Lam, "Tacit Knowledge, Organizational Learning and Societal Institutions: An Integrated Framework," *Organization Studies* 21, no. 3 (2000): 487–513.

7. Ericka Johnson, "Surgical Simulators and Simulated Surgeons: Reconstituting Medical Practice and Practitioners in Simulations," *Social Studies of*

Science 37, no. 4 (2007): 585–608, https://doi.org/10.1177/0306312706072179; Anna Harris, *A Sensory Education* (Routledge, 2021).

8. Recent reforms in medical education have seen a shift toward competency-based education to place greater focus on the synthesis of skills and attitudes and de-emphasize time spent training. For an overview of competency-based medical education, see Jason R. Frank et al., "Competency-Based Medical Education: Theory to Practice," *Medical Teacher* 32, no. 8 (2010): 638–45, https://doi.org/10.3109/0142159X.2010.501190. Critics of this approach question the extent to which it facilitates the development of expert understanding and competence in practice; see Olle ten Cate and Fedde Scheele, "Viewpoint: Competency-Based Postgraduate Training: Can We Bridge the Gap Between Theory and Clinical Practice?," *Academic Medicine* 82, no. 6 (2007): 542–47, https://doi.org/10.1097/ACM.0b013e31805559c7; Martin Talbot, "Monkey See, Monkey Do: A Critique of the Competency Model in Graduate Medical Education," *Medical Education* 38, no. 6 (2004): 587–92, https://doi.org/10.1046/j.1365-2923.2004.01794.x. Medical education reforms have also resulted in more formalized methods of supervising and assessing residents; see Iris Wallenburg et al., "Learning to Doctor: Tinkering with Visibility in Residency Training," *Sociology of Health & Illness* 35, no. 4 (2013): 544–59, https://doi.org/10.1111/j.1467-9566.2012.01512.x.

9. Tom Rice described a group of medical students who stood speechless when asked to describe normal heart sounds. They were taught the language of "lub dub" in an effort to make stethoscopic listening communal. See Tom Rice, "Learning to Listen: Auscultation and the Transmission of Auditory Knowledge," *Journal of the Royal Anthropological Institute* 16 (2010): S45, S54, https://doi.org/10.1111/j.1467-9655.2010.01609.x.

10. In the 1960s, a decade during which some of the doctors I spoke with were medical students, three-quarters of clinical education happened at the bedside. Rounds were an important forum for learning for all the doctors I spoke with, who all completed their training before 1990. A lot has changed in medical education since then, just as medical advances have supported a radical transformation in health care provision. Patients are in hospital for considerably less time, and hospitalized patients are more unwell. These changes present challenges for learning through rounds; there are simply not the patients in hospital beds to visit in the same way that there were previously. Technological advancements and shifts toward laboratory testing over clinical diagnosis have also changed how medicine is practiced and by extension how it is taught. In addition, the shift toward patient-oriented medicine

has prompted questions about the impact of bedside teaching on patients. In the last decade, rounds have been reduced; estimates suggest they now represent as little as 8 percent of clinical education. While this way of learning now plays a minor role when measured as a proportion of training time, its virtues are still touted, and it remains critical for the development of medical hearing to the extent that, without it, medical students and residents are mostly unable to hear and diagnose a heart murmur using their clinical skills. See Franz Reichsman et al., "Observations of Undergraduate Clinical Teaching in Action," *Academic Medicine* 39, no. 2 (1964): 147–63, http://journals.lww .com/academicmedicine/Fulltext/1964/02000/Observations_of_Undergraduate _Clinical_Teaching_in.8.aspx; Balakrishnan R. Nair et al., "Impediments to Bed-Side Teaching," *Medical Education* 32, no. 2 (1998): 159–62, https://doi .org/10.1046/j.1365-2923.1998.00185.x; George E. Thibault "Bedside Rounds Revisited," *New England Journal of Medicine* 336, no. 16 (1997): 1174–75, https:// doi.org/10.1056/nejm199704173361610; Faith Fitzgerald, "Physical Diagnosis Versus Modern Technology: A Review," *Western Journal of Medicine* 152, no. 4 (1990): 377–82, http://www.ncbi.nlm.nih.gov/pmc/articles/PMC1002356/; Tom Rice, "'Beautiful Murmurs': Stethoscopic Listening and Acoustic Objectification," *Senses and Society* 3, no. 3 (2008): 293–306; M. A. LaCombe, "On Bedside Teaching," *Annals of Internal Medicine* 127, no. 2 (1997): 173–73, https:// doi.org/10.7326/0003-4819-127-2-199707150-00047; Faith Fitzgerald, "Bedside Teaching," *Western Journal of Medicine* 158, no. 4 (1993): 418–20, http:// www.ncbi.nlm.nih.gov/pmc/articles/PMC1022080/; Keith N. Williams et al., "Improving Bedside Teaching: Findings from a Focus Group Study of Learners," *Academic Medicine* 83, no. 3 (2008): 257–64, https://doi.org/10.1097 /ACM.0b013e3181637f3e; Max Peters and Olle ten Cate, "Bedside Teaching in Medical Education: A Literature Review," *Perspectives on Medical Education* 3, no. 2 (2014): 76–88, https://doi.org/10.1007/s40037-013-0083-y; Bernard Favrat et al., "Teaching Cardiac Auscultation to Trainees in Internal Medicine and Family Practice: Does It Work?," *Medical Education* 4, no. 5 (2004): 1–7.

11. See also Rice, "Learning to Listen," S49.

12. Teaching stethoscopes with two or more ear pieces and a single diaphragm can also be used for this purpose.

13. This challenge has endured from the nineteenth century practice of medicine into the present. See Jonathan Sterne, "Mediate Auscultation, the Stethoscope, and the 'Autopsy of the Living': Medicine's Acoustic Culture," *Journal of Medical Humanities* 22, no. 2 (2001): 130, https://doi.org/10.1023/a:1009067628620.

14. René Laënnec, *A Treatise on Diseases of the Chest and on Mediate Auscultation*, trans. John Forbes (Samuel Wood & Sons and Collins and Hannay, 1830), 52.

15. Laënnec, *A Treatise on Diseases*, 56.

16. Laënnec, *A Treatise on Diseases*, 588.

17. George Lakoff and Mark Johnson, *Metaphors We Live By* (University of Chicago Press, 1980), 3.

18. Laënnec, *A Treatise on Diseases*, 588.

19. Lakoff and Johnson, *Metaphors We Live By*, 157.

20. Rice, "'Beautiful Murmurs.'"

21. Sergio Mondillo et al., "Seagulls Flying in the Echo Lab," *Heart* 90, no. 11 (2004): 1247, https://doi.org/10.1136/hrt.2004.037200.

22. Lakoff and Johnson, *Metaphors We Live By*, 10.

23. Hinton and colleagues have described metaphors as "sensation scripts" that can both rely on and induce certain sensory experiences. In this account from Matthew, we see that metaphor can more foundationally *construct* sensation. See Devon E. Hinton et al., "Toward a Medical Anthropology of Sensations: Definitions and Research Agenda," *Transcultural Psychiatry* 45, no. 2 (2008): 142–62, https://doi.org/10.1177/1363461508089763.

24. The use of metaphor to approximate experience is not limited to hearing. David, the general surgeon, explained that the stools of a person with cholera are visually like rice water.

25. Anna Harris, "Listening-Touch, Affect and the Crafting of Medical Bodies Through Percussion," *Body & Society* 22, no. 1 (2016): 31–61, https://doi.org/10.1177/1357034X15604031. On auto-auscultation, see Tom Rice, *Hearing and the Hospital: Sound, Listening, Knowledge and Experience* (Sean Kingston, 2013). Studies of medical education often emphasize learning from the bodies of patients, as well as from corpses and mannequin simulators. For analyses of the latter, see Ruth Richardson, *Death, Dissection and the Destitute*, 2nd ed. (University of Chicago Press, 2001); Jeffery B. Cooper and Viviany Rodrigues Taqueti, "A Brief History of the Development of Mannequin Simulators for Clinical Education and Training," *BMJ Quality and Safety in Health Care* 13 (2004): i11–i18, https://doi.org/10.1136/qshc.2004.009886.

26. Harris similarly gives an example of hearing the contrast between the sounds of the stomach and chest. She writes, "The body is a walking fleshy textbook of comparisons." See Harris, "Listening-Touch," 44, 46.

27. Maurice Merleau-Ponty, *Phenomenology of Perception*, trans. Colin Smith (Routledge, 2002), 176–78.

28. In her account of teaching a medical student to use a drill in a hand surgery, Rachel Prentice describes how the surgeon must simultaneously pass on their embodied knowledge of surgical work while managing "the student's unhandiness to prevent errors." The surgeon tells the student which hand to use, and they give "silent feedback" by guiding the student's body with their own. In effect, it is the surgeon's hands that are placing the screw, but at the same time the student experiences "the correct feel of drilling." See Rachel Prentice, "Drilling Surgeons: The Social Lessons of Embodied Surgical Learning," *Science, Technology & Human Values* 32, no. 5 (2007): 542–46, https://doi.org/10.1177/0895904805303201.

29. Sociologies of health and illness mostly neglect this physiological diversity. See Stefan Timmermans and Steven Haas, "Towards a Sociology of Disease," *Sociology of Health & Illness* 30, no. 5 (2008): 659–76, https://doi.org/10.1111/j.1467-9566.2008.01097.x.

30. Comparative feeling has been identified as a learning strategy for blind medical massage students; see Gili Hammer, "'You Can Learn Merely by Listening to the Way a Patient Walks Through the Door': The Transmission of Sensory Medical Knowledge," *Medical Anthropology Quarterly* 32, no. 1 (2018): 138–54, https://doi.org/10.1111/maq.12366.

31. Christian Heath, "Body Work: The Collaborative Production of the Clinical Object." In *Communication in Medical Care: Interaction Between Primary Care Physicians and Patients*, ed. John Heritage and Douglas Maynard (University of Cambridge Press, 2006), 208.

32. On diagnosis through hearing gait, see Hammer, "'You Can Learn Merely by Listening.'"

33. Merleau-Ponty, *Phenomenology of Perception*, 264.

34. David Armstrong, "Clinical Sense and Clinical Science," *Social Science & Medicine (1967)* 11, nos. 11–13 (1977): 599–601, https://doi.org/10.1016/0037-7856(77)90041-5; Marc Berg, *Rationalizing Medical Work: Decision-Support Techniques and Medical Practices* (MIT Press, 1997); Stefan Timmermans and Marc Berg, *The Gold Standard: The Challenge of Evidence-Based Medicine and Standardization in Healthcare* (Temple University Press, 2003); Joel D. Howell, *Technology in the Hospital: Transforming Patient Care in the Early Twentieth Century* (Johns Hopkins University Press, 1995).

35. See Veit Erlmann, ed., *Hearing Cultures: Essays on Sound, Listening and Modernity* (Berg, 2004); David Howes and Constance Classen, *Ways of Sensing: Understanding the Senses in Society* (Routledge, 2013); Martin Jay,

Downcast Eyes: The Denigration of Vision in Twentieth-Century French Thought (University of California Press, 1993).

36. Lisa Cartwright, *Screening the Body: Tracing Medicine's Visual Culture* (University of Minnesota Press, 1995); José van Dijck, *The Transparent Body: A Cultural Analysis of Medical Imaging* (University of Washington Press, 2011); Barbara Duden, *Disembodying Women: Perspectives on Pregnancy and the Unborn*, trans. Lee Hoinacki (Harvard University Press, 1993).

37. Abraham Verghese, "Culture Shock—Patient as Icon, Icon as Patient," *New England Journal of Medicine* 359, no. 26 (2008): 2748–51, https://doi.org/10.1056 /NEJMp0807461.

38. Gardner and Williams, "Corporal Diagnostic Work"; Goodwin, "Sensing the Way"; Anna Harris, "In a Moment of Mismatch: Overseas Doctors' Adjustments in New Hospital Environments," *Sociology of Health & Illness* 33, no. 2 (2011), https://doi.org/10.1111/j.1467-9566.2010.01307.x; Prentice, "Drilling Surgeons"; Schubert, "Making Sure."

39. Many studies have reported a decline in clinical skills such as auscultation among younger generations of doctors; see Uazman Alam et al., "Cardiac Auscultation: An Essential Clinical Skill in Decline," *British Journal of Cardiology* 17, no. 1 (2010): 8–10; Favrat et al., "Teaching Cardiac Auscultation"; Salvatore Mangione, "Cardiac Auscultatory Skills of Physicians-in-Training: A Comparison of Three English-Speaking Countries," *American Journal of Medicine* 110 (2001): 210–16. In response, some medical education researchers have argued for training in operating handheld echocardiography devices to ensure the efficacy of this technology rather than returning to a focus on developing the medical ear for auscultation; see Lori B. Croft et al., "A Pilot Study of the Clinical Impact of Hand-Carried Cardiac Ultrasound in the Medical Clinic," *Echocardiography: A Journal of Cardiovascular Ultrasound and Allied Techniques* 23, no. 6 (2006): 439–46; Jeanne M. DeCara et al., "The Hand-Carried Echocardiographic Device as an Aid to the Physical Examination," *Echocardiography: A Journal of Cardiovascular Ultrasound and Allied Techniques* 20, no. 5 (2003): 477–85.

40. More than being "hybrids of machine and organism" as in Donna Haraway's original theorization in which we could observe a doctor using a tool disconnected from themselves, hearing with the echocardiogram reflects a fundamental entanglement of subject and object closer to Karen Barad's articulation of intraaction. Donna Haraway, "A Cyborg Manifesto: Science, Technology, and Socialist-Feminism in the Late Twentieth Century," in *Simians, Cyborgs*

and Women: The Reinvention of Nature (Routledge, 1991), 149–82; Karen Barad, *Meeting the Universe Halfway: Quantum Physics and the Entanglement of Matter and Meaning* (Duke University Press, 2007).

41. Simon Carmel, "The Craft of Intensive Care Medicine," *Sociology of Health & Illness* 35, no. 5 (2013): 731–45, https://doi.org/10.1111/j.1467-9566.2012.01524.x.

42. Our senses can process as many as 11.2 million "bits" of information per second unconsciously, whereas information gained via conscious tasks such as reading aloud or multiplication is processed at about 10 to 60 bits per second. For a review, see Ap Dijksterhuis and Loran F. Nordgren, "A Theory of Unconscious Thought," *Perspectives on Psychological Science* 1, no. 2 (2006): 95–109, https://doi.org/10.1111/j.1745-6916.2006.00007.x.

43. Timothy D. Wilson et al., "Introspecting About Reasons Can Reduce Post-choice Satisfaction," *Personality and Social Psychology Bulletin* 19, no. 3 (1993): 331–39, https://doi.org/10.1177/0146167293193010; Ap Dijksterhuis and Zeger van Olden, "On the Benefits of Thinking Unconsciously: Unconscious Thought Can Increase Post-choice Satisfaction," *Journal of Experimental Social Psychology* 42, no. 5 (2006): 627–31, https://doi.org/https://doi.org/10.1016/j.jesp.2005.10.008.

44. Dijksterhuis and Nordgren, "A Theory of Unconscious Thought."

45. Pierre Bourdieu, *Outline of a Theory of Practice*, trans. Richard Nice (Cambridge University Press, 1977).

46. Harris, *A Sensory Education*; Rice, *Hearing and the Hospital*.

47. Harris, "Listening-Touch."

2. HOW MUSICIANS HEAR

1. Valerie Ann Malhotra, "The Social Accomplishment of Music in a Symphony Orchestra: A Phenomenological Analysis," *Qualitative Sociology* 4, no. 2 (1981): 102–25, https://doi.org/10.1007/BF00987214.

2. Gunther Schuller, *The Compleat Conductor* (Oxford University Press, 1997), 9.

3. Jonna K. Vuoskoski and Dee Reynolds, "Music, Rowing, and the Aesthetics of Rhythm," *Senses and Society* 14, no. 1 (2019): 1–14, https://doi.org/10.1080/17458927.2018.1525201; Peter Weeks, "Musical Time as a Practical Accomplishment: A Change in Tempo," *Human Studies* 13, no. 4 (1990): 323–59, http://www.jstor.org/stable/20009106.

4. For example, see Peter Weeks, "A Rehearsal of a Beethoven Passage: An Analysis of Correction Talk," *Research on Language and Social Interaction* 29,

no. 3 (1996): 247–90, https://doi.org/10.1207/s15327973rlsi2903_3; John B. Haviland, "Master Speakers, Master Gesturers: A String Quartet Master Class," in *Gesture and the Dynamic Dimension of Language: Essays in Honor of David McNeill*, ed. Susan D. Duncan et al. (John Benjamins, 2007), 147–72; Peter Tolmie et al., "Playing in Irish Music Sessions," in *Ethnomethodology at Play*, ed. Peter Tolmie and Mark Rouncefield (Ashgate, 2013), 227–56.

5. See also John Holt, *Never Too Late: A Musical Life Story* (Merloyd Lawrence, 1978), 167–68.

6. Malhotra, "The Social Accomplishment of Music," 111.

7. Howard Becker, "A School Is a Lousy Place to Learn Anything In," *American Behavioral Scientist* 16, no. 1 (1972): 85.

8. This problem in formal education is common to many fields. See Rosalie Goldsmith et al., "Investigating Invisible Writing Practices in the Engineering Curriculum Using Practice Architectures," *European Journal of Engineering Education* (2017): 1–14, https://doi.org/10.1080/03043797.2017.14 05241; David Boud et al., "Does Student Engagement in Self-Assessment Calibrate Their Judgement Over Time?," *Assessment & Evaluation in Higher Education* 38, no. 8 (2013): 941–56, https://doi.org/10.1080/02602938.2013.76 9198; Noble Christy and Billett Stephen, "Learning to Prescribe Through Co-working: Junior Doctors, Pharmacists and Consultants," *Medical Education* 51, no. 4 (2017): 442–51, https://doi.org/10.1111/medu.13227; Billett Stephen, "Workplace Participatory Practices: Conceptualising Workplaces as Learning Environments," *Journal of Workplace Learning* 16, no. 6 (2004): 312–24, https://doi.org/10.1108/13665620410550295.

9. Both Michael and Lachlan described elements of classical and jazz training in their formal education. Professionally, they also move between disciplines. Michael plays jazz and Latin music, while Lachlan composes in conversation with the classical tradition and performs Latin, jazz, folk, and popular music.

10. However, both Michael and Hannah reenrolled and completed different music programs later.

11. Daniel Barenboim, *A Life in Music*, rev. ed., ed. Michael Lewin and Phillip Huscher (Weidenfeld & Nicolson, 2002), 52. The classical pianist James Rhodes similarly emphasized fingering as the most important aspect of learning a piece. Fingering is connected to the sound, but the process of hearing to evaluate whether one's fingering is correct is not Rhodes's focus: "What combination of fingers will make the melody sound clearest, smoothest, joined up and voiced as the composer intended . . . some fingers are weaker or stronger

than others and shouldn't be used in certain places; the thumb, for example, is heaviest and will make whichever note it hits sound louder than, say, the fourth finger." See James Rhodes, *Instrumental: A Memoir of Madness, Medication and Music* (Canongate, 2015), 40.

12. Lois Choksy, *The Kodály Method I: Comprehensive Music Education*, 3rd ed. (Prentice-Hall, 1999); Mary Shamrock, "Orff Schulwerk: An Integrated Foundation," *Music Educators Journal* 72, no. 6 (1986): 51–55, https://doi.org/10.2307/3401278; Joy Yelin, *Movement That Fits: Dalcroze Eurhythmics and the Suzuki Method* (Summy-Brichard, 1990).

13. Steven Demorest, *Building Choral Excellence: Teaching Sight-Singing in the Choral Rehearsal* (Oxford University Press, 2003). Despite the widespread application of solfège and Curwen hand signs, their efficacy in improving pitch recognition is contentious. For a review, see Marta Frey-Clark, "Pitch Systems and Curwen Hand Signs: A Review of Literature," *Update: Applications of Research in Music Education* 36, no. 1 (2017): 59–65, https://doi.org/10.1177/8755123316689812.

14. In an amateur taiko drumming class, students similarly work off the exaggerated body movements of the teacher, who may bounce on a tire to suggest whole-body movement in producing the right drumming sound, showing right and wrong body position as being linked to the different sounds that these stances and movements generate. See Jennifer Winther, "The Embodiment of Sound and Cohesion in Music," *American Behavioral Scientist* 48, no. 11 (2005): 1414–16, https://doi.org/10.1177/0002764205277362.

15. Holt, *Never Too Late*, 123.

16. Pantelis Vassilakis, *Auditory Roughness as a Means of Musical Expression* (Department of Ethnomusicology, University of California, Los Angeles, 2005).

17. George Herbert Mead, *Mind, Self, and Society: From the Standpoint of a Social Behaviorist* (University of Chicago Press, 1934).

18. Maurice Merleau-Ponty, *The Visible and the Invisible*, trans. Alphonso Lingis (Northwestern University Press, 1968), 144. David Sudnow similarly observed that, in piano tuning, hearing pitch involves feeling the pulsating strings. See David Sudnow, *Ways of the Hand: The Organization of Improvised Conduct* (Harvard University Press, 1978), 44.

19. Quoted in Paul F. Berliner, *Thinking in Jazz: The Infinite Art of Improvisation* (University of Chicago Press, 1994), 58. In the classical context, James Rhodes similarly reflected, "I found recordings by Grigory Sokolov, the greatest living pianist, that taught me more about music, life, commitment and passion than anything before or since has managed to do." See Rhodes, *Instrumental*, 62–63.

20. Berliner, *Thinking in Jazz*, 104–5.

21. Sudnow, *Ways of the Hand*, 17.

22. Weeks, "A Rehearsal of a Beethoven Passage."

23. See also Berliner, *Thinking in Jazz*, 508.

24. While here Amy is describing learning from looking at others, she later clarified that she had only audio recordings as a resource in her early education and did not attend her first live performance until she was in her twenties.

25. Weeks, "A Rehearsal of a Beethoven Passage"; Jackson Tolins, "Assessment and Direction Through Nonlexical Vocalizations in Music Instruction," *Research on Language and Social Interaction* 46, no. 1 (2013): 247–90, https://doi.org/10.1080/08351813.2013.753721.

26. Metal often uses "power chords," which are based on a dyad of the tonic (first) and dominant (fifth) only.

27. Patricia Greenfield, "Children, Material Culture and Weaving: Historical Change and Developmental Change," in *Children and Material Culture*, ed. Joanna Sofaer Derevenski (Routledge, 2000).

28. Mead, *Mind, Self, and Society*, 151–52.

29. Merleau-Ponty, *The Visible and the Invisible*.

30. Sarah Maslen, "Hearing Like a Musician: Integrating Sensory Perception of Self Into a Social Theory of Self-Reflexivity," *Social Psychology Quarterly* 85, no. 1 (2022): 65–83, https://doi.org/10.1177/01902725211071106.

31. Hubert L. Dreyfus and Stuart E. Dreyfus, *Mind Over Machine* (Free Press, 1986).

32. Robert R. Faulkner and Howard S. Becker, *"Do You Know . . . ?" The Jazz Repertoire in Action* (University of Chicago Press, 2009).

33. Faulkner and Becker, *"Do You Know . . . ?"*, 31.

34. Berliner, *Thinking in Jazz*, 67.

35. Berliner, *Thinking in Jazz*, 67.

36. Schuller, *The Compleat Conductor*; Christopher Small, *Musicking: The Meanings of Performing and Listening* (University Press of New England, 1998).

37. Fanny Gribenski, "Tuning Forks as Time Travel Machines: Pitch Standardisation and Historicism," *Sound Studies* 6, no. 2 (2020): 153–73, https://doi.org/10.1080/20551940.2020.1794628.

38. Garfinkel demonstrated that practitioners do not make unambiguous judgments as a result of the rigorous application of rational decision-making techniques. Even in contexts that outsiders may expect are the domain of absolute judgments, such as the assignment of mode of death, practitioners seek only an "account of how a particular person died in society that is adequately told,

sufficiently detailed, clear, etc., for all practical purposes." The employment terms, lines of reporting and supervision, and organizational priorities all serve to position this work as "what 'realistically,' 'practically,' or 'reasonably' needed to be done and could be done, how quickly, with what resources, seeing whom, talking about what, for how long, and so on." See Harold Garfinkel, *Studies in Ethnomethodology* (Prentice-Hall, 1967), 11–24.

39. Tongue position also affects pitch formation, but this is not what Mark means here.

40. Schuller, *The Compleat Conductor*, 6, 17–18.

41. Schuller, *The Compleat Conductor*, 4.

42. Robert R. Faulkner, "Orchestra Interaction: Some Features of Communication and Authority in an Artistic Organization," *Sociological Quarterly* 14, no. 2 (1973): 147–57, https://doi.org/10.1111/j.1533-8525.1973.tb00850.x.

43. Schuller, *The Compleat Conductor*, 16–17.

44. Small, *Musicking*, 68.

45. Schuller, *The Compleat Conductor*, 18.

46. Schuller, *The Compleat Conductor*, 6.

47. Berliner, *Thinking in Jazz*, 314–36.

48. Gary Burton, *Learning to Listen: The Jazz Journey of Gary Burton*, ed. Neil Tesser (Berklee, 2013), 21.

49. Schuller, *The Compleat Conductor*, 7.

50. Schuller, *The Compleat Conductor*, 9.

51. Winther, "The Embodiment of Sound."

52. Michal Pagis, "Producing Intersubjectivity in Silence: An Ethnographic Study of Meditation Practice," *Ethnography* 11, no. 2 (2010): 309–28, https://doi.org/10.1177/1466138109339041.

53. Tolins, "Assessment and Direction"; Weeks, "A Rehearsal of a Beethoven Passage."

54. Drew Foster, "Fighters Who Don't Fight: The Case of Aikido and Somatic Metaphorism," *Qualitative Sociology* 38, no. 2 (2015): 165–83, https://doi.org/10.1007/s11133-015-9305-4.

3. HOW ADVENTURERS HEAR

1. For example, see *127 Hours*, directed by Danny Boyle (2010; Warner Bros., Fox Searchlight); *Touching the Void*, directed by Kevin Macdonald (2003; Pathé).

2. Ralph Storer, *The Joy of Hillwalking* (Luath, 2004), 117. For a discussion of this argument in the context of walking, see Jo Lee Vergunst, "Taking a Trip and

Taking Care in Everyday Life," in *Ways of Walking: Ethnography and Practice on Foot*, ed. Tim Ingold and Jo Lee Vergunst (Ashgate, 2008), 120.

3. Lisa M. Bogardus, "The Bolt Wars: A Social Worlds Perspective on Rock Climbing and Intragroup Conflict," *Journal of Contemporary Ethnography* 41, no. 3 (2011): 283–308, https://doi.org/10.1177/0891241611426429; Matthew Bunn, "Habitus and Disposition in High-Risk Mountain-Climbing," *Body & Society* 22, no. 1 (2016): 92–114, https://doi.org/10.1177/1357034x15612897; Ian Heywood, "Climbing Monsters: Excess and Restraint in Contemporary Rock Climbing," *Leisure Studies* 25, no. 4 (2006): 455–67, https://doi .org/10.1080/02614360500333911; Amanda West and Linda Allin, "Chancing Your Arm: The Meaning of Risk in Rock Climbing," *Sport in Society* 13, nos. 7–8 (2010): 1234–48, https://doi.org/10.1080/17430431003780245; Jennifer Lois, "Peaks and Valleys: The Gendered Emotional Culture of Edgework," *Gender and Society* 15, no. 3 (2001): 381–406, http://www.jstor.org/stable/3081890; J. A. Walter, "Death as Recreation: Armchair Mountaineering," *Leisure Studies* 3, no. 1 (1984): 67–76, https://doi.org/10.1080/02614368400390051.

4. Benjamin C. Ingman, "Bigger Experiences and the Meaning of Adventure," *Journal of Adventure Education and Outdoor Learning* 17, no. 4 (2017): 338–52, https://doi.org/10.1080/14729679.2017.1291356; Leif Inge Magnussen, "Play— The Making of Deep Outdoor Experiences," *Journal of Adventure Education and Outdoor Learning* 12, no. 1 (2012): 25–39, https://doi.org/10.1080/14729679 .2010.532995; Marcus Morse, "Being Alive to the Present: Perceiving Meaning on a Wilderness River Journey," *Journal of Adventure Education and Outdoor Learning* 15, no. 2 (2015): 168–80, https://doi.org/10.1080/14729679.2014.9084 01; James Hardie-Bick and Penny Bonner, "Experiencing Flow, Enjoyment and Risk in Skydiving and Climbing," *Ethnography* 17, no. 3 (2016): 369–87, https://doi.org/10.1177/1466138115609377.

5. Margarethe Kusenbach, "Street Phenomenology: The Go-Along as Ethnographic Research Tool," *Ethnography* 4, no. 3 (2003): 455–85, https://doi .org/10.1177/146613810343007.

6. Jon Krakauer, *Into the Wild* (Anchor, 1996).

7. Catherine Kohler Riessman, *Divorce Talk: Women and Men Make Sense of Personal Relationships* (Rutgers University Press, 1990); Arthur Frank, *The Wounded Storyteller: Body, Illness, and Ethics* (University of Chicago Press, 1995); Calvin Morrill et al., "Telling Tales in School: Youth Culture and Conflict Narratives," *Law & Society Review* 34, no. 3 (2000): 521–65, https:// doi.org/10.2307/3115137.

8. Brian Wattchow, "Moving on an Effortless Journey: Paddling, River-Places and Outdoor Education," *Australian Journal of Outdoor Education* 12, no. 2 (2008): 15; Hannah Macpherson, "Articulating Blind Touch: Thinking Through the Feet," *Senses and Society* 4, no. 2 (2009): 184.

9. Hayden White, "The Value of Narrativity in the Representation of Reality," *Critical Inquiry* 7, no. 1 (1980): 5–27, http://www.jstor.org/stable/1343174; Wolfgang Iser, "The Reading Process: A Phenomenological Approach," *New Literary History* 3, no. 2 (1972): 279–99, https://doi.org/10.2307/468316.

10. Michael Polanyi, *The Tacit Dimension* (University of Chicago Press, 1966), 5.

11. Michael Bull, *Sound Out the City: Personal Stereos and the Management of Everyday Life* (Berg, 2000).

12. For a detailed analysis, see Sarah Maslen, "'You Have Got Such a Beautiful Symphony in Front of You!' Use and Resistance to mobile music Devices Among Adventurers," *Poetics* (2021): 101640, https://doi.org/10.1016/j.poetic .2021.101640.

13. Murray Schafer, "Open Ears," in *The Auditory Culture Reader*, ed. Michael Bull and Les Black (Berg, 2003), 25–39.

14. Aat Vervoorn, *Mountain Solitudes: Solo Journeys in the Southern Alps of New Zealand* (Craig Potton, 2000), 134.

15. Laurence Gonzales, *Deep Survival: Who Lives, Who Dies, and Why* (Norton, 2003); Arno Ilgner, *The Rock Warrior's Way: Mental Training for Climbers* (Desiderata Institute, 2003).

16. Bogardus, "The Bolt Wars"; Bunn, "Habitus and Disposition"; Heywood, "Climbing Monsters"; West and Allin, "Chancing Your Arm"; Lois, "Peaks and Valleys"; Walter, "Death as Recreation."

17. Others have also critiqued the degree to which risk-taking is central to adventuring identity and practice. See Ingman, "Bigger Experiences"; Magnussen, "Play"; Morse, "Being Alive to the Present"; Lee Davidson, "The Calculable and the Incalculable: Narratives of Safety and Danger in the Mountains," *Leisure Sciences* 34, no. 4 (2012): 298–313, https://doi.org/10.1080/01490400.2012.687617.

18. Alex Honnold and David Roberts, *Alone on the Wall: The Ultimate Limits of Adventure* (Pan, 2020).

19. Stephen Lyng, ed., *Edgework: The Sociology of Risk-Taking* (Routledge, 2004).

20. Honnold and Roberts, *Alone on the Wall*.

21. John Geiger, *The Third Man Factor: The Secret to Survival in Extreme Environments* (Text, 2009).

22. Joe Simpson, *Touching the Void* (Jonathan Cape, 1988).

4. HOW MORSE CODE OPERATORS HEAR

1. This idea is discussed in Tom Standage, *The Victorian Internet: The Remarkable Story of the Telegraph and the Nineteenth Century's Online Pioneers* (Walker, 1998). See also Jane Curtis, "The First Internet," *ABC Central Victoria*, March 21, 2011. Morse abbreviations have also been described as precursors to SMS. See Terri-Anne Kingsley, "Dot-Dot Memories," *ABC Central Victoria*, August 23, 2007.

2. McGowan had worked with Samuel Morse.

3. This was only a couple of years after the Colony of Victoria was established as separate from the Colony of New South Wales in 1851. Each had their own independent governments as part of the British Empire. The Commonwealth of Australia was not established until 1901.

4. The last transmission in the eastern state of New South Wales occurred five years earlier, in 1963.

5. A woman named Mrs. Mackenzie made it her personal mission to train women in signaling as part of the war effort. For more on Mrs. Mac and her "girls in green," see David Dufty, *The Secret Code-Breakers of Central Bureau: How Australia's Signals-Intelligence Network Helped Win the Pacific War* (Scribe, 2017).

6. Morse code has long had a connection to the railway network; some of the first lines were installed following the laying-down of the railway lines to address time and traffic management issues.

7. The Perth-to-Eucla line was 2,529 kilometers in length, providing a critical connection between Western Australia and South Australia, which at the time were separate colonies. The Overland Telegraph line that ran from Darwin to Adelaide was 2,896 kilometers long. Perth and Wyndham was perhaps the longest direct line in Australia at around 3,218 kilometers in length.

8. Following Federation in 1901, most Australian Morse equipment was manufactured locally, resulting in variation in design and materials among the PMG, railways, and other networks. Before 1901, most equipment was imported from either Britain or the United States.

9. Operators were susceptible to what was called "glass arm" or "telegraphist's cramp," and the development of a semiautomatic key, the jigger, reduced the strain on operators' hands and arms. With the jigger, operators move their hand and arm side to side rather than up and down.

10. There was also a fully automatic key that formed both dots and dashes, but this was not in common use.

11. Toward the midtwentieth century on this electrical telegraph system, messages transmitted via Morse could also be sent using teletype, teleprinter, and the Murray Multiplex system. These went on to gradually replace Morse transmissions using a key and sounder. Though there are various iterations in machine telegraphy, they have some common features. On the sending end, there was a move away from the Morse key toward a keyboard with keys for each character, which increased the potential sending speed considerably. On the receiving end, the code was printed as perforations on paper tape, which were then translated into alphanumeric characters by an operator.

12. The first wireless message transmitted in Australia occurred in 1918, but the technology was not in common use until World War II.

13. There is also automatic radiotelegraphy which makes use of teleprinters to translate the signals into typed text.

14. This is not the case with numbers, where there is an internal logic.

15. Vanina Leschziner and Gordon Brett, "Beyond Two Minds: Cognitive, Embodied, and Evaluative Processes in Creativity," *Social Psychology Quarterly* 82, no. 4 (2019): 340–66, https://doi.org/10.1177/0190272519851791.

16. Cf. Michal Pagis, *Inward: Vipassana Meditation and the Embodiment of the Self* (University of Chicago Press, 2019).

17. Standage, *The Victorian Internet*, 129–30.

18. This is in keeping with Bryan and Harter's finding that an expert operator could use Morse with "automatic perfection," having the ability to "sense" the message or give it "practically no attention at all." See William Lowe Bryan and Noble Harter, "Studies on the Telegraphic Language: The Acquisition of a Hierarchy of Habits," *Psychological Review* 6, no. 4 (1899): 352.

19. See also Standage, *The Victorian Internet*, 130.

20. Harold Garfinkel, *Studies in Ethnomethodology* (Prentice-Hall, 1967), 11–24.

5. TURNING TO THE SENSED UNCONSCIOUS

1. Jack Katz described what he terms the "visible unconscious" in his analysis of human emotion; see Jack Katz, "Mundane Metamorphoses," chap. 7 in *How Emotions Work* (University of Chicago Press, 1999). See also Jack Katz, "Emotion's Crucible," in *Emotions Matter: A Relational Approach to Emotions*, ed. Dale Spencer et al. (University of Toronto Press, 2012), 15–39.

2. "Ethnomethods" is a nod to Harold Garfinkel and Aaron Cicourel's "ethnomethodology," the study of the practices employed as natural, indispensable, and universal ways to act competently in social life.

3. For a discussion of the use of the term *habitus* by Mauss and Bourdieu and of *habit* by Merleau-Ponty and Dewey, see Nick Crossley, "Habit and Habitus," *Body & Society* 19, nos. 2–3 (2013): 136–61, https://doi.org/10.1177/1357034X12472543.

4. William James, "What Is an Emotion?," *Mind* 9, no. 34 (1884): 195, http://www.jstor.org/stable/2246769.

5. John Dewey, *Human Nature and Conduct* (Dover, 2002), 177.

6. Mauss, "Techniques of the Body," *Economy and Society* 2, no. 1 (1973): 70–88, https://doi.org/10.1080/03085147300000003.

7. Norbert Elias, *The Civilizing Process: Sociogenetic and Psychogenetic Investigations*, 2nd ed., ed. Eric Dunning et al., trans. Edmund Jephcott (Wiley-Blackwell, 2000).

8. Maurice Merleau-Ponty, "Indirect Languages and the Voices of Silence," in *Signs*, trans. Richard C. McCleary (Northwestern University Press, 1964), 39–83.

9. David McNeill, *Hand and Mind: What Gestures Reveal About Thought* (University of Chicago Press, 1992).

10. Michael Polanyi, *The Tacit Dimension* (University of Chicago Press, 1966), 18.

11. Polanyi, *The Tacit Dimension*, 15.

12. Maurice Merleau-Ponty, *Phenomenology of Perception*, trans. Colin Smith (Routledge, 2002), 166.

13. Pierre Bourdieu, *Distinction: A Social Critique of the Judgement of Taste*, trans. Richard Nice (Harvard University Press, 1984).

14. Pierre Bourdieu, *Outline of a Theory of Practice*, trans. Richard Nice (Cambridge University Press, 1977), 94.

15. Loïc Wacquant, *Body and Soul: Notebooks of an Apprentice Boxer* (Oxford University Press, 2004), 59.

16. Wacquant, *Body and Soul*, 59.

17. Wacquant, *Body and Soul*, 64.

18. Wacquant, *Body and Soul*, 65.

19. Wacquant, *Body and Soul*, 117.

20. Matthew Desmond, *On the Fireline: Living and Dying with Wildland Firefighters* (University of Chicago Press, 2007), 170.

21. Desmond, *On the Fireline*, 171.

22. Pierre Bourdieu, *The Logic of Practice*, trans. Richard Nice (Stanford University Press, 1990), 59.

23. Polanyi, *The Tacit Dimension*, 18.

24. Erving Goffman, *Behavior in Public Places: Notes on the Social Organization of Gatherings* (Free Press, 1963), 43.

25. Gary Klein, *Sources of Power: How People Make Decisions* (MIT Press, 1998), 31–32.

26. Merleau-Ponty, *Phenomenology of Perception*, 166.

27. David Sudnow, *Ways of the Hand: The Organization of Improvised Conduct* (Harvard University Press, 1978), 3.

28. Sudnow, *Ways of the Hand*, 8–9.

29. Sudnow, *Ways of the Hand*, xiii.

30. Erin O'Connor, "Embodied Knowledge: The Experience of Meaning and the Struggle Towards Proficiency in Glassblowing," *Ethnography* 6, no. 2 (2005): 189, https://doi.org/10.1177/1466138105057551.

31. Einat Bar-On Cohen, "Kibadachi in Karate: Pain and Crossing Boundaries Within the 'Lived Body' and Within Sociality," *Journal of the Royal Anthropological Institute* 15, no. 3 (2009): 615–16, http://www.jstor.org/stable/40541702.

32. Polanyi, *The Tacit Dimension*, 18.

33. Maurice Merleau-Ponty, *The Visible and the Invisible*, trans. Alphonso Lingis (Northwestern University Press, 1968), 133.

34. Brian Lande, "Breathing Like a Soldier: Culture Incarnate," *Sociological Review* 55, no. S1 (2007): 101, https://doi.org/10.1111/j.1467-954X.2007.00695.x.

35. Michal Pagis, "Producing Intersubjectivity in Silence: An Ethnographic Study of Meditation Practice," *Ethnography* 11, no. 2 (2010): 309–28, https://doi.org/10.1177/1466138109339041.

36. Lev Vygotsky, *Mind in Society: The Development of Higher Psychological Processes* (Harvard University Press, 1978).

37. Patricia Greenfield, "Children, Material Culture and Weaving: Historical Change and Developmental Change," in *Children and Material Culture*, ed. Joanna Sofaer Derevenski (Routledge, 2000), 76.

38. Rachel Prentice, "Drilling Surgeons: The Social Lessons of Embodied Surgical Learning," *Science, Technology & Human Values* 32, no. 5 (2007): 534–53, https://doi.org/10.1177/0895904805303201.

39. Giovanni Buccino et al., "Neural Circuits Underlying Imitation Learning of Hand Actions: An Event-Related fMRI Study," *Neuron* 42, no. 2 (2004): 323, https://doi.org/10.1016/S0896-6273(04)00181-3.

40. Greg Downey, "Scaffolding Imitation in Capoeira: Physical Education and Enculturation in an Afro-Brazilian Art," *American Anthropologist* 110, no. 2 (2008): 204–13, https://doi.org/10.1111/j.1548-1433.2008.00026.x.

41. Frederick Turner and Ernst Pöppel, "The Neural Lyre: Poetic Meter, the Brain, and Time," *Poetry* 142, no. 5 (1983): 277–309, http://www.jstor.org/stable/20599567; Barbara Tillmann and W. Jay Dowling, "Memory Decreases for

Prose, but Not for Poetry," *Memory & Cognition* 35, no. 4 (2007): 628–39, https://doi.org/10.3758/BF03193301.

42. Catherine Robson, "Standing on the Burning Deck: Poetry, Performance, History," *PMLA* 120, no. 1 (2005): 159, http://www.jstor.org/stable/25486150.

43. Robson, "Standing on the Burning Deck," 150–51.

44. Anna Harris, *A Sensory Education* (Routledge, 2021), 52.

45. Geneviève Teil, "Amateurs' Exploration of Wine: A Pragmatic Study of Taste," *Theory, Culture & Society* 38, no. 5 (2021): 143, https://doi.org/10.1177/02632764211029347.

46. Amateurs use similar analogical tasting strategies in the case of coffee; see Giolo Fele and Kenneth Liberman, "Some Discovered Practices of Lay Coffee Drinkers," *Symbolic Interaction* 44, no. 1 (2021): 40–62, https://doi.org/10.1002/symb.486.

47. Marcus Aldredge, "Negotiating and Practicing Performance: An Ethnographic Study of a Musical Open Mic in Brooklyn, New York," *Symbolic Interaction* 29, no. 1 (2006): 109–17, https://doi.org/10.1525/si.2006.29.1.109.

48. Sibyl Kleiner, "Thinking with the Mind, Syncing with the Body: Ballet as Symbolic and Nonsymbolic Interaction," *Symbolic Interaction* 32, no. 3 (2009): 236–59, https://doi.org/10.1525/si.2009.32.3.236.

49. On runners' seeing of self in shop windows, see John Hockey, "Knowing the 'Going': The Sensory Evaluation of Distance Running," *Qualitative Research in Sport, Exercise and Health* 5, no. 1 (2013): 127–41, https://doi.org/10.1080/2159676X.2012.693531.

50. John Hockey, "Sensing the Run: The Senses and Distance Running," *Senses and Society* 1, no. 2 (2006): 183–201.

51. Peter Weeks, "A Rehearsal of a Beethoven Passage: An Analysis of Correction Talk," *Research on Language and Social Interaction* 29, no. 3 (1996): 247–90, https://doi.org/10.1207/s15327973rlsi2903_3.

52. Charles Goodwin, "The Blackness of Black: Color Categories as Situated Practice," in *Discourse, Tools and Reasoning: Essays on Situated Cognition*, ed. Lauren B. Resnick et al. (Springer, 1997), 127.

53. For an analysis of historical medical textbooks, see Melissa Van Drie, "Training the Auscultative Ear," *Senses and Society* 8, no. 2 (2013): 165–91, https://doi.org/10.2752/174589313X13589681981019.

54. Tony Bennett et al., *Accounting for Tastes: Australian Everyday Cultures* (Cambridge University Press, 1999).

55. For example, see Katz, *How Emotions Work*.

56. Erving Goffman, *Interaction Ritual: Essays on Face-to-Face Behavior* (Pantheon, 1967), 3; Harvey Sacks, *Lectures on Conversation*, vols. 1–2, ed. Gail Jefferson (Wiley-Blackwell, 1992), 26.

57. Michael F. DeLand, "Men and Their Moments: Character-Driven Ethnography and Interaction Analysis in a Park Basketball Rule Dispute," *Social Psychology Quarterly* (2021): 01902725211004894, https://doi.org/10.1177/01902725211004894.

58. Jackson Tolins, "Assessment and Direction Through Nonlexical Vocalizations in Music Instruction," *Research on Language and Social Interaction* 46, no. 1 (2013): 47–64, https://doi.org/10.1080/08351813.2013.753721; Lorenza Mondada, *Sensing in Social Interaction: The Taste for Cheese in Gourmet Shops* (Cambridge University Press, 2021).

59. Weeks, "A Rehearsal of a Beethoven Passage"; Christian Heath, "Body Work: The Collaborative Production of the Clinical Object," in *Communication in Medical Care: Interaction Between Primary Care Physicians and Patients*, ed. John Heritage and Douglas Maynard (University of Cambridge Press, 2006), 185–213.

60. DeLand, "Men and Their Moments."

REFERENCES

Abath, André J. "Merleau-Ponty and the Problem of Synaesthesia." In *Sensory Blending: On Synaesthesia and Related Phenomena*. Ed. Ophelia Deroy. Oxford University Press, 2017.

Alam, Uazman, Omar Asghar, Sohail Q. Khan, Sajad Hayat, and Rayaz A. Malik. "Cardiac Auscultation: An Essential Clinical Skill in Decline." *British Journal of Cardiology* 17, no. 1 (2010): 8–10.

Aldredge, Marcus. "Negotiating and Practicing Performance: An Ethnographic Study of a Musical Open Mic in Brooklyn, New York." *Symbolic Interaction* 29, no. 1 (2006): 109–17. https://doi.org/10.1525/si.2006.29.1.109.

Armstrong, David. "Clinical Sense and Clinical Science." *Social Science & Medicine (1967)* 11, nos. 11–13 (1977): 599–601. https://doi.org/10.1016/0037-7856(77)90041-5.

Barad, Karen. *Meeting the Universe Halfway: Quantum Physics and the Entanglement of Matter and Meaning*. Duke University Press, 2007.

Barenboim, Daniel. *A Life in Music*. Rev. ed. Ed. Michael Lewin and Phillip Huscher. Weidenfeld & Nicolson, 2002.

Beauchamp, Michael S., and Tony Ro. "Neural Substrates of Sound–Touch Synesthesia After a Thalamic Lesion." *Journal of Neuroscience* 28, no. 50 (2008): 13696. https://doi.org/10.1523/JNEUROSCI.3872-08.2008.

Becker, Howard. "A School Is a Lousy Place to Learn Anything In." *American Behavioral Scientist* 16, no. 1 (1972): 85.

Becker, Howard S. *Outsiders: Studies in the Sociology of Deviance*. Free Press, 1963.

Bennett, Tony, Michael Emmison, and John Frow. *Accounting for Tastes: Australian Everyday Cultures*. Cambridge University Press, 1999.

Berg, Marc. *Rationalizing Medical Work: Decision-Support Techniques and Medical Practices*. MIT Press, 1997.

Berger, Harris. *Metal, Rock, and Jazz: Perception and Phenomenology of Musical Experience*. Wesleyan University Press, 1999.

Berliner, Paul F. *Thinking in Jazz: The Infinite Art of Improvisation*. University of Chicago Press, 1994.

Bijsterveld, Karin. "Breaking Into a World of Perfection: Innovation in Today's Classical Musical Instruments." *Social Studies of Science* 34, no. 5 (2004): 649–74.

——. *Mechanical Sound: Technology, Culture, and Public Problems of Noise in the Twentieth Century*. MIT Press, 2008.

Billett, Stephen. "Workplace Participatory Practices: Conceptualising Workplaces as Learning Environments." *Journal of Workplace Learning* 16, no. 6 (2004): 312–24. https://doi.org/10.1108/13665620410550295.

Blume, Stuart S. "Histories of Cochlear Implantation." *Social Science & Medicine* 49, no. 9 (1999): 1257–68. https://doi.org/10.1016/S0277-9536(99)00164-1.

Bogardus, Lisa M. "The Bolt Wars: A Social Worlds Perspective on Rock Climbing and Intragroup Conflict." *Journal of Contemporary Ethnography* 41, no. 3 (2011): 283–308. https://doi.org/10.1177/0891241611426429.

Boud, David, Romy Lawson, and Darrall G. Thompson. "Does Student Engagement in Self-Assessment Calibrate Their Judgement Over Time?" *Assessment & Evaluation in Higher Education* 38, no. 8 (2013): 941–56. https://doi.org/10.1080/02602938.2013.769198.

Bourdieu, Pierre. *Distinction: A Social Critique of the Judgement of Taste*. Trans. Richard Nice. Harvard University Press, 1984.

——. *The Logic of Practice*. Trans. Richard Nice. Stanford University Press, 1990.

——. *Outline of a Theory of Practice*. Trans. Richard Nice. Cambridge University Press, 1977.

Boyle, Danny, dir. *127 Hours*. Warner Bros., Fox Searchlight, 2010.

Brang, D., E. M. Hubbard, S. Coulson, M. Huang, and V. S. Ramachandran. "Magnetoencephalography Reveals Early Activation of V4 in Grapheme-Color Synesthesia." *NeuroImage* 53, no. 1 (2010): 268–74. https://doi.org/10.1016/j.neuroimage.2010.06.008.

Brown, John Seely, and Paul Duguid. "Organizational Learning and Communities of Practice: Toward a Unified View of Working, Learning, and Innovation." *Organization Science* 2, no. 1 (1991): 40–57.

Bryan, William Lowe, and Noble Harter. "Studies on the Telegraphic Language: The Acquisition of a Hierarchy of Habits." *Psychological Review* 6, no. 4 (1899): 345–75.

Buccino, Giovanni, Stefan Vogt, Afra Ritzl, et al. "Neural Circuits Underlying Imitation Learning of Hand Actions: An Event-Related fMRI Study." *Neuron* 42, no. 2 (2004): 323–34. https://doi.org/10.1016/S0896-6273(04)00181-3.

Bull, Michael. *Sound Out the City: Personal Stereos and the Management of Everyday Life.* Berg, 2000.

Bunn, Matthew. "Habitus and Disposition in High-Risk Mountain-Climbing." *Body & Society* 22, no. 1 (2016): 92–114. https://doi.org/10.1177/1357034x15612897.

Burton, Gary. *Learning to Listen: The Jazz Journey of Gary Burton.* Ed. Neil Tesser. Berklee, 2013.

Butler, Judith. *Bodies That Matter: On the Discursive Limits of "Sex."* Routledge, 1993.

——. *Gender Trouble: Feminism and the Subversion of Identity.* Routledge, 1999.

Cahill, Spencer E., William Distler, Cynthia Lachowetz, Andrea Meaney, Robyn Tarallo, and Teena Willard. "Meanwhile Backstage: Public Bathrooms and the Interaction Order." *Urban Life* 14, no. 1 (1985): 33–58. https://doi.org/10.1177/0098303985014001002.

Carmel, Simon. "The Craft of Intensive Care Medicine." *Sociology of Health & Illness* 35, no. 5 (2013): 731–45. https://doi.org/10.1111/j.1467-9566.2012.01524.x.

Carter, Paul. "Ambiguous Traces, Mishearing and Auditory Space." In *Hearing Cultures: Essays on Sound, Listening and Modernity.* Ed. Veit Erlmann. Berg, 2004.

Cartwright, Lisa. *Screening the Body: Tracing Medicine's Visual Culture.* University of Minnesota Press, 1995.

Choksy, Lois. *The Kodály Method I: Comprehensive Music Education.* 3rd ed. Prentice Hall, 1999.

Christy, Noble, and Billett Stephen. "Learning to Prescribe Through Co-working: Junior Doctors, Pharmacists and Consultants." *Medical Education* 51, no. 4 (2017): 442–51. https://doi.org/10.1111/medu.13227.

Cohen, Einat Bar-On. "Kibadachi in Karate: Pain and Crossing Boundaries Within the 'Lived Body' and Within Sociality." *Journal of the Royal Anthropological Institute* 15, no. 3 (2009): 610–29. http://www.jstor.org/stable/40541702.

Collins, Harry. *Tacit and Explicit Knowledge.* University of Chicago Press, 2010.

Collins, Harry, and Robert Evans. *Rethinking Expertise.* University of Chicago Press, 2007.

Cooper, J. B., and V. R. Taqueti. "A Brief History of the Development of Mannequin Simulators for Clinical Education and Training." *BMJ Quality and Safety in Health Care* 13 (2004): i11–i18. https://doi.org/10.1136/qshc.2004.009886.

Corbin, Alain. *The Foul and the Fragrant: Odor and the French Social Imagination.* Harvard University Press, 1988.

——. *Village Bells: Sound and Meaning in the Nineteenth-Century French Countryside.* Ed. Lawrence D. Kritzman. Trans. Martin Thom. Columbia University Press, 1998.

Croft, Lori B., W. Lane Duvall, and Martin E. Goldman. "A Pilot Study of the Clinical Impact of Hand-Carried Cardiac Ultrasound in the Medical Clinic." *Echocardiography: A Journal of Cardiovascular Ultrasound and Allied Techniques* 23, no. 6 (2006): 439–46.

Crossley, Nick. "Habit and Habitus." *Body & Society* 19, nos. 2–3 (2013): 136–61. https://doi.org/10.1177/1357034X12472543.

Curtis, Jane. "The First Internet." *ABC Central Victoria*, March, 21, 2011.

Cytowic, Richard. *Synaesthesia: A Union of the Senses.* Springer-Verlag, 1989.

Davidson, Lee. "The Calculable and the Incalculable: Narratives of Safety and Danger in the Mountains." *Leisure Sciences* 34, no. 4 (2012): 298–313. https://doi.org/10.1080/01490400.2012.687617.

DeCara, Jeanne M., Roberto M. Lang, and Kirk T. Spencer. "The Hand-Carried Echocardiographic Device as an Aid to the Physical Examination." *Echocardiography: A Journal of Cardiovascular Ultrasound and Allied Techniques* 20, no. 5 (2003): 477–85.

DeLand, Michael F. "Men and Their Moments: Character-Driven Ethnography and Interaction Analysis in a Park Basketball Rule Dispute." *Social Psychology Quarterly* (2021): 0190272521004894. https://doi.org/10.1177/0190272521004894.

Demorest, Steven. *Building Choral Excellence: Teaching Sight-Singing in the Choral Rehearsal.* Oxford University Press, 2003.

DeNora, Tia. *Music in Everyday Life.* Cambridge University Press, 2000.

Desmond, Matthew. *On the Fireline: Living and Dying with Wildland Firefighters.* University of Chicago Press, 2007.

Dewey, John. *Human Nature and Conduct.* Dover, 2002.

Dijck, José van. *The Transparent Body: A Cultural Analysis of Medical Imaging.* University of Washington Press, 2011.

Dijksterhuis, Ap, and Loran F. Nordgren. "A Theory of Unconscious Thought." *Perspectives on Psychological Science* 1, no. 2 (2006): 95–109. https://doi.org/10.1111/j.1745-6916.2006.00007.x.

Dijksterhuis, Ap, and Zeger van Olden. "On the Benefits of Thinking Unconsciously: Unconscious Thought Can Increase Post-choice Satisfaction." *Journal of Experimental Social Psychology* 42, no. 5 (2006): 627–31. https://doi.org/10.1016/j.jesp.2005.10.008.

Dixon, Mike J., Daniel Smilek, and Philip M. Merikle. "Not All Synaesthetes Are Created Equal: Projector Versus Associator Synaesthetes." *Cognitive, Affective & Behavioral Neuroscience* 4, no. 3 (2004): 335–43. https://doi.org/10.3758/CABN.4.3.335.

Downey, Greg. "Scaffolding Imitation in Capoeira: Physical Education and Enculturation in an Afro-Brazilian Art." *American Anthropologist* 110, no. 2 (2008):
204–13. https://doi.org/10.1111/j.1548-1433.2008.00026.x.

Dreyfus, Hubert L., and Stuart E. Dreyfus. *Mind Over Machine*. Free Press, 1986.

Driver, Rosalind, Hilary Asoko, John Leach, Philip Scott, and Eduardo Mortimer.
"Constructing Scientific Knowledge in the Classroom." *Educational Researcher* 23,
no. 7 (1994): 5–12. https://doi.org/10.3102/0013189X023007005.

Duden, Barbara. *Disembodying Women: Perspectives on Pregnancy and the Unborn.*
Trans. Lee Hoinacki. Harvard University Press, 1993.

Dufty, David. *The Secret Code-Breakers of Central Bureau: How Australia's Signals-
Intelligence Network Helped Win the Pacific War.* Scribe, 2017.

Eisler, Hanns, and Theodor Adorno. "The Politics of Hearing." In *Audio Culture:
Readings in Modern Music.* Ed. Christoph Cox and Daniel Warner. Continuum, 2007.

Elias, Norbert. *The Civilizing Process: Sociogenetic and Psychogenetic Investigations.*
2nd ed. Ed. Eric Dunning, Johan Goudsblom, and Stephen Mennell. Trans.
Edmund Jephcott. Wiley-Blackwell, 2000.

Emerson, Joan. "Behavior in Private Places: Sustaining Definitions of Reality in Gynecological Examinations." In *Readings on Ethical and Social Issues in
Biomedicine.* Ed. Richard Wertz. Prentice-Hall, 1973.

Eraut, Michael. "Transfer of Knowledge Between Education and Workplace
Settings." In *Knowledge, Values and Educational Policy: A Critical Perspective.*
Ed. Harry Daniels, Hugh Lauder, and Jill Porter. Routledge, 2009.

Erlmann, Veit, ed. *Hearing Cultures: Essays on Sound, Listening and Modernity.*
Berg, 2004.

Faulkner, Robert R. "Orchestra Interaction: Some Features of Communication and
Authority in an Artistic Organization." *Sociological Quarterly* 14, no. 2 (1973):
147–57. https://doi.org/10.1111/j.1533-8525.1973.tb00850.x.

Faulkner, Robert R., and Howard S. Becker. *"Do You Know . . . ?" The Jazz Repertoire
in Action.* University of Chicago Press, 2009.

Favrat, Bernard, Alain Pecoud, and Andres Jaussi. "Teaching Cardiac Auscultation
to Trainees in Internal Medicine and Family Practice: Does It Work?" *Medical
Education* 4, no. 5 (2004): 1–7.

Fele, Giolo, and Kenneth Liberman. "Some Discovered Practices of Lay Coffee
Drinkers." *Symbolic Interaction* 44, no. 1 (2021): 40–62. https://doi.org/10.1002
/symb.486.

Fitzgerald, Faith. "Bedside Teaching." *Western Journal of Medicine* 158, no. 4 (1993):
418–20. http://www.ncbi.nlm.nih.gov/pmc/articles/PMC1022080/.

——. "Physical Diagnosis Versus Modern Technology: A Review." *Western Journal of Medicine* 152, no. 4 (1990): 377–82. http://www.ncbi.nlm.nih.gov/pmc/articles /PMC1002356/.

Foster, Drew. "Fighters Who Don't Fight: The Case of Aikido and Somatic Metaphorism." *Qualitative Sociology* 38, no. 2 (2015): 165–83. https://doi.org/10.1007 /s11133-015-9305-4.

Foucault, Michel. *Discipline and Punish: The Birth of the Prison*. Trans. Alan Sheridan. Penguin, 1977.

——. *The History of Sexuality*, vol. 1. Trans. Robert Hurley. Pantheon, 1978.

——. *Madness and Civilization: A History of Insanity in the Age of Reason*. Trans. Richard Howard. Routledge, 1967.

Frank, Arthur. *The Wounded Storyteller: Body, Illness, and Ethics*. University of Chicago Press, 1995.

Frank, Jason R., Linda S. Snell, Olle Ten Cate, et al. "Competency-Based Medical Education: Theory to Practice." *Medical Teacher* 32, no. 8 (2010): 638–45. https:// doi.org/10.3109/0142159X.2010.501190.

Frey-Clark, Marta. "Pitch Systems and Curwen Hand Signs: A Review of Literature." *Update: Applications of Research in Music Education* 36, no. 1 (2017): 59–65. https://doi.org/10.1177/8755123316689812.

Gallagher, Shaun. *How the Body Shapes the Mind*. Oxford University Press, 2012.

Garcia, Luis-Manuel. "Beats, Flesh, and Grain: Sonic Tactility and Affect in Electronic Dance Music." *Sound Studies* 1, no. 1 (2015): 59–76. https://doi.org/10.1080 /20551940.2015.1079072.

Gardner, John, and Clare Williams. "Corporal Diagnostic Work and Diagnostic Spaces: Clinicians' Use of Space and Bodies During Diagnosis." *Sociology of Health & Illness* 37, no. 5 (2015): 765–81. https://doi.org/10.1111/1467-9566.12233.

Garfinkel, Harold. *Studies in Ethnomethodology*. Prentice-Hall, 1967.

Geiger, John. *The Third Man Factor: The Secret to Survival in Extreme Environments*. Text, 2009.

Glennie, Evelyn. *Good Vibrations: My Autobiography*. Hutchinson, 1990.

Goffman, Erving. *Behavior in Public Places: Notes on the Social Organization of Gatherings*. Free Press, 1963.

——. *Forms of Talk*. University of Pennsylvania Press, 1981.

——. *Interaction Ritual: Essays on Face-to-Face Behavior*. Pantheon, 1967.

——. *The Presentation of Self in Everyday Life*. Anchor, 1959.

——. "Where the Action Is." In *Interaction Ritual: Essays on Face-to-Face Behaviour*. Penguin, 1967.

Goldman, Alvin I. "A Moderate Approach to Embodied Cognitive Science." *Review of Philosophy and Psychology* 3, no. 1 (2012): 71–88. https://doi.org/10.1007/s13164-012-0089-0.

Goldsmith, Rosalie, Keith Willey, and David Boud. "Investigating Invisible Writing Practices in the Engineering Curriculum Using Practice Architectures." *European Journal of Engineering Education* (2017): 1–14. https://doi.org/10.1080/03043797.2017.1405241.

Gonzales, Laurence. *Deep Survival: Who Lives, Who Dies, and Why*. Norton, 2003.

González-Grandón, Ximena, Andrea Falcón-Cortés, and Gabriel Ramos-Fernández. "Proprioception in Action: A Matter of Ecological and Social Interaction." *Frontiers in Psychology* 11 (2021). https://doi.org/10.3389/fpsyg.2020.569403.

Goodwin, Charles. "The Blackness of Black: Color Categories as Situated Practice." In *Discourse, Tools and Reasoning: Essays on Situated Cognition*. Ed. Lauren B. Resnick, Roger Säljö, Clotilde Pontecorvo, and Barbara Burge. Springer, 1997.

——. "Professional Vision." *American Anthropologist* 96, no. 3 (1994): 606–33. https://doi.org/10.1525/aa.1994.96.3.02a00100.

Goodwin, Dawn. "Sensing the Way: Embodied Dimensions of Diagnostic Work." In *Ethnographies of Diagnostic Work: Dimensions of Transformative Practice*. Ed. Monika Buscher, Dawn Goodwin, and Jessica Mesman. Palgrave Macmillan, 2010.

Greenfield, Patricia. "Children, Material Culture and Weaving: Historical Change and Developmental Change." In *Children and Material Culture*. Ed. Joanna Sofaer Derevenski. Routledge, 2000.

Gribenski, Fanny. "Tuning Forks as Time Travel Machines: Pitch Standardisation and Historicism." *Sound Studies* 6, no. 2 (2020): 153–73. https://doi.org/10.1080/20551940.2020.1794628.

Grossenbacher, Peter G., and Christopher T. Lovelace. "Mechanisms of Synesthesia: Cognitive and Physiological Constraints." *Trends in Cognitive Sciences* 5, no. 1 (2001): 36–41. https://doi.org/10.1016/S1364-6613(00)01571-0.

Grosz, Elizabeth. *Volatile Bodies: Towards a Corporeal Feminism*. Allen & Unwin, 1994.

Hammer, Gili. "'You Can Learn Merely by Listening to the Way a Patient Walks Through the Door': The Transmission of Sensory Medical Knowledge." *Medical Anthropology Quarterly* 32, no. 1 (2018): 138–54. https://doi.org/10.1111/maq.12366.

Haraway, Donna. "A Cyborg Manifesto: Science, Technology, and Socialist-Feminism in the Late Twentieth Century." In *Simians, Cyborgs and Women: The Reinvention of Nature*. Routledge, 1991.

Hardie-Bick, James, and Penny Bonner. "Experiencing Flow, Enjoyment and Risk in Skydiving and Climbing." *Ethnography* 17, no. 3 (2016): 369–87. https://doi.org/10.1177/1466138115609377.

Harris, Anna. "In a Moment of Mismatch: Overseas Doctors' Adjustments in New Hospital Environments." *Sociology of Health & Illness* 33, no. 2 (2011): 308–20. https://doi.org/10.1111/j.1467-9566.2010.01307.x.

——. "Listening-Touch, Affect and the Crafting of Medical Bodies Through Percussion." *Body & Society* 22, no. 1 (2016): 31–61. https://doi.org/10.1177/1357034X15604031.

——. *A Sensory Education*. Routledge, 2021.

Harrison, John. *Synaesthesia: The Strangest Thing*. Oxford University Press, 2001.

Haviland, John B. "Master Speakers, Master Gesturers: A String Quartet Master Class." In *Gesture and the Dynamic Dimension of Language: Essays in Honor of David McNeill*. Ed. Susan D. Duncan, Elena T. Levy, and Justine Cassell. John Benjamins, 2007.

Hayward, Eva. "Fingeryeyes: Impressions of Cup Corals." *Cultural Anthropology* 25, no. 4 (2010): 577–99. https://doi.org/10.1111/j.1548-1360.2010.01070.x.

Heath, Christian. "Body Work: The Collaborative Production of the Clinical Object." In *Communication in Medical Care: Interaction Between Primary Care Physicians and Patients*. Ed. John Heritage and Douglas Maynard. University of Cambridge Press, 2006.

——. "Pain Talk: The Expression of Suffering in the Medical Consultation." *Social Psychology Quarterly* 52, no. 2 (1989): 113–25. https://doi.org/10.2307/2786911.

Hegarty, Paul. *Noise/Music: A History*. Continuum, 2007.

Hennion, Antoine. "Music Lovers: Taste as Performance." *Theory, Culture & Society* 18, no. 5 (2001): 1–22. https://doi.org/10.1177/02632760122051940.

Heywood, Ian. "Climbing Monsters: Excess and Restraint in Contemporary Rock Climbing." *Leisure Studies* 25, no. 4 (2006): 455–67. https://doi.org/10.1080/02614360500333911.

Hinton, Devon E., David Howes, and Laurence J. Kirmayer. "Toward a Medical Anthropology of Sensations: Definitions and Research Agenda." *Transcultural Psychiatry* 45, no. 2 (2008): 142–62. https://doi.org/10.1177/1363461508089763.

Hockey, John. "Knowing the 'Going': The Sensory Evaluation of Distance Running." *Qualitative Research in Sport, Exercise and Health* 5, no. 1 (2013): 127–41. https://doi.org/10.1080/2159676X.2012.693531.

——. "Sensing the Run: The Senses and Distance Running." *Senses and Society* 1, no. 2 (2006): 183–201.

Holt, John. *Never Too Late: A Musical Life Story*. Merloyd Lawrence, 1978.

Honnold, Alex, and David Roberts. *Alone on the Wall: The Ultimate Limits of Adventure*. Pan, 2020.

Howell, Joel D. *Technology in the Hospital: Transforming Patient Care in the Early Twentieth Century*. Johns Hopkins University Press, 1995.

Howes, David, and Constance Classen. *Ways of Sensing: Understanding the Senses in Society*. Routledge, 2013.

Hubbard, Edward M., and V. S. Ramachandran. "Neurocognitive Mechanisms of Synesthesia." *Neuron* 48, no. 3 (2005): 509–20. https://doi.org/10.1016/j.neuron.2005.10.012.

Ihde, Don. *Listening and Voice: Phenomenologies of Sound*. 2nd ed. State University of New York Press, 2007.

Ilgner, Arno. *The Rock Warrior's Way: Mental Training for Climbers*. Desiderata Institute, 2003.

Ingersoll, Brooke, and Anna Dvortcsak. *Teaching Social Communication to Children with Autism: A Practitioner's Guide to Parent Training*. Guilford, 2010.

Ingman, Benjamin C. "Bigger Experiences and the Meaning of Adventure." *Journal of Adventure Education and Outdoor Learning* 17, no. 4 (2017): 338–52. https://doi.org/10.1080/14729679.2017.1291356.

Ingold, Tim. *The Perception of the Environment: Essays on Livelihood, Dwelling, and Skill*. Routledge, 2000.

Iser, Wolfgang. "The Reading Process: A Phenomenological Approach." *New Literary History* 3, no. 2 (1972): 279–99. https://doi.org/10.2307/468316.

James, William. "What Is an Emotion?" *Mind* 9, no. 34 (1884): 188–205. http://www.jstor.org/stable/2246769.

Jay, Martin. *Downcast Eyes: The Denigration of Vision in Twentieth-Century French Thought*. University of California Press, 1993.

Johnson, Ericka. "Surgical Simulators and Simulated Surgeons: Reconstituting Medical Practice and Practitioners in Simulations." *Social Studies of Science* 37, no. 4 (2007): 585–608. https://doi.org/10.1177/0306312706072179.

Katz, Jack. "Emotion's Crucible." In *Emotions Matter: A Relational Approach to Emotions*. Ed. Dale Spencer, Kevin Walby, and Alan Hunt. University of Toronto Press, 2012.

——. *How Emotions Work*. University of Chicago Press, 1999.

——. "On Becoming an Ethnographer." *Journal of Contemporary Ethnography* 48, no. 1 (2018): 16–50. https://doi.org/10.1177/0891241618777801.

——. *Seductions of Crime: Moral and Sensual Attractions in Doing Evil*. Basic Books, 1988.

Kingsley, Terri-Anne. "Dot-Dot Memories." *ABC Central Victoria*, August 23, 2007.

Klein, Gary. *Sources of Power: How People Make Decisions*. MIT Press, 1998.

Kleiner, Sibyl. "Thinking with the Mind, Syncing with the Body: Ballet as Symbolic and Nonsymbolic Interaction." *Symbolic Interaction* 32, no. 3 (2009): 236–59. https://doi.org/10.1525/si.2009.32.3.236.

Krakauer, Jon. *Into the Wild*. Anchor, 1996.

Kusenbach, Margarethe. "Street Phenomenology: The Go-Along as Ethnographic Research Tool." *Ethnography* 4, no. 3 (2003): 455–85. https://doi.org/10.1177/14661381034343007.

LaCombe, M. A. "On Bedside Teaching." *Annals of Internal Medicine* 127, no. 2 (1997): 173–73. https://doi.org/10.7326/0003-4819-127-2-199707150-00047.

Laënnec, René. *A Treatise on Diseases of the Chest and on Mediate Auscultation*. Trans. John Forbes. Samuel Wood & Sons and Collins and Hannay, 1830.

Lakoff, George, and Mark Johnson. *Metaphors We Live By*. University of Chicago Press, 1980.

Lam, Alice. "Tacit Knowledge, Organizational Learning and Societal Institutions: An Integrated Framework." *Organization Studies* 21, no. 3 (2000): 487–513.

Lande, Brian. "Breathing Like a Soldier: Culture Incarnate." *Sociological Review* 55, no. S1 (2007): 95–108. https://doi.org/10.1111/j.1467-954X.2007.00695.x.

——. "'Laying Hands' and Learning to Touch and Grab in the Police Academy." In *The Oxford Handbook of the Sociology of Body and Embodiment*. Ed. Natalie Boero and Katherine Mason. Oxford University Press, 2020.

Leschziner, Vanina, and Gordon Brett. "Beyond Two Minds: Cognitive, Embodied, and Evaluative Processes in Creativity." *Social Psychology Quarterly* 82, no. 4 (2019): 340–66. https://doi.org/10.1177/0190272519851791.

Levitin, Daniel. *This Is Your Brain on Music: The Science of a Human Obsession*. Dutton, 2006.

Lois, Jennifer. "Peaks and Valleys: The Gendered Emotional Culture of Edgework." *Gender and Society* 15, no. 3 (2001): 381–406. http://www.jstor.org/stable/3081890.

Lyng, Stephen, ed. *Edgework: The Sociology of Risk-Taking*. Routledge, 2004.

Macdonald, Kevin, dir. *Touching the Void*. Pathé, 2003.

Macpherson, Hannah. "Articulating Blind Touch: Thinking Through the Feet." *Senses and Society* 4, no. 2 (2009): 179–94.

Magnussen, Leif Inge. "Play—The Making of Deep Outdoor Experiences." *Journal of Adventure Education and Outdoor Learning* 12, no. 1 (2012): 25–39. https://doi.org/10.1080/14729679.2010.532995.

Malhotra, Valerie Ann. "The Social Accomplishment of Music in a Symphony Orchestra: A Phenomenological Analysis." *Qualitative Sociology* 4, no. 2 (1981): 102–25. https://doi.org/10.1007/BF00987214.

Mangione, Salvatore. "Cardiac Auscultatory Skills of Physicians-in-Training: A Comparison of Three English-Speaking Countries." *American Journal of Medicine* 110 (2001): 210–16.

Mann, Anna, Annemarie Mol, Priya Satalkar, et al. "Mixing Methods, Tasting Fingers: Notes on an Ethnographic Experiment." *HAU: Journal of Ethnographic Theory* 1, no. 1 (2011): 221–43. https://doi.org/10.14318/hau1.1.009.

Maslen, Sarah. "Hearing Like a Musician: Integrating Sensory Perception of Self Into a Social Theory of Self-Reflexivity." *Social Psychology Quarterly* 85, no. 1 (2022): 65–83. https://doi.org/10.1177/01902725211071106.

——. "Sensory Work of Diagnosis: A Crisis of Legitimacy." *Senses & Society* 11, no. 2 (2016): 158–76. https://doi.org/10.1080/17458927.2016.1190065.

——. "'You Have Got Such a Beautiful Symphony in Front of You!' Use and Resistance to Mobile Music Devices Among Adventurers." *Poetics* (2021): 101640. https://doi.org/ 10.1016/j.poetic.2021.101640.

Mauldin, Laura. *Made to Hear: Cochlear Implants and Raising Deaf Children*. University of Minnesota Press, 2016.

Mauss, Marcel. "Techniques of the Body." *Economy and Society* 2, no. 1 (1973): 70–88. https://doi.org/10.1080/03085147300000003.

McNeill, David. *Hand and Mind: What Gestures Reveal About Thought*. University of Chicago Press, 1992.

Mead, George Herbert. *Mind, Self, and Society: From the Standpoint of a Social Behaviorist*. University of Chicago Press, 1934.

Merleau-Ponty, Maurice. "Indirect Languages and the Voices of Silence." In *Signs*. Trans. Richard C. McCleary. Northwestern University Press, 1964.

——. *Phenomenology of Perception*. Trans. Colin Smith. Routledge, 2002.

——. *The Visible and the Invisible*. Trans. Alphonso Lingis. Northwestern University Press, 1968.

Mondada, Lorenza. *Sensing in Social Interaction: The Taste for Cheese in Gourmet Shops*. Cambridge University Press, 2021.

Mondillo, S., P. Ballo, and V. Zacà. "Seagulls Flying in the Echo Lab." *Heart* 90, no. 11 (2004): 1247. https://doi.org/10.1136/hrt.2004.037200.

Morrill, Calvin, Christine Yalda, Madelaine Adelman, Michael Musheno, and Cindy Bejarano. "Telling Tales in School: Youth Culture and Conflict Narratives." *Law & Society Review* 34, no. 3 (2000): 521–65. https://doi.org/10.2307/3115137.

Morse, Marcus. "Being Alive to the Present: Perceiving Meaning on a Wilderness River Journey." *Journal of Adventure Education and Outdoor Learning* 15, no. 2 (2015): 168–80. https://doi.org/10.1080/14729679.2014.908401.

Munz, Hervé. "Les doigts fertiles." *Socio-anthropologie* 35 (2017): 75–91.

Nair, B. R., J. L. Coughlan, and M. J. Hensley. "Impediments to Bed-Side Teaching." *Medical Education* 32, no. 2 (1998): 159–62. https://doi.org/10.1046/j.1365-2923.1998.00185.x.

Neufeld, J., C. Sinke, M. Zedler, et al. "Disinhibited Feedback as a Cause of Synesthesia: Evidence from a Functional Connectivity Study on Auditory-Visual Synesthetes." *Neuropsychologia* 50, no. 7 (2012): 1471–77. https://doi.org/10.1016/j.neuropsychologia.2012.02.032.

Nishizaka, Aug. "Touch Without Vision: Referential Practice in a Non-technological Environment." *Journal of Pragmatics* 43, no. 2 (2011): 504–20. https://doi.org/10.1016/j.pragma.2009.07.015.

Noble, Greg, and Megan Watkins. "So, How Did Bourdieu Learn to Play Tennis? Habitus, Consciousness and Habituation." *Cultural Studies* 17, nos. 3–4 (2003): 520–39. https://doi.org/10.1080/0950238032000083926.

Noë, Alva. *Action in Perception*. MIT Press, 2004.

Nylander, Erik. "Mastering the Jazz Standard: Sayings and Doings of Artistic Valuation." *American Journal of Cultural Sociology* 2, no. 1 (2014): 66–96.

O'Connor, Erin. "Embodied Knowledge: The Experience of Meaning and the Struggle Towards Proficiency in Glassblowing." *Ethnography* 6, no. 2 (2005): 183–204. https://doi.org/10.1177/1466138105057551.

O'Regan, J. Kevin, and Alva Noë. "The Origin of 'Feel.'" In *From Animals to Animats*. Ed. Hallam Bridget, Floreano Dario, Meyer Jean-Arcady, and Hayes Gillian. MIT Press, 2002.

Oudshoorn, Nelly. "Diagnosis at a Distance: The Invisible Work of Patients and Healthcare Professionals in Cardiac Telemonitoring Technology." *Sociology of Health & Illness* 30, no. 2 (2008): 272–88. https://doi.org/10.1111/j.1467-9566.2007.01032.x.

Pagis, Michal. *Inward: Vipassana Meditation and the Embodiment of the Self*. University of Chicago Press, 2019.

——. "Producing Intersubjectivity in Silence: An Ethnographic Study of Meditation Practice." *Ethnography* 11, no. 2 (2010): 309–28. https://doi.org/10.1177/1466138109339041.

Penn, Sean. "127 Hours." USA: Twentieth Century Fox Film Corporation 2011.

Pentimalli, Barbara, and Giampietro Gobo. "'Hearing with the Eyes': Visual Hearing in (a Trio) Music Rehearsals." *Senses and Society* 18, no. 3 (2023): 254–72. https://doi.org/10.1080/17458927.2023.2232621.

Perlman, Marc. "Golden Ears and Meter Readers: The Contest for Epistemic Authority in Audiophilia." *Social Studies of Science* 34, no. 5 (2004): 783–807. https://doi.org/10.1177/0306312704047613.

Peters, Max, and Olle ten Cate. "Bedside Teaching in Medical Education: A Literature Review." *Perspectives on Medical Education* 3, no. 2 (2014): 76–88. https://doi.org/10.1007/s40037-013-0083-y.

Peterson, Richard. *Creating Country Music: Fabricating Authenticity.* University of Chicago Press, 1997.

Polanyi, Michael. *Personal Knowledge: Towards a Postcritical Philosophy.* Routledge and Kegan Paul, 1958.

——. *The Tacit Dimension.* University of Chicago Press, 1966.

Prentice, Rachel. *Bodies in Formation: An Ethnography of Anatomy and Surgery Education.* Duke University Press, 2013.

——. "Drilling Surgeons: The Social Lessons of Embodied Surgical Learning." *Science, Technology & Human Values* 32, no. 5 (2007): 534–53. https://doi.org/10.1177/0895904805303201.

Proske, Uwe, and Simon C. Gandevia. "The Proprioceptive Senses: Their Roles in Signaling Body Shape, Body Position and Movement, and Muscle Force." *Physiological Reviews* 92, no. 4 (2012): 1651–97. https://doi.org/10.1152/physrev.00048.2011.

Ramachandran, V. S., and E. M. Hubbard. "Synaesthesia—A Window Into Perception, Thought and Language." *Journal of Consciousness Studies* 8, no. 12 (2001): 3–34. https://www.ingentaconnect.com/content/imp/jcs/2001/00000008/00000012/1244.

Reichsman, Franz, Francis E. Browning, and J. Raymond Hinshaw. "Observations of Undergraduate Clinical Teaching in Action." *Academic Medicine* 39, no. 2 (1964): 147–63. http://journals.lww.com/academicmedicine/Fulltext/1964/02000/Observations_of_Undergraduate_Clinical_Teaching_in.8.aspx.

Rhodes, James. *Instrumental: A Memoir of Madness, Medication and Music.* Canongate, 2015.

Rice, Tom. "'Beautiful Murmurs': Stethoscopic Listening and Acoustic Objectification." *Senses and Society* 3, no. 3 (2008): 293–306.

——. *Hearing and the Hospital: Sound, Listening, Knowledge and Experience.* Sean Kingston, 2013.

——. "Learning to Listen: Auscultation and the Transmission of Auditory Knowledge." *Journal of the Royal Anthropological Institute* 16 (2010): S41–S61. https://doi.org/10.1111/j.1467-9655.2010.01609.x.

Richardson, Ruth. *Death, Dissection and the Destitute.* 2nd ed. University of Chicago Press, 2001.

Riessman, Catherine Kohler. *Divorce Talk: Women and Men Make Sense of Personal Relationships*. Rutgers University Press, 1990.

Robson, Catherine. "Standing on the Burning Deck: Poetry, Performance, History." *PMLA* 120, no. 1 (2005): 148–62. http://www.jstor.org/stable/25486150.

Rosch, Eleanor, Lydia Thompson, and Francisco J. Varela. *The Embodied Mind: Cognitive Science and Human Experience*. MIT Press, 1991.

Rouw, Romke, and H. Steven Scholte. "Increased Structural Connectivity in Grapheme-Color Synesthesia." *Nature Neuroscience* 10, no. 6 (2007): 792–97. https://doi.org/10.1038/nn1906.

Sacks, Harvey. *Lectures on Conversation*, vols. 1–2. Ed. Gail Jefferson. Wiley-Blackwell, 1992.

Scarry, Elaine. *The Body in Pain: The Making and Unmaking of the World*. Oxford University Press, 1988.

Schafer, Murray. "Open Ears." In *The Auditory Culture Reader*. Ed. Michael Bull and Les Black. Berg, 2003.

Schubert, Cornelius. "Making Sure: A Comparative Micro-analysis of Diagnostic Instruments in Medical Practice." *Social Science & Medicine* 73, no. 6 (2011): 851–57. https://doi.org/10.1016/j.socscimed.2011.05.032.

Schuller, Gunther. *The Compleat Conductor*. Oxford University Press, 1997.

Shamrock, Mary. "Orff Schulwerk: An Integrated Foundation." *Music Educators Journal* 72, no. 6 (1986): 51–55. https://doi.org/10.2307/3401278.

Simpson, Joe. *Touching the Void*. Jonathan Cape, 1988.

Small, Christopher. *Musicking: The Meanings of Performing and Listening*. University Press of New England, 1998.

Smith, Bruce R. "Listening to the Wild Blue Yonder: The Challenges of Acoustic Ecology." In *Hearing Cultures: Essays on Sound, Listening and Modernity*. Ed. Viet Erlmann. Berg, 2004.

Standage, Tom. *The Victorian Internet: The Remarkable Story of the Telegraph and the Nineteenth Century's Online Pioneers*. Walker, 1998.

Sterne, Jonathan. *The Audible Past: Cultural Origins of Sound Reproduction*. Duke University Press, 2003.

——. "Mediate Auscultation, the Stethoscope, and the 'Autopsy of the Living': Medicine's Acoustic Culture." *Journal of Medical Humanities* 22, no. 2 (2001): 115–36. https://doi.org/10.1023/a:1009067628620.

Storer, Ralph. *The Joy of Hillwalking*. Luath, 2004.

Strong, Catherine. *Grunge: Music and Memory*. Ashgate, 2011.

Sudnow, David. *Ways of the Hand: The Organization of Improvised Conduct*. Harvard University Press, 1978.

Talbot, Martin. "Monkey See, Monkey Do: A Critique of the Competency Model in Graduate Medical Education." *Medical Education* 38, no. 6 (2004): 587–92. https://doi.org/10.1046/j.1365-2923.2004.01794.x.

Tavory, Iddo. *Summoned: Identification and Religious Life in a Jewish Neighborhood.* University of Chicago Press, 2016.

Teil, Geneviève. "Amateurs' Exploration of Wine: A Pragmatic Study of Taste." *Theory, Culture & Society* 38, no. 5 (2021): 137–57. https://doi.org/10.1177/02632764211029347.

ten Cate, Olle, and Fedde Scheele. "Viewpoint: Competency-Based Postgraduate Training: Can We Bridge the Gap Between Theory and Clinical Practice?" *Academic Medicine* 82, no. 6 (2007): 542–47. https://doi.org/10.1097/ACM.0b013e31805559c7.

Terhune, Devin Blair, Sarah Tai, Alan Cowey, Tudor Popescu, and Roi Cohen Kadosh. "Enhanced Cortical Excitability in Grapheme-Color Synesthesia and Its Modulation." *Current Biology* 21, no. 23 (2011): 2006–9. https://doi.org/10.1016/j.cub.2011.10.032.

Thibault, George E. "Bedside Rounds Revisited." *New England Journal of Medicine* 336, no. 16 (1997): 1174–75. https://doi.org/10.1056/nejm199704173361610.

Tillmann, Barbara, and W. Jay Dowling. "Memory Decreases for Prose, but Not for Poetry." *Memory & Cognition* 35, no. 4 (2007): 628–39. https://doi.org/10.3758/BF03193301.

Timmermans, Stefan, and Marc Berg. *The Gold Standard: The Challenge of Evidence-Based Medicine and Standardization in Healthcare.* Temple University Press, 2003.

Timmermans, Stefan, and Steven Haas. "Towards a Sociology of Disease." *Sociology of Health & Illness* 30, no. 5 (2008): 659–76. https://doi.org/10.1111/j.1467-9566.2008.01097.x.

Tolins, Jackson. "Assessment and Direction Through Nonlexical Vocalizations in Music Instruction." *Research on Language and Social Interaction* 46, no. 1 (2013): 47–64. https://doi.org/10.1080/08351813.2013.753721.

Tolmie, Peter, Steve Benford, and Mark Rouncefield. "Playing in Irish Music Sessions." In *Ethnomethodology at Play.* Ed. Peter Tolmie and Mark Rouncefield. Ashgate, 2013.

Turner, Frederick, and Ernst Pöppel. "The Neural Lyre: Poetic Meter, the Brain, and Time." *Poetry* 142, no. 5 (1983): 277–309. http://www.jstor.org/stable/20599567.

van Bohemen, Samira, Luna den Hertog, and Liesbet van Zoonen. "Music as a Resource for the Sexual Self: An Exploration of How Young People in the Netherlands Use Music for Good Sex." *Poetics* 66 (2018): 19–29. https://doi.org/10.1016/j.poetic.2017.12.001.

Van Drie, Melissa. "Training the Auscultative Ear." *Senses and Society* 8, no. 2 (2013): 165–91. https://doi.org/10.2752/174589313X13589681981019.

Vassilakis, Pantelis. *Auditory Roughness as a Means of Musical Expression*. Department of Ethnomusicology, University of California, Los Angeles, 2005.

Verghese, Abraham. "Culture Shock—Patient as Icon, Icon as Patient." *New England Journal of Medicine* 359, no. 26 (2008): 2748–51. https://doi.org/10.1056/NEJMp0807461.

Vergunst, Jo Lee. "Taking a Trip and Taking Care in Everyday Life." In *Ways of Walking: Ethnography and Practice on Foot*. Ed. Tim Ingold and Jo Lee Vergunst. Ashgate, 2008.

Vervoorn, Aat. *Mountain Solitudes: Solo Journeys in the Southern Alps of New Zealand*. Craig Potton, 2000.

Vuoskoski, Jonna K., and Dee Reynolds. "Music, Rowing, and the Aesthetics of Rhythm." *Senses and Society* 14, no. 1 (2019): 1–14. https://doi.org/10.1080/17458927.2018.1525201.

Vygotsky, Lev. *Mind in Society: The Development of Higher Psychological Processes*. Harvard University Press, 1978.

Wacquant, Loïc. *Body and Soul: Notebooks of an Apprentice Boxer*. Oxford University Press, 2004.

Wallenburg, Iris, Antoinette Bont, Maas-Jan Heineman, Fedde Scheele, and Pauline Meurs. "Learning to Doctor: Tinkering with Visibility in Residency Training." *Sociology of Health & Illness* 35, no. 4 (2013): 544–59. https://doi.org/10.1111/j.1467-9566.2012.01512.x.

Walser, Robert. *Running with the Devil: Power, Gender, and Madness in Heavy Metal Music*. Wesleyan University Press, 1993.

Walter, J. A. "Death as Recreation: Armchair Mountaineering." *Leisure Studies* 3, no. 1 (1984): 67–76. https://doi.org/10.1080/02614368400390051.

Wattchow, Brian. "Moving on an Effortless Journey: Paddling, River-Places and Outdoor Education." *Australian Journal of Outdoor Education* 12, no. 2 (2008): 12–23.

Weeks, Peter. "Musical Time as a Practical Accomplishment: A Change in Tempo." *Human Studies* 13, no. 4 (1990): 323–59. http://www.jstor.org/stable/20009106.

——. "A Rehearsal of a Beethoven Passage: An Analysis of Correction Talk." *Research on Language and Social Interaction* 29, no. 3 (1996): 247–90. https://doi.org/10.1207/s15327973rlsi2903_3.

West, Amanda, and Linda Allin. "Chancing Your Arm: The Meaning of Risk in Rock Climbing." *Sport in Society* 13, nos. 7–8 (2010): 1234–48. https://doi.org/10.1080/17430431003780245.

White, Hayden. "The Value of Narrativity in the Representation of Reality." *Critical Inquiry* 7, no. 1 (1980): 5–27. http://www.jstor.org/stable/1343174.

Williams, Keith N., Subha Ramani, Bruce Fraser, and Jay D. Orlander. "Improving Bedside Teaching: Findings from a Focus Group Study of Learners." *Academic Medicine* 83, no. 3 (2008): 257–64. https://doi.org/10.1097/ACM.0b013e3181637f3e.

Wilson, Timothy D., Douglas J. Lisle, Jonathan W. Schooler, Sara D. Hodges, Kristen J. Klaaren, and Suzanne J. LaFleur. "Introspecting About Reasons Can Reduce Post-choice Satisfaction." *Personality and Social Psychology Bulletin* 19, no. 3 (1993): 331–39. https://doi.org/10.1177/0146167293193010.

Winther, Jennifer. "The Embodiment of Sound and Cohesion in Music." *American Behavioral Scientist* 48, no. 11 (2005): 1410–21. https://doi.org/10.1177/0002764205277362.

Wyse, Elizabeth, ed. *Debrett's Handbook*. Debrett's, 2014.

Yelin, Joy. *Movement That Fits: Dalcroze Eurhythmics and the Suzuki Method*. Summy-Brichard, 1990.

Young, Iris Marion. *Throwing Like a Girl and Other Essays in Feminist Philosophy and Social Theory*. Indiana University Press, 1990.

Zamm, Anna, Gottfried Schlaug, David M. Eagleman, and Psyche Loui. "Pathways to Seeing Music: Enhanced Structural Connectivity in Colored-Music Synesthesia." *NeuroImage* 74 (2013): 359–66. https://doi.org/10.1016/j.neuroimage.2013.02.024.

INDEX

GPSR Authorized Representative: Easy Access System Europe, Mustamäe tee
50, 10621 Tallinn, Estonia, gpsr.requests@easproject.com